HOT DESK

HOT DESK

A Novel

Laura Dickerman

GALLERY BOOKS
New York   Amsterdam/Antwerp   London
Toronto   Sydney/Melbourne   New Delhi

G

Gallery Books
An Imprint of Simon & Schuster, LLC
1230 Avenue of the Americas
New York, NY 10020

For more than 100 years, Simon & Schuster has championed authors and the stories they create. By respecting the copyright of an author's intellectual property, you enable Simon & Schuster and the author to continue publishing exceptional books for years to come. We thank you for supporting the author's copyright by purchasing an authorized edition of this book.

No amount of this book may be reproduced or stored in any format, nor may it be uploaded to any website, database, language-learning model, or other repository, retrieval, or artificial intelligence system without express permission. All rights reserved. Inquiries may be directed to Simon & Schuster, 1230 Avenue of the Americas, New York, NY 10020 or permissions@simonandschuster.com.

This book is a work of fiction. Any references to historical events, real people, or real places are used fictitiously. Other names, characters, places, and events are products of the author's imagination, and any resemblance to actual events or places or persons, living or dead, is entirely coincidental.

Copyright © 2025 by Laura Dickerman

All rights reserved, including the right to reproduce this book or portions thereof in any form whatsoever. For information, address Gallery Books Subsidiary Rights Department, 1230 Avenue of the Americas, New York, NY 10020.

First Gallery Books hardcover edition September 2025

GALLERY BOOKS and colophon are registered trademarks of Simon & Schuster, LLC

Simon & Schuster strongly believes in freedom of expression and stands against censorship in all its forms. For more information, visit BooksBelong.com.

For information about special discounts for bulk purchases, please contact Simon & Schuster Special Sales at 1-866-506-1949 or business@simonandschuster.com.

The Simon & Schuster Speakers Bureau can bring authors to your live event. For more information or to book an event, contact the Simon & Schuster Speakers Bureau at 1-866-248-3049 or visit our website at www.simonspeakers.com.

Manufactured in the United States of America

10   9   8   7   6   5   4   3   2   1

Library of Congress Control Number: 2025936079

ISBN 978-1-6680-8109-9
ISBN 978-1-6682-1216-5 (Int Exp)
ISBN 978-1-6680-8111-2 (ebook)

Excerpt from "Let It Snow! Let It Snow! Let It Snow!": Words by Sammy Cahn; Music by Jule Styne; © 1945 (Renewed) PRODUCERS MUSIC PUBLISHING CO., INC. and CAHN MUSIC COMPANY; All Rights for PRODUCERS MUSIC PUBLISHING CO., INC.; Administered by CHAPPELL & CO., INC.; All Rights for CAHN MUSIC COMPANY; Administered by CONCORD SOUNDS c/o CONCORD MUSIC PUBLISHING; All Rights Reserved; Used by Permission; Reprinted by Permission of Hal Leonard LLC.

"The Snow Is Deep on the Ground": By Kenneth Patchen, from COLLECTED POEMS OF KENNETH PATCHEN, copyright ©1943 by Kenneth Patchen. Reprinted by permission of New Directions Publishing Corp.

Excerpt from BANG A GONG (Get It On): Words and Music by Marc Bolan; © Copyright 1971 (Renewed) Westminster Music Ltd., London, England R B Investments 1, Beverly Hills, CA controls all publication rights for the United States (administered by TRO-Essex Music International, Inc., New York, NY); TRO-Essex Music International, Inc., New York, controls all rights for Canada; International Copyright Secured Made In U.S.A; All Rights Reserved Including Public Performance For Profit; Used by Permission.

For Bill, of course

HOT DESK

CHAPTER ONE

MONDAY
WORK, REBECCA

Rebecca glared at her new shared desk, bare except for a sad cactus in a green plastic pot. How had it come to this? She used to have her own office. Yes, it had been fabricated from a file closet when she first started at Avenue Publishing five years ago. But it had a door she could close. And, after two long years of living in and working from her grandmother's apartment on West Ninety-Third Street, Rebecca had actually looked forward to going back into work, to seeing colleagues without having to parse their Zoom backgrounds, to gossiping in the company kitchen, and to wearing clothes with zippers.

But Leesen, the larger company that owned Avenue, Hawk Mills, and a handful of other publishing divisions, had moved to open plan, which their CEO, Frank French, had tried to pass off as an exciting opportunity for team spirit building. Then, just as she was adjusting to the lack of privacy, Leesen had subleased the fourth floor, capped her in-office days to Mondays and Tuesdays, and moved Hawk Mills to Avenue's floor, where they would be working Wednesdays and Thursdays, at the very same desks she and her colleagues now inhabited. Rebecca's tiny office had been rebranded as the "Synergy Room." She had only ever seen Paul from Production use it to eat his chopped kale Caesar salads that she knew from sad experience tasted exactly the same as the chopped buffalo chicken salad.

She eased the heavy bag from her shoulder onto the chair, which rolled away as she dropped a box of belongings onto the desk: her blue Marimekko mug; the company laptop; her other mug, which had a croissant for a handle (a beloved, hideous gift from her nephews) into which she dumped her favorite pens; a framed photo of Stella (her best friend from college) and her grandma, Mimi, with champagne glasses held high; a bag of chocolate-covered almonds; a bottle of cherry kombucha to store in the company fridge; her Julia Child mouse pad; and a postcard from the Hungarian Pastry Shop that she propped against the back of the desk.

Seriously, everyone knew the cactus was the worst of plants: an ugly, prickly copout for people who enjoyed sand and heat and Westerns, who had given up on lushness, on green, on life. If she, Monday–Tuesday Desk, had to sweep all her belongings into a locked file cabinet every Tuesday night and haul everything out again on Monday mornings, couldn't Mister Wednesday–Thursday Desk store his pathetic cactus out of sight? Maybe, Rebecca thought churlishly, office life was not the life for her. Dragging the chair back, she collapsed into it to survey the lay of the land in her new, decidedly untenable situation. Working from home, even from her dad's childhood bedroom, was looking pretty good.

Mrs. Singh of Human Resources was lording over everyone from her dedicated Monday–Friday desk, which boasted an electric kettle, her inspirational word-of-the-day calendar, and a veritable jungle of healthy, flowering plants. Chloe, Rebecca's cheerful assistant, motioned wildly to indicate that she was, obviously, on a Zoom call. Rebecca waved, hoping Chloe would keep her cheer away until Rebecca could get more settled into what felt like a demotion. It wasn't a demotion! It was the new world! An "agile seating" world, as Frank French had unfortunately called it. She was only twenty-eight and already she felt old, cranky, and out of touch. Was Chloe wearing leopard print Crocs? Why? Were Crocs back? She had fervently hoped they were gone forever. She opened the top desk drawer and pulled out a new package of neon Post-its. Was neon back? What was wrong with the old yellow ones? Had her "hot desking" (seriously, Frank French?) deskmate bought neon Post-its and a cactus? She knew nothing about this person except that his name was Ben and he was a new editor at Hawk Mills, and therefore her enemy: Hawk Mills and Avenue were in direct competition for the same projects, fighting over literary fiction, memoirs, and the occasional $250 coffee table book about tulips.

"I hear the new guy might be a ginger!" Gabe, who ran the marketing department, gave Rebecca a kiss on the cheek and a donut wrapped in a napkin. Last week there was a great display of welcome to the new desk sharing life, with breakfast burritos in the kitchen and a cheese-cubes-and-cheap-wine reception at 4 p.m. Predictably, the fanfare had dwindled to two dozen donuts this week. Gabe half propped himself on the desk, his long legs crossed at the ankles so that she could admire his brightly striped, no doubt shockingly expensive socks. Gabe was the main reason Rebecca wanted to be in the office at all; they had arrived at Avenue around the same time to become not just work friends but real friends. She had read a Cavafy poem at his wedding last year to his party planner husband, Thanapob, who everyone called Tor.

"A ginger! That tracks." Rebecca could guess that Gabe's source was Mrs. Singh, whose interest in office gossip dovetailed serendipitously with Gabe's. She took a bite of the donut with the optimism of her grandmother Mimi scratching off a lottery ticket. This time it would yield millions! This time it would not be stale! It was stale. Rebecca allowed herself yet another wistful memory of chatting on speaker and using her phone camera to check her teeth, and yes, of also being able to concentrate on her actual job in peace and quiet behind a closed door. She waved her hand to encompass the desk but also the general unacceptable state of things. "Gingers are the worst."

"There are hot gingers and problem gingers." Gabe gave the cactus a pitying glance and moved it pointedly out of his way.

"That is not my cactus," Rebecca explained. "That is the ginger's decor. He left it there against all rules."

"For instance," Gabe said, ignoring her. "Prince Harry, were he not a prince, might be a problem ginger. But his prince-ness makes him subjectively hot. A hot ginger."

"Prince-ness?" Rebecca took another disappointing bite of the donut. "Also, I thought you were seeking treatment for your unreasonable rage at our losing out on the Prince Harry book. As if Avenue was going to give anyone untold millions."

"It wasn't untold! It was told! It was twenty-five million! Worth every penny, and I could have marketed the fuck out of it with Meghan."

"So you've mentioned before." Rebecca turned on her computer and pushed the cactus to the far edge of the desk behind the monitor. "Fact: there is no hot ginger in the world who wouldn't also be just as hot as a non-ginger. What do we know about this Ben?" Ben didn't seem like a good name for a redhead. Rebecca imagined her deskmate as a freckled Prince Harry but not a prince, therefore bereft of the hotness conferred upon him by prince-ness. "Ben like Benjamin, a strapping preppy blue blood from Boston who wears deck shoes and flies kites. Wait, that's Benjamin Franklin. He's ancient and wears Ben Franklin knickers."

"Not knickers. Breeches," Gabe corrected her. "Or Ben like Benny, a scrappy kid from Jersey who rolls a pack of cigarettes in his T-shirt sleeve and fixes cars. Or maybe both . . . like scrappy and strapping. Strapping and scrappy."

Rebecca tore a yellow Post-it from the pack and wrote, "**CACTI ARE THE WORST OF PLANTS.**" Too aggressive? She crumpled it and tore off another. "**IS A CACTUS APPROPRIATE DESK DECOR?**" Too passive-aggressive? Crumpled. "**I HATE YOUR CACTUS.**" Too aggressive-aggressive? Crumpled. She swept the Post-its debris into the gray bin beneath her shared desk. "Come get me later. I have shit to do now."

Gabe returned to his neat desk across the room. (His deskmate was the inoffensive Carlotta, who worked his mirror job in marketing at Hawk Mills, the imprint interloper now sharing their space two days a week.) Always a diligent rule follower, Gabe had immediately contacted Carlotta with gentle suggestions about a smattering of tasteful desk accessories that she had immediately approved, not a cactus among them. Carlotta knew without asking to remove high school graduation photos of her niece, and on Tuesday nights Gabe locked away his Tizio task lamp from the MoMA Design Store to "protect" Carlotta from accidentally breaking it.

Rebecca checked her email. Should she contact Ben and make it clear the cactus was a no-go? And that she would like to leave her black work sweater neatly folded in the bottom drawer in case the air conditioning was on full blast? She preferred not to cram it in the locker with her mugs. Forget it! She had much more important things to attend to right now. Case in point: an email with the latest edits from Lady Paulette (not really a Lady, not born a Paulette), whose memoir about being a companion to one of the twentieth century's lesser-known philosophers had inexplicably caught the eye of Rebecca's boss, Ami, and had subsequently landed on Rebecca's desk to shepherd through publication. "*Rebecca*"—Lady Paulette used script font in all her correspondence, which was highly annoying—"*it is imperative that these changes make their way into the finished book. I know it's late, I know it's beastly of me. But the book would be absolute rubbish without them. If these modifications are not incorporated, I cannot promise*

I shall be able to stand behind The Lady and the Brain *and do the agreed-upon publicity and media. Ja."* Rebecca opened the attachment. Lady Paulette had changed the spelling of her cat's name from Catherine to Katherine, which involved a lot of find-and-replace. Rebecca sighed and forwarded it to Richard, the long-suffering managing editor, who would, Rebecca knew, have a tantrum, tell her it wasn't possible, and then make it happen. She sent Gabe a quick email to see if he thought Liberty London would be interested in swaddling Lady Paulette in scarves for her tour. Perhaps they had a feline print?

Further down in her inbox was an announcement from Frank French himself, welcoming everyone to their second shared desk week with jargon about "home/office flexibility," "streamlined efficiency," and a suspicious-sounding "boundaryless workplace."

There was an all-company email, also from Frank French, about the recent death of literary lion Edward David Adams, the last of the New York cohort of terrible but gifted men who had ruled the writing world—the ones whose exploits had not quite yet overshadowed their brilliant war novels, prize-winning depictions of suburban infidelity, and tome after tome chronicling their privileged white struggle against mortality. EDA, a.k.a. the Lion, had finally gone raging into that dark night, and Rebecca had studied enough of his glittering, flinty sentences in college to grant him a grudging respect. "A singular, towering talent whose lifetime of achievement will, in the record of his written word, live on"—which, to be honest, was laying it on a bit thick. The company had never even published any of the Lion's many novels, making this heartfelt remembrance superfluous, but Rebecca knew, from having been cornered at a cocktail party by Frank French (back when they had cocktail parties!), that he had once spent a drunken evening with the Lion at the legendary Bread Loaf Writers' Conference, an annual literary-star-studded summer gathering in Vermont that used to be known as "Bed Loaf" but was now more of a networking scene and less of a Bacchanalian romp among the Green Mountains. The Lion's death was the end of an era, to be sure. An era, Rebecca thought, whose end was certainly due.

She quickly checked Instagram to see if the menu for her best friend Stella's monthly supper club, *salute!*, had dropped. She had been helping Stella put on the dinner parties and was thrilled with their success. Rebecca had big plans for Stella. She had been researching different media strategies in her goal to rocket Stella to fame and fortune. Pasta primavera, strawberry shortcake. Rebecca flipped her phone face down before she got too distracted, turned back to her computer, took a hopeful bite of donut. Still stale.

She continued going through her emails, the usual mash-up of pitches from agents she was no longer supposed to take out to lunch (her meager travel and expenses budget had been frozen as the company reeled from the post-pandemic economic storm) and requests from the various authors under her care. After the stress of moving the stubbornly old-fashioned business of publishing fully remote, with management calling into meetings from their upstate houses or hastily winterized Maine retreats, and the younger staff tuning in from the basements of their childhood homes or their shared bedrooms in Bushwick, it was shocking when book sales actually increased. Fine, it was mostly adult coloring books, but even literary fiction had seen a bump. Now, though, as people ventured out into the world again, sales were tanking. Hence the sublet of the fourth floor, lack of book parties, fewer agent lunches, and Rebecca's current desk debacle.

Rebecca's phone vibrated. It was her mom, Jane, calling from Rebecca's childhood home in Philadelphia. "Good morning," Rebecca whispered, so her mother would understand that she was hard at work and also so that Mrs. Singh wouldn't notice she was on a personal call. On the one hand, working at a not-only-hers desk out in the open was terrible. On the other hand, being under Mrs. Singh's gaze and wanting to prove she was not the kind of person perusing Hinge, making an appointment for eyebrow threading, or researching hot new restaurants in Brooklyn, Rebecca found she got more work done more quickly. Was it sustainable? Who knew? It helped to retreat into one of the numerous space-age-looking phone booths positioned around the perimeter of the office when necessary. Every single person who saw them for the first time said exactly the same thing with no exception: "Beam me up, Scotty." People who had never seen *Star Trek*. People who didn't know that "Beam me up, Scotty" was a reference to *Star Trek*. Rebecca (she could kick herself) had said it. She clambered in and closed the spaceship door.

"Good morning, sweetheart," her mom said briskly. "I was just checking in to see if you had wrapped up the final edits for Lady Paulette. I'm taking a walk this afternoon with Peggy from the library, and you know what an Anglophile she is."

"First of all, you know Lady Paulette's not really English, right?" Rebecca couldn't help but think that her mom used the ancient royal watcher Peggy as an excuse to keep tabs on Rebecca's work projects. Her mother started every day with a call, "just checking in" with her. She had always taken what Rebecca felt was an inordinate interest in Rebecca's job, which was ironic, since Jane herself had never had a career. Having sacrificed the best years of her life to raising twin boys (Rebecca's brothers, Ethan and Andrew, ten years older, both now happily married and gainfully employed, had spent their childhood hurling balls, falling from trees, dragging each other in headlocks from room to room, and leaving muddy cleats on every surface), Rebecca's mother turned her attention to Rebecca. Professor (as the boys called their father) was a distracted, gentle man, bemused by and removed from both the chaos of the boys and his wife's project that was Rebecca.

"She enjoys any details at all, you know," Jane chided.

"Fine! Their cat has been renamed Katherine with a *K*."

"Thank you. Have you followed up with Alice Gottlieb about her next book?"

"Oh my god, Mom! I already have a boss. Also, I have to get to work. I'll talk to you later."

"Talk to you later," Jane said, unperturbed. "When you speak to Alice, let her know that our book club is starting the trilogy this month."

Rebecca rolled her eyes. "Love you. Bye!" She left the pod, stored her phone out of sight, and made a big show of returning emails.

A few hours later, Chloe, who had been cheerfully working away, no doubt making Rebecca's life easier, popped up in her leopard Crocs, about which Rebecca was determined not to speak. "Ami wants to see you in her office!"

"Do you know why?" Being summoned by Ami still gave her the anxiety and defensiveness of being caught breaking school rules involving cigarettes or a plaid skirt hiked too high.

Chloe, ever obtuse to Rebecca's moods, unloaded a pile of bound manuscripts onto her desk. "I adore your cactus! So Southwest chic! I just thrifted this presh poncho and I'm making it into a minidress!" As usual, Rebecca had no response to Chloe's relentless positivity. Would the no doubt so-ugly-it-was-fabulous repurposed poncho that Chloe would wear to work next week be ironic? Or worn earnestly? Would she wear it with Crocs? Was Chloe judging her for wearing expensive jeans? Did Chloe adore the cactus, or did "adore" mean she hated it? How was twenty-eight already old? "Don't forget the marketing meeting later, and Ami is waiting." Chloe vanished in a waft of dewberry lotion.

Ami Ito, editorial director, Rebecca's boss, had, like Frank French, hung on to an actual office, though she made a big show of leaving the door open as an egalitarian gesture. Whenever Rebecca passed by, gazing covetously inside, Ami was clacking the keyboard one hundred miles an hour, speaking softly into her headset, her shiny swoop of black hair obscuring one perfectly mascaraed eye, her impossibly high heel swinging from the toes of her crossed foot. Ami had a beautiful wife, a ceramicist whose vases sold at galleries, and a small dog, Trinket, whom they dressed in seasonal outfits. Rebecca knew this because Ami had a large digital frame facing outward so all who peered in could see the often-updated photos of Trinket and remember it was almost Valentine's Day (pink heart sweater) or had just been Mardi Gras (purple-and-green top hat and gold bead necklace). Ami continued murmuring into her headset, all the while typing furiously, but she gave Rebecca a quick nod and motioned her into the cream leather Barcelona chair, a vestige from another, richer time in the company's history. Rebecca sank nervously into the seat, gazing at the latest photo. Was it okay for dogs to celebrate Cinco de Mayo? Rebecca wondered. Could a half-Japanese, half-Venezuelan dog with its paw on festive-looking maracas be accused of cultural appropriation?

"Rebecca. I received the oddest call this morning. About you." Ami affixed her gaze on Rebecca. It didn't happen often, but Rebecca was speechless. Words flew out of her head, leaving only guilt and sorrow for whatever crime she had unknowingly committed. She was sorry. She was sorry she had complained bitterly to all who would listen about the shared desk. A shared desk was better than no desk, she thought sadly, as she imagined piling all her belongings back into the box and leaving everything in accordance with the Clean Desk Policy, which she would absolutely, positively read for real this time before schlepping her fired ass out of the office for good. "What connection do you have to Edward David Adams?" Ami continued as Rebecca's brain sputtered to keep up.

"The Lion? EDA? Edward David Adams?" Ami waited patiently while Rebecca listed all his monikers. "Edward David Adams, the writer who just died?" she added for good measure. "Um. Well, I took a class on him, Philip Roth, and Norman Mailer that was required for my major?" Rebecca stopped herself from explaining that she would have gotten an A and not an A– had her professor (in her opinion, a wannabe disciple of the very writers he taught) not been put off by her application of post-structural feminist theory to examine the role of housewives in their novels. Distracted, Rebecca thought fondly of her rousing conclusion in which she took the Lion and the others to task for their reinforcement of gendered roles and how white women were both oppressed by and benefited from the system upheld in the books. Yes, it was seven years after graduation, and she could almost recite that unjustly underappreciated essay from memory. She was that proud.

"I don't think that solves the mystery," Ami stated dryly. She was often bracingly dry, and Rebecca wished they could be friends and that Ami and Elena would invite her over to their fabulous loft and feed her canapés, smiling indulgently at her charming tales of dating and amusing nightlife while she cuddled Trinket in her lap. But she knew better. Ami existed in a world of unwrinkled linen, dainty gold jewelry, and season tickets to Lincoln Center. "I had a call from Rose Adams this morning. The Lion's widow. I'm sure you're aware that the Lion died without a literary agent. He worked directly with his editor, Maury Kantor?"

Rebecca knew who Maury Kantor was, the *K* of PK Publishing, last seen a few years ago shuffling around the National Book Awards ceremony in a tuxedo that reeked of mothballs and a forbidden lit pipe clenched between his khaki-colored teeth. Aside from his relationship with the Lion, he was famous for chastising women editors for not wearing lipstick.

"PK Publishing handled everything connected to the Lion's work, an arrangement that, I'm sure you know, is highly unusual. So, as you can imagine, his estate is complicated. You might say a mess. And Mrs. Adams intimated there might be unpublished short stories and the like. She told me she wants younger, fresher eyes on the Lion's work, both old and new."

Rebecca uttered what she hoped was an appropriate murmur to convey polite interest. How was any of this connected to her?

"Maury Kantor is no longer able to continue his, shall we say, 'unorthodox shepherding' of the estate." Ami used delicate finger quotes to make "unorthodox shepherding" sound like the name of a hipster band of which she disapproved. "And now that the Lion has died, there will be an inevitable frenzy of lawyers, agents, and publishers circling it. It's a very unusual situation. PK Publishing is neither young nor fresh, and it seems Mrs. Adams shares her late husband's aversion to agents, so we're in the running for control of the estate. I think you understand how huge this could be for us." Ami crossed her barre-toned arms and leaned forward. "Rebecca. Can you think of any reason why Mrs. Adams would specifically ask for you, by name, to meet with her to discuss the estate?"

Rebecca could not.

"I would, of course, usually suggest a more senior editor to meet with Mrs. Adams, but she was very clear about her desire to meet with you. You, Rebecca. She insisted. The only other division at Leesen that makes sense is Hawk Mills, so you can be sure they will be trying to land the estate too. It might not matter to Frank French who brings it in, as long as it doesn't end up at Random House. But I don't have to tell you how much it matters to me, do I?" Ami's gaze was as steely as her arms. "Do you have any connection to Rose Adams?"

Rebecca racked her brain. She considered the phrase and substituted "rake" for "rack." She imagined raking the folds of her brain but with a soft rake so it wouldn't hurt, like one of those tiny ones that came with the soothing Japanese sand gardens that fancy people used to keep on their desks. Their private, personal desks. Into a pile of Edward David Adams knowledge went her undeniably brilliant essay that had pulled her grade down; a controversial short story he had written in *The New Yorker* a few years ago that had gone viral, something people had read as a covert defense of Roman Polanski; the bright spines of the literary magazine the Lion had started, the *East River Review*, packed into the guest room bookcase of her childhood home in Philadelphia. Rebecca halted and backed up, tiny rake in hand. Why did they have those old copies of the *East River Review*? "My mom was an intern or an assistant at the *East River Review* when she was young? I think she was in the city for a year or two, a really long time ago. She never mentioned the Lion or talked about any of it. But that's it."

"So no connection that you know of to his widow, Rose Adams? And no reason to think your mother had any relationship to the family? To the estate?" Ami was tapping one pearly nail on her desk, the only outward sign of agitation she betrayed.

"Absolutely not," Rebecca declared, with a certainty she might later regret but seemed necessary to the occasion. *Was* there something to her mother's connection with the magazine? Why hadn't they ever talked about it beyond the bare minimum? "I mean, I can ask my mom, but, honestly, it was way before I was born." Ami gazed at her impassively, but Rebecca was sure she was considering a demand for a DNA test to determine if Rebecca was the unclaimed child of the most famous no-longer-living lascivious writer in America. She was 100 percent her father's daughter: thick hair unwieldy, check; statement nose, check; pond water–green eyes, but fitted with contact lenses instead of the wire-rimmed glasses her father had sported since the early '60s, check; and his mother Mimi's large breasts and wide feet. Not a trace of the Lion!

"Curious." Ami and Rebecca looked at each other, the only sound Ami's manicure testing itself on the desk, *tap tap tap*. Ami abruptly clapped her hands, startling Rebecca and signaling her decision to move forward. "Well, Rebecca, you're a talented editor. Your writers trust you. You did do impressive work on the Alice Gottlieb trilogy," Ami mused aloud, trying, it seemed, to convince herself. Rebecca wished she were wearing her recently purchased Theory blazer, bought under her mother's insistent supervision to look more "polished." She was somewhere between Ami's impeccable sleeveless pussy bow top and Chloe's Crocs and clashing plaids, neither sophisticated chic nor confidently outrageous. The most she could hope for was casually cool, and that was only if Gabe took pity on her and steered her around vintage boutiques.

Yes, she was a talented editor! But maybe it wasn't just her lack of seniority Ami was pondering. She liked her job. Really liked it, was grateful for her successes, for her connection to her writers (Lady Paulette not included), for sharing her office (not her desk!) with people who cared so deeply about books, who believed in reading. Did she absolutely love it? The way Gabe loved marketing, how he sang his perfect taglines or pressed an excellent debut novel into Ann Patchett's hands to feature at her Nashville bookstore? Did she love it with the fierce competitive passion of Ami, even now pinning her to the Barcelona chair with the intensity of her gaze? Maybe not—though, if pushed, she couldn't really say why. Was it, as her mother suggested, a lack of ambition? No "fire in the belly," as was unfortunately the phrase she often repeated about Rebecca's career? "I'll call my mother to check," Rebecca said, and Ami nodded.

"We need to get you over there as soon as possible. But you'll need a briefing. I can get that set up once I talk to Frank French."

"'Over there'?"

"Mrs. Adams wants to meet you at the East End Avenue town house."

Rebecca was again at a loss for words. Ami hadn't even bothered to add *I'm sure you've heard of it.* Every culturally literate person in

New York knew that the Lion had founded the *East River Review* out of his parents' palatial town house in the 1960s when he graduated from Columbia and had inherited money to invest in both the literary magazine and the raucous parties that celebrated every issue. After a few wives, a son whose name Rebecca had on the tip of her tongue (Huck? Holden?), and great literary success, the Lion had turned over the daily running of the magazine to a succession of editors, who still worked out of his town house, and focused on writing novels, spending more time in old age at his Hamptons estate, where, recently, he had died, apparently leaving Rebecca (Rebecca!) somehow (how?) entangled in the aftermath.

"We'll get to the bottom of this mystery," Ami said briskly as an old photo of Trinket flashed before Rebecca. Easter bonnet. "I'll let you know what comes next. But you should expect to head over there soon. We need to get you up to speed: as I said, there will be extreme interest, both in our publishing house and from all over town. Rose Adams's peculiar interest in you might give us an advantage, but I don't doubt the competition will be fierce. I want this for Avenue, Rebecca. No pressure."

Was Ami making a joke? "No pressure," Rebecca repeated weakly. "Peculiar interest" didn't sound promising. Backing out of the office, Rebecca gave Ami a regrettable little wave, but Ami was already in a hushed conversation with her headset. Rebecca went directly to Gabe's spotless desk. "You. Will. Never. Believe. What. Just. Happened."

Gabe looked up from his computer. "You broke it off with Max?"

"What?" Rebecca had to search around to remember who Max was: the perfectly fine guy she was seeing.

"What?" Gabe asked innocently.

"Seriously? Why do you hate Max?" Rebecca liked Max; she did! She found that she doubled down on liking him in direct proportion to everyone else disliking him.

"I don't hate him! I don't have any feelings about him whatsoever," Gabe claimed dramatically.

Rebecca lowered her voice to a stage whisper as she caught sight of Mrs. Singh staring at them over her oversize reading glasses. "Come to the kitchen." She bared her teeth in what she hoped was a calming smile at Mrs. Singh and strode to the kitchen, assuming Gabe would follow her—which, of course, he did.

There were no donuts left, just a box of crumbs, a small mercy. Out of habit, Rebecca opened the fridge and examined the contents: everyone's labeled salads and yogurts; one sad person had even written their initials, in black Sharpie, on three hard-boiled eggs. She took out her cherry kombucha and held it over the sink to open gingerly, recalling, even in her excitement to tell all to Gabe, the one time she had sprayed kombucha all over herself and reeked of vinegar the rest of the day. Fine, two times. "Okay, so Ami just told me that the Lion's widow, Rose Adams, called her to ask that I, Rebecca, me, go over to the East End town house to talk to her about the estate."

Gabe raised one dark eyebrow and cocked his head. "To talk to her about the estate."

"Correct." She swigged the kombucha a little too enthusiastically and coughed.

"You, Rebecca."

"I, Rebecca."

"The title of your memoir, naturally." Gabe couldn't resist.

"Naturally."

"Curious."

"That's exactly what Ami said!"

"Rose Adams asked for you by name."

Rebecca could sense a subtle shift in her internal narrative as Gabe expressed his admittedly warranted disbelief. Really, was it so unthinkable that she would be in the running? Alice Gottlieb's trilogy—years of painstaking editing and coaxing—had won the National Book Critics Circle Award. But now she, Rebecca, was in competition with probably every editor in town. Fine, it *was* unthinkable. She would be eaten alive. Worse, she would disappoint Ami and never enjoy canapés in her (Rebecca imagined) warm-walnut-and-cool-steel kitchen. "I don't even like the Lion! He's problematic. He's like *The Merchant of Venice*. Yes, it's Shakespeare and he tries with the mercy, but still, at the end of the day: antisemitic. Or Picasso. And Hemingway was a dick!"

"D. H. Lawrence was a homophobe," Gabe added sympathetically. "And maybe closeted? The wrestling in *Women in Love* was a seminal scene for teenage me. Literally."

"Focus!" Rebecca reminded them both.

"Hold the fuck up. What in god's name will you wear?"

"All hands on deck, obviously." Rebecca tossed her empty kombucha bottle into the recycling bin, where it clanked loudly. Just then Mrs. Singh strolled in, casually opening the cupboard where all the tea was stored, as if she didn't have an entire setup fit for the queen of England on her own desk.

"Hello, dears," she said, fake rummaging in the canister of sugars and NutraSweet packages. Of course, Rebecca liked Mrs. Singh, and understood it wasn't her fault that Rebecca had shared-desk rage. Everyone knew you befriended HR, and Mrs. Singh, with her homey desk and passion for veganism and knitting, was not difficult to like. She had offered to help reimburse Rebecca for her mostly unused Pilates studio pass. But Mrs. Singh knew too much about everyone, Rebecca thought, and absolute power could corrupt even a lady who crafted her own tea cozies. And besides, sometimes she and Gabe went out to lunch and didn't invite Rebecca.

"Sahila," Gabe said fondly, like the traitor he was. "You'll never guess what's going on with Rebecca."

"She has decided to end things with Max?" Mrs. Singh stopped pretending that she was in the kitchen for any other reason than to gossip.

"Come on!" Rebecca glared at Gabe, who busied himself wiping down the counter and tossing the empty donut box away. "Why does everyone hate Max?"

"He's just not the right one for you, dear." Rebecca considered reporting Mrs. Singh to HR for her flagrant and inappropriate use of endearments, but of course Mrs. Singh *was* HR. Rebecca and Max had only been dating for three months, but he had met Gabe, her grandmother, and Stella, and now Rebecca was going to invite him to Stella's dinner club, *salute!*, next week. After there was a mention of it in *Eater*, the tickets were a hot commodity and sold out in minutes, but since Stella threw the dinner parties at Mimi's apartment, Rebecca always had a seat at the table. She had actually been hesitating about inviting Max, who tragically didn't seem as interested in food as he should be, but Mrs. Singh and Gabe's disapproval had pushed her over the edge. She would invite him! He was perfectly fine.

"The Lion's widow wants Rebecca to go to East End to discuss the estate and no one knows why," Gabe blurted. He avoided Rebecca's accusatory eyes.

"Yessss," Mrs. Singh said slowly. "I am aware. Perplexing." So Mrs. Singh already knew (how?) but had no helpful further information. "I have some extra vegan lasagna that I made last night. Right in the refrigerator. Please take and reheat for about sixty seconds."

Rebecca felt herself wavering but stayed strong. "Thank you but no," she said frostily. "I already had a donut." With that, resisting the lure of Mrs. Singh's homemade and obviously delicious vegan lasagna, she marched out of the kitchen, leaving Gabe and Mrs. Singh no doubt with their heads together, plotting. She sat down at her desk and texted Max to spite them.

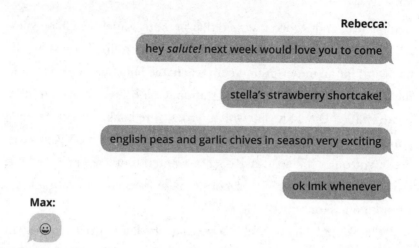

Granted, Max was a lazy texter, and that was good, right? He preferred FaceTime so they could see each other, he had once explained, which was kind of romantic. Emojis, unless used with a tinge of irony or the necessary heart/broken heart shorthand, were a pale substitute for writing. Max was a lawyer who had grown up outside Chicago; he got along with his parents and wore sneakily stylish glasses. Gabe's annoying resistance notwithstanding, Rebecca had high hopes that Max would continue to grow on her. Max was mature and good at explaining international law treaties. She had taught him how to use a semicolon on bar napkins with a Clinique Chubby Stick and that had been good drunk fun.

"Rebecca?" Chloe materialized so suddenly that Rebecca's phone clattered to her desk before she could grill her mother about why Rose Adams had summoned her to the town house. "Don't forget the marketing meeting. I sent the agenda on Blabber." She smiled. She knew full well that Rebecca had deleted Blabber, the interoffice communication tool that no one had asked for. Rebecca found it particularly offensive that a publishing company that prided itself on elevating language would welcome Blabber into its fold. Last she checked, "blabber" meant witless prattle. "I know what you need now." Chloe paused with significance, and Rebecca hoped that perhaps somehow Chloe knew why the Lion's widow had summoned her. After all, Chloe knew the password for an underground club reachable only by descending into the Twenty-Third Street subway station. Chloe knew how to authenticate vintage Dior. She knew that Crocs were back. "Ta-da!" Chloe pulled a paper bag from behind her back and placed it on Rebecca's desk. Not quite the answer Rebecca wanted, but she knew without looking that it was a piece of house-made focaccia, burrata added, from Eataly. Honestly, she loved Chloe.

"Thank you! Thank you!" Rebecca gushed, and stuck her nose in the bag, inhaling deeply enough to mask the enticing smell of Mrs. Singh's lasagna being reheated in the kitchen.

"I got your back, girl!" Chloe handed Rebecca a wad of napkins and tapped her enormous white plastic Swatch. "Ten minutes till go time. And here's your seltzer, duh!" Chloe, the only person who truly understood and cared for Rebecca, put a sweaty bottle of lemon seltzer on the desk like the angel she was and flitted away. Rebecca Venmoed her twenty dollars. Then she left a message for her mom, who was probably walking or reading in her blue chair with her phone annoyingly off.

Rebecca was almost on time for the marketing meeting, still clutching a napkin in one hand and her seltzer in the other. Chloe was already at the conference table. Ami entered, laptop in hand, with Richard, the managing editor. Everything Richard said sounded smart and sarcastic because he was British. His patience for Lady Paulette had worn dangerously thin and her wavering posh accent irked him beyond measure. He and Ami, usually quite collegial, circled each other warily on this book, and Rebecca, who had, in her opinion, suffered the most by her almost daily acquaintance with Lady Paulette, was left trying to please all three of them.

Ami's spindly assistant Greg, one foot already out the door on his way to graduate school, fiddled with the conference room's AV pad, trying to link up the giant monitor that dominated the entire back wall. After several fumbles (Greg) and a few high-pitched squeaks (the equipment), the squares of people calling in remotely sharpened into view. There was a mix of salespeople and assistants, mid-level marketing and publicity associates who were, for whatever reason, still working from home. Some had their cameras off, and Rebecca analyzed the choices. Not having your camera on immediately made you suspect. Were you answering work emails, thereby signaling your lack of commitment to this particular project (Rebecca's)? Were you sexting while your coworkers saw nothing but your awkward professional headshot? Were you folding laundry or eating an enchilada? There was the true story from Simon & Schuster early in the pandemic in which a clueless assistant had actually left her camera on as she began a nearly naked (and impressively acrobatic) yoga practice in full view of her slack-jawed and paralyzed colleagues. What about the blurred background people? What were they hiding? And then there were the people who had, from the very first day, simply never put their cameras on at all, their surroundings remaining completely, maddeningly mysterious. Rebecca admired these people most of all. She would have never dared, and instead welcomed her coworkers to what she hoped was the effortlessly attractive background of her bedroom bookcase, painstakingly staged for hours with input from Gabe and Stella regarding book titles, photographs, tasteful vases, and flattering light.

And how was it humanly possible that in the year 2022 people still didn't remember to unmute? Yet somehow, at every meeting, someone would forget to turn their microphone on. And that someone was usually Susan from Corporate Sales. Years in and Rebecca suspected that maybe Susan was performing some kind of experimental art piece.

When Rebecca joined from home, she kept her finger hovering anxiously over the unmute button in case someone asked her a question. It was stressful, yes, but didn't human beings adapt? Didn't they learn from their mistakes? And Rebecca had seen more cat buttholes than a person could bear. Cats rubbing their butts on the computer, their owners tsk-tsking in a "He's incorrigible!" singsong and everyone else shielding their eyes in horror while yet another cat butthole presented itself ON. A. WORK. CALL. Sometimes Ami logged on remotely while she was physically *at* the meeting, so that she was both virtual and present, a kind of time travel physics voodoo that freaked out Rebecca so much she almost preferred cat buttholes.

The thunk of Ami's laptop on the table signaled the start of the meeting, and Gabe began in his most full-throated movie trailer voice: "*The Lady and the Brain* offers a unique perspective on philosophy, love, and fame as seen by a woman who shared her life with the brilliant Chester Wineskin." He paused for emphasis and started again: "Or: Discover the insightful and thought-provoking musings of a renowned philosopher through the eyes of his droll lover in this season's must-read memoir, *The Lady and the Brain*. Think *A Brief History of Time* crossed with *The Saga of the Mitford Sisters*. If you liked *The Genius and the Goddess* about Arthur Miller and Marilyn Monroe . . ."

Lady Paulette would very much like the sound of being compared to Marilyn Monroe. She was probably more akin to a Mitford sister, and most likely a Nazi sympathizer one. Sadly, Chester Wineskin was dead and gone, so his lofty theories were being strained through the shallow celebrity gossip of an expat from Iowa with long legs, an iron will, and a shameless propensity to say "rubbish" at least once in every conversation. Lady Paulette treated Rebecca as she might a slightly dim-witted nanny: she could be trusted with the children but needed to be corrected, instructed, and expected at every turn to do tasks not agreed upon in the original contract.

Ami was laser focused on Gabe. "How much of the salon aspect will we stress? And I think her almost childlike grasp of his most complex doctrine will endear her to readers more fascinated by social mores than theoretics."

"Come for the ethics, stay for the aesthetics," Gabe enthused.

"Would love to do a tie-in with the Schopenhauer festival in Poland," someone said from the screen, and everyone ignored the comment. Lady Paulette would certainly not approve travel to Poland. Rebecca caught sight of Susan talking animatedly, silently. "Mother of God, woman, unmute yourself," Richard muttered under his breath, while Ami patiently pointed to her ear and Gabe yelled, "Susan! You're on mute!" Everyone was treated to the familiar sight of Susan's face looming into the foreground while she adjusted her glasses in order to find the unmute button. Her voice burst into the room, mid-sentence with no apology, no starting back at the beginning. Susan, that provocateur, that character from a lost Beckett play; the only certainty here was that she would remember to mute herself with emphasis after a diatribe about not forgetting about independent bookstores, and that she would begin the charade all over again at least once more. Rebecca was already exhausted. But she had to look perky so as not to give Ami any reason to doubt her ability to edit newly discovered work by the Lion. Perhaps she was not quite the obvious choice to handle his considerable and complex estate. But maybe she could establish herself and make Ami proud. She could make her mother proud.

"I said: Rebecca, would you take the lead when Lady Paulette joins the call?" Ami asked, apparently not for the first time.

"Of course!" Rebecca could make Ami proud right now. Granted, she would have to draw on every reserve of patience to balance standing firm in the face of Lady Paulette's ultimatums with coddling her enough so that she didn't hang up in a huff or, worse, weep into a handkerchief ostentatiously embroidered with Chester Wineskin's initials.

"Rebecca? Rebecca?" The plaintive yet pitiless voice of Lady Paulette, forged in the tornadoes of Iowa, honed in the regional theaters of Milwaukee, and refined in the graceful streets of Kensington, pierced the conference room. "Ah, there you are! How marvelous!" Not unlike Rebecca's own grandmother, Lady Paulette felt compelled to comment on the magic of technology during each video call. Though Mimi didn't say "And all the way across the pond!" every single time. Greg tentatively pushed another button on the AV pad, and Lady Paulette's face suddenly filled the entire screen.

"Hallo, hallo!" Lady Paulette was in an excellent mood, buoyed by having a larger audience than usual. She lifted a teacup from its saucer and took a reverberating slurp. "Cheers from all the way across the pond!"

"Good evening, Lady Paulette. Thank you for joining us and welcome stateside! I think you know everyone here? We're so excited to discuss our plans for *The Lady and the Brain*. I'm going to let Gabe Tatlock from Marketing take it away. You're in good hands," Rebecca said. The rest of the meeting passed with only one more unmuting routine from Susan, who inquired about how many copies they expected to sell during Lady Paulette's high tea reception at Liberty London; Gabe's unflagging enthusiasm as he outlined the specifics of how Avenue would transform Lady Paulette's story from that of a snob with a suspect genesis to that of a starry-eyed muse whose innocent-American-abroad take on the brilliant man was as resonant as his take on ethical procreation; and one brief, hideous moment when it appeared that Catherine—strike that—Katherine with a *K* would indeed present her ancient hindquarters to the group.

After debriefing with Gabe in the kitchen, Rebecca couldn't wait to get home after this strange day. She went to retrieve her bag, much lighter on Monday nights than it was on Monday mornings or Tuesday nights. It was her one time to leave her belongings freely scattered on the desk—the desk that would be hers all the livelong night. Even one incongruous cactus couldn't mar her mood.

CHAPTER TWO

MONDAY
HOME, REBECCA

After it became clear that the pandemic was not a two-week staycation inside her cozy Cobble Hill apartment with her roommates (one of whom was a paranoid germophobe who wore a face shield in their shared space, and the other an old high school acquaintance who acquired a lot of dubious medical "expertise" on the internet), Rebecca packed up and moved into her grandmother Mimi's rent-controlled apartment on the Upper West Side.

It was not at all weird that she had commandeered her father's childhood bedroom (all vestiges of him scrubbed and painted away), nor was it social suicide to live with an eighty-two-year-old who kept two pet budgies (Noodle and Pookie), and it was certainly not an issue that it had been over two years and Rebecca had made no serious effort to find her own place. She was saving a lot of money! She had her own "wing": a hallway, a full bath, and a bedroom flooded with natural light. Mimi was, considerately, hard of hearing. The kitchen had a full-size refrigerator. There was a separate dining room with a long table around which her friend Stella squeezed twelve happy people once a month for her supper club. There were original herringbone floors and crown molding. No matter that there was no central air, the lobby smelled of cabbage, and Tibor, the part-time doorman, never stopped talking. Rebecca had always been close to Mimi, but quarantine, in all its horror and beauty, had truly bonded them. It would be really hard to leave, but she must at some point. Before she turned thirty, definitely. Because living with your grandmother at thirty? Now, that might be a problem.

Rebecca knew she should call her mom again, but first there was the subway; the deli stop for tonic water, a lottery ticket, and kale (Mimi's list); Tibor's predictions for the NBA playoffs; and Mimi's daily 6 p.m. cocktail hour. Turning the key in the lock, turning another key in another lock, jolting the door against the chain that Mimi often forgot to undo, leaning on the doorbell long enough to enrage the Yorkshire terrier in the apartment across the way and to alert Mimi, Rebecca pushed away thoughts of the day. For now. Until she had an olive, a Ritz cracker with a thick slice of extra-sharp cheddar, a handful of lightly salted peanuts, and a few sips of Sapphire gin and tonic in a tiny etched glass, she would empty her mind. Mimi sorted out the chain lock and offered her soft, papery cheek for a kiss. "And how was your day, my darling? Come, come, I've put out provisions, but I'm misting the boys before dinner."

"Good! I'll tell you." Rebecca draped her sweater over the hat rack. "Just let me wash my hands and change." Once you had seen one bird bath, you had seen them all, and there was always the chance that Noodle, who had bonded with Mimi long before Rebecca had arrived and who disapproved of any other human, would bite her. Pookie was definitely the brighter bird and liked to perch on Rebecca's finger during their hour of supervised exercise. He had two words—"Hello, Pookie"—which was two more than Noodle did. All in all, Rebecca preferred the cage covered and the constant peeping silenced. Mimi had always had parakeets, always two budgies, always named Pookie and Noodle; some Noodles and Pookies lived a mere year or so; and the next Noodle or Pookie might live a decade. It was a flawed system whereby occasionally there were two Noodles or two Pookies in the cage at the same time, but Mimi seemed unbothered.

After Rebecca "freshened up," as Mimi called it, she joined her grandmother in the living room, where they had their cocktail hour, Rebecca on the uncomfortable, high-backed sofa and Mimi in her blue toile chair, its seat cushion worn shiny. Mimi Katz, daughter of a wealthy haberdasher, had married a poor medical student for love: Rebecca's grandfather, Nathan Blume. Rebecca had only snatches of memory of her grandfather, who sang "Wake Up Little Susie," and let her listen through the stethoscope that dangled out of his overcoat pocket. Mimi was still in mourning, Rebecca thought, twenty-five years later. Dr. Blume, as Mimi sometimes referred to him, had been known to enjoy a home-cooked meal, and although she had come to the marriage not knowing how to boil water (as she liked to say), she had modeled herself on Julia Child, also a tall lady who adored her husband and could manhandle a chicken into a perfect coq au vin.

It had done Mimi a world of good to have someone to cook for (she said it herself!), and in that way Rebecca was a generous, altruistic soul. These days Mimi was good for at least two meals a week. Stella had been working for a wealthy family on the Upper East Side, and her perks included a room that she crashed in whenever she wasn't staying with her boyfriend Miles and a crazy budget to grocery shop with when the family was in town. Stella came over to pick up Mimi's slack every Sunday. Mondays were the leftovers, and Rebecca filled in where she could, following Stella's recipes or ordering take-out Thai, because they were, after all, New Yorkers.

Rebecca lifted her tiny etched glass and made a "Cheers" motion at Mimi, who did the same. She had a blissful swallow of the stiff drink. (Mimi's mixology skills skewed heavy on the alcohol and light on the mixer, though her antique glasses meant that Rebecca would need to have at least four drinks before getting mildly drunk.) "I have to call Mom before dinner," Rebecca reminded herself out loud, tossing a few peanuts into her mouth and trying to relax against the stiff, awkward back of the couch.

"I'm heating up Stella's leftover white bean stew," Mimi declared. Stella was the only person who called Mimi "Grandma," and Mimi was the only person who allowed Stella to smoke her one cigarette a day on the narrow balcony outside Mimi's bedroom window. "Grandma, show me the view!" Stella would say after dinner while Rebecca rolled her eyes and did the dishes. They would disappear into Mimi's room, where Stella would grapple the window up, crawl out of it, and turn sideways to fit on the wrought iron slats while Mimi pulled up her ottoman and puffed daintily on the offered cigarette, blowing smoke out the window, and handing it half finished for Stella to toss into the empty planter, kept for this very purpose. Rebecca disapproved: Stella was trying to quit! Mimi had already quit! No one cared what Rebecca had to say on this topic, but she continued to register her disappointment every time.

"Do tell Jane hello for me, please." Mimi and her daughter-in-law got along extremely well in absentia, less well in proximity, but with age came acceptance: they had worn each other down to a slightly reluctant respect and real love. The crux of their issue, as Rebecca observed it, was her mother's exasperation that Mimi had "waited on the men in her life hand and foot," thereby creating a model and expectation that Jane herself had resented but not successfully resisted.

"Ami asked me to go over to Edward David Adams's town house to talk to his widow about possibly working with her on his estate," Rebecca announced. No use introducing the "curious" request from Mrs. Adams herself.

"She asked who, dear?" Rebecca couldn't tell if this question was due to Mimi's incredulity or her increasing deafness.

"Ami asked *me* to go over. You know the Lion just died, right?"

"That dreadful man. Very full of himself! I never cared for his books." Mimi gestured toward the living room bookcase. "Of course, we own them all. How old was he? Eighty-four, I believe?" Mimi rattled her ice in agitation, and Rebecca understood that she knew full well how old he was and was doing some unfavorable math. Luckily, the Lion was older, and by everyone's calculations Mimi had a few more years at least. No more cigarettes! One of Mimi's favorite darkly comic routines was to make Rebecca sit next to her on the terrible couch while she flipped through her address book, examining the names written in her distinctive script: "Dead. Dead. Dead. Dead to me! Dead. Dead. Dead to me!"

"Yes, he was really old," Rebecca assured her grandmother. "He never got out anymore. Hibernated in the Hamptons. Certainly not living a robust, fulfilling life hanging with millennials and becoming an Instagram star like some people." Stella featured Mimi in most of her livestreams, and Mimi's deadpan takes on cooking had been very well received. The broadcast where she explained (wearing a whole raw chicken on her upheld hand like an oven mitt) that when she first roasted a chicken for Dr. Blume, she didn't know there was a heart, neck, and gizzards crammed "up there" in plastic, which resulted in a visit from the fire department, had garnered thousands of delighted comments.

"I am a natural, Stella says." Mimi stabbed an olive with a toothpick and waved it theatrically.

"'Stella says, Stella says.'" Rebecca pretended to be jealous of the outsize influence her best friend had on Mimi, but she was thrilled that they loved each other, and she thought their partnership in the kitchen and on social media would lead to big things for Stella, whose charisma and talent Rebecca believed were destined to catapult her to fame. As for Mimi, if fisting a chicken and sucking the marrow out of lamb shank bones with the vigor of a vampire kept her young, that was a bonus.

She balanced the glasses on the empty cheese tray and headed into the kitchen. Even after two years, she still sent up a silent gratitude mantra for an actual separate kitchen instead of the dollhouse appliances that had lined the entrance wall in her Brooklyn apartment. She rinsed everything in the sink, then opened the fridge and admired the bouquets of Italian parsley, sealed container of SCOBY (Stella was on a fermenting kick), cartons of oat milk for her and half-and-half for Mimi, stacks of neatly labeled containers filled with chicken and fish and pre-chopped mirepoix, a few bottles of decent wine, a bottle of celebration champagne, a jumble of speckled eggs from the farmers market, fancy mustard, Mimi's probiotic yogurt, an amber jar of face cream, and a flame-orange Le Creuset Dutch oven (a wedding present and heirloom) that contained the rest of Stella's stew. Rebecca lifted it onto the counter along with the bag of kale for the budgies.

When she dug her phone out of her bag, she saw that Mrs. Singh had sent her an email with the heading "A Great Honor!" Was she referring to Rebecca's rapidly advancing career as posthumous editor to literary lions, the Lion in particular? She was not.

"Dear Rebecca," the email read. "You have been nominated to serve on the Desk Share Cooperative Community Group Committee. Please see below for more information on this exciting new opportunity!" She read on, recognizing parts of the attachment from Frank French's original announcement.

"In these evolving times, Leesen has reacted with nimble readjustment, bringing the hybrid work model to life. Of course, hot desking is new to all of us, and to help us improve its rollout we are forming a **COOPERATIVE COMMUNITY GROUP COMMITTEE** comprising representatives from all publishing divisions and departments. The committee will meet to process employee feedback from the Office

Life Inbox, and to update our desk sharing guidance with the goal of improving desk sharing practices for everyone. If you are receiving this email, congratulations on your nomination. We appreciate your dedication to helping Leesen maintain the efficiency and collaboration that has always imbued our company. —The Management"

Nominated, my ass, Rebecca thought. Scowling, she took her phone into her room and called her mom.

"Hello, sweetheart! I'm so glad you called. How was work? Did you send me a link to Avenue's spring catalog yet? Remember to mark all the books that you edited, please."

"Oh my god, okay, okay." Rebecca often regressed into a sullen teenager when faced with her mother's relentless barrage of inquiries and expectations. On her last trip back to Philadelphia, she was not proud of the fact she had actually stomped up the stairs and slammed the door to her childhood bedroom, now a combination home gym and storage closet. There was nowhere to sit but on her mom's Peloton.

"I hope you'll be able to come down for the boys' party. Ethan and Emma are renting a bouncy castle. Did you have the marketing meeting with Lady Paulette today?"

"What? Yes." How did she know about that? Rebecca hadn't said anything about it this morning, had she? It would not be beyond Jane to have a spy monitoring Rebecca at work, making sure that she asserted herself and didn't spill food on her shirt. Wait, did her mom have Gabe's number?

"I remember that you mentioned it was scheduled for today. And now that you go in so rarely . . ." Jane disapproved of the new hybrid office plan; she made it clear that, when Rebecca was working from home, she imagined her in pajamas or idly thumbing through *Cook's Illustrated* in the bathtub. Well, the joke was on her, because Rebecca didn't own pajamas. She slept in oversize concert and sports T-shirts she had "borrowed" from her brothers over the years.

The smell of reheated white bean stew and the distant clatter of Mimi setting the table reminded Rebecca to get to the point. "Mom, the craziest thing happened today. You know that Edward David Adams died, right? Well, Ami called me in and said that his widow, Rose Adams, asked for me to meet with her to discuss his estate. I mean, it's a huge deal; he died without an agent, so the whole thing is a big free-for-all. And get this: she said there might be unpublished stories."

There was a long, uncharacteristic silence on Jane's end.

"I know you used to work at the magazine, right? The *East River Review*?"

"Briefly." Rebecca could hear the unmistakable sound of her mother slamming the dishwasher shut, the little beeps of her turning it on.

"So can you think of any reason she would ask for me? I mean, strange, right? Did you know Rose Adams?"

"Fergus! Get out of there!" There was some scuffling; obviously Fergus was underfoot, as always. "This dog is on his last legs, I'm telling you! If it weren't for your father, I'd take him to the vet tomorrow."

"Mom, stop trying to murder Fergus. Why are you being so weird?"

"I don't like your tone, Rebecca. Did it ever occur to you that you're an excellent editor? Is it inconceivable that your reputation might be the reason you were requested?"

It was pretty much inconceivable. Rebecca appreciated her mother's faith while chafing under the pressure. "I feel like you're not telling me something. *Did* you know Rose Adams?"

"Rebecca. We can talk about this later. It's dinnertime. Your father can't find the ketchup because he is apparently incapable of moving a single thing in the refrigerator. My lord, Sam, you're helpless!"

Rebecca heard her father's rumble and could imagine him staring haplessly into the fridge, waiting for her mother to elbow him aside and triumphantly retrieve the ketchup. "Wait! Is there something you're not telling me? Mom!"

"Goodbye, sweetheart—see you at the boys' party. Give our love to Mimi." There was a decisive silence, and Rebecca, stunned, had the sudden realization that her mother rarely (never?) hung up first when they were on the phone. What the fuckety fuck was going on? She texted Stella.

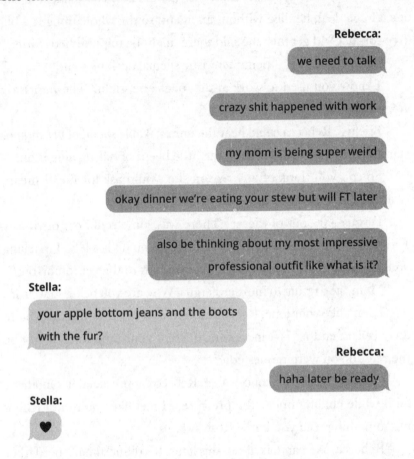

Rebecca checked her email once more and impulsively pulled up the instructions for posting on the Office Life Inbox. She needed a screen name. Was "Bartleby" too obvious? He was the OG passive resister of the corporate grind. Had they tried to extinguish her humanity by forcing her to share a desk? Kind of. Hold on. Using a clever literary reference was exactly what they would expect Rebecca to do.

She remembered all the unfortunate terms Frank French had thrown around in his memo: "What is Hot Desking?" What indeed. There were two comments already. Rebecca's would be the third.

Rebecca googled, typed quickly, and—without even editing—pressed "send."

OFFICE LIFE INBOX:

AGIRLHASNODESK:

Where do we find the End Cap Shelf Replacement Request Form?

paul:

why all the higher ups have dedicated desk :/

HOT DESK:

"reach for the stars, even if you have to stand on a cactus" —unknown

Rebecca closed her computer with satisfaction. But the moment was short-lived. *Was* Jane involved somehow with Rose Adams? How could it be that the biggest break of her literary career was a mystery possibly involving her mother? Rebecca thought of the manuscripts she had to read through for work. Everyone knew she did not care for mysteries.

CHAPTER THREE

WEDNESDAY
WORK, BEN

Ben could not be happier. After five years that included online graduate school, bartending gigs, coaching high school basketball, working in that lonely bookstore in Burlington, and a recent stint as an assistant at Champlain Press, a local Vermont publisher that specialized in environmental books, he was finally starting a real job in a real city. Hawk Mills had an efficient desk sharing setup. He'd never thought of himself as a corporate tool, as his younger sister, Ava, had accused him of being, but the emails from the CEO, Frank French, made him feel part of something important. Champlain Press was run by an ex-hippie who made it big investing early in Ben & Jerry's, but that noble, chaotic passion project was light-years away from the professional vibe at Hawk Mills. He had a few new button-down shirts from J.Crew and some excellent boots from Varvatos that probably cost more than anything he had ever owned. Growing up in Vermont, going to school in Vermont (public high school and UVM, then an MA at Dartmouth that might as well have been in Vermont), Ben was ready to get his new life started.

When he was first offered the editor job, the salary had sounded low but, if he was careful, manageable. Then this morning he had checked his bank balance after a week of orientation and a week of hybrid work and after taxes and rent and health care insurance and paying for insanely good Thai takeout every night, Ben was in shock at the meager amount he had left from his first paycheck. There was a bar, Betty Jack's, on the same block as his apartment, and Ben had already clocked the "Help Wanted" sign. With his experience (he had basically written his senior thesis during the lull before the college student rush at What Ales You in Burlington), he figured he could pick up some shifts and at least pay to keep the electricity on.

Last week Ben had left his desk spotless, smelling faintly of lemon disinfectant. So when he pulled out his XL Hydro Flask, his only desk accessory, he was surprised to see a cactus. Ben looked around but, yeah, this was definitely his desk. Bizarrely, there was a smear of what, on closer inspection, looked to be olive oil. Ben sat down in the desk chair, pulling his laptop from his bag. There was something small and hard in the seat. Ben retrieved what could have been an actual pellet of rat dropping. What did he know? He was from Vermont, but city rats were a whole other breed, strolling casually down the streets, owning the fucking place.

It was a chocolate-covered almond. What the hell? He was okay with the cactus, though it was a questionable choice in terms of bringing good vibes to the shared workspace. But either Rebecca Blume, his deskmate, hadn't read the memo (not to be a nerd, but there were rules, right?) or she was kind of inconsiderate. The email had explicitly said: "All desk sharing partners are expected to abide by the Clean Desk Policy, which requires you to leave your desk surface clean, wiped down, and ready for use by your desk sharing partner at the end of each day. If you have concerns about desk hygiene, please discuss them with your desk sharing partner." Did he have concerns about Rebecca Blume's desk hygiene? He did a little, but while communication was clearly encouraged by the Clean Desk Policy, Rebecca had not yet emailed him, and she was the one with the seniority, while Ben was brand-new. But he would get over it, because he was just glad to be at Hawk Mills, about to do what he loved: read manuscripts, edit amazing authors, bring new books into the world.

He moved the cactus to the back of his desk and noticed a Post-it attached to its plastic pot. "**WHAT IS THIS ABOUT?**" was written on it in black pen. Had the note come with the cactus? Was the note to do with something else altogether, stuck to the cactus and forgotten? Was the note some kind of existential query? The Post-it couldn't be for him, could it? Why would she (he assumed that, since it was Rebecca's cactus, it was Rebecca's Post-it) leave him a note when she hadn't bothered to email him?

"Dude! Good morning!" Josh Howard ("Call me Howie!") came out of nowhere with the same complicated bro shake he had tried to teach Ben unsuccessfully last week. Howie was an intern assigned to help Ben get acclimated. Howie smelled like smoke, had dark circles under his eyes, was wearing the same shapeless red sweater every time Ben had seen him, and, according to his résumé, which Ben found on LinkedIn, had graduated summa cum laude from Harvard and spent a few years "kickin' it" in Nepal. Ben had to admire the balls it took to write "kickin' it" on your résumé. Howie was "couch surfing," "dating an actress," but it was "chill," and he was "doing the thing until grad school next year." Howie's plan involved a PhD in the philosophy of language, and Ben already knew more about Howie's past, present, and future than he did about most of his oldest, closest friends. Ben was giving him the benefit of the doubt. He and Howie *had* had a seriously deep conversation about the brilliance of Cormac McCarthy's *All the Pretty Horses* and the disappointment they both endured when the next two books of the trilogy did not measure up.

"Hashtag Girlboss said to remind you about the meeting at eleven," Howie announced. Ben didn't think it was okay to call the middle-aged editorial director of Hawk Mills, Caro Nowak, "Hashtag Girlboss," but he wasn't exactly sure how to best convey that to Howie. He made a mental note to put a stop to it as soon as he figured out exactly when and where he was supposed to be giving Howie formal feedback.

"Sure. I have to return a call from an agent about this linked collection of short stories; the writer's a former Google exec and they're set in the future where algorithms determine everything. I think it sounds cool—a cross between Jennifer Egan and George Saunders, maybe."

"Short stories are a hard sell, man." Howie shook his head.

"But kind of making a comeback," Ben replied. "And they're linked. You know, connected?" Were short stories, linked or otherwise, a hard sell? Should he trust his instincts or defer to Howie, who was wearing plastic slides and sweat socks?

"But also kind of a hard sell. Like, you have to already be famous and at least 60 percent of the collection has to have already been published in *The New Yorker*."

"I'm not sure that's completely accurate."

"It's pretty accurate."

"Lorrie Moore. Walter Mosley. Ben Lerner. Emma Cline. All with new collections."

"You do you, man!" Howie put his palms up and made a great show of backing down. "You've been introduced to the phone pods?" Howie was quick to move on, which Ben recognized as a positive trait. He looked at the row of phone pods, someone's idea of making phone booths futuristic and moving them indoors. They looked like spaceship capsules. "Yeah, beam me up, Scotty," Ben found himself saying.

"You know, that's a misquote. It's never been said in any of the television episodes or films. I mean, Kirk says, 'Scotty, beam us up,' and 'Mr. Scott, beam us up,' but that's it."

Ben's *Star Trek* trivia knowledge began and ended with what was, according to Howie, a near miss.

"Also, Darth Vader never said 'Luke, I am your father.'"

"Oh yeah?" Ben was not a *Star Trek* guy. He was not a *Star Wars* guy. He just wanted to make a phone call. And maybe work with the next Raymond Carver.

"Think how the relationship between meaning and truth is related to both reality and perceived reality. Like, what's more real, what everybody thinks Kirk says, or what he actually says?"

"Right." Ben looked around for something to wipe the olive oil off the desk so he could plug his laptop into the monitor. He opened one of the desk drawers, fished out a packet of neon (?) Post-its, a few napkins, one of which was definitely used (lip gloss?), and a black pen. He wiped off the desk and threw the napkins into the recycle bin. How hard was that?

"Okay, so eleven a.m. Good luck with your call. To boldly go where no man, etc., etc." Howie headed to the elevator, miming sucking on a vape pen.

On his way to the phone pod, Ben was waved over by Mrs. Singh, the head of Human Resources at Leesen, who had been incredibly nice to him during orientation while trying to explain the difference between in-network and out-of-network medical plans. Ben had selected the absolute cheapest, which probably meant he was covered if he was hit by a bus (honestly, more of a possibility than he had anticipated), but everything else was coming out of his pocket. He thought again about picking up some shifts at the bar in his neighborhood. "Anytime you want a cup of tea," Mrs. Singh promised him, "I can brew you loose leaf. You don't have to drink that Lipton."

Ben was a coffee drinker but didn't like to say no to Mrs. Singh, who reminded him of his favorite aunt. Last week he had eaten about four free breakfast burritos each morning, but this week there were only some picked-over donuts, and he did much better on protein than pure sugar and carbs. He wondered what that meant for the future of those afternoon platters of cheese and salami and if he should save some money by not eating lunch and making up for it later or if there were to be no platters of cheese and salami and he would starve to death.

After his phone call with the agent, Ben checked his email. He scrolled back through Frank French's communications about the desk sharing policies and pulled up his moving tribute to Edward David Adams, a.k.a. the Lion, a.k.a. the very reason why Ben was here at Hawk Mills. He clicked the link to the Lion's obituary and read it for maybe the fourth time. He lingered on the photos, his favorite the one from when the Lion was a young man, patrician and windswept, more like a famous actor than one of the greatest writers who had ever lived. There he was in Sweden with his beautiful third wife, maybe twenty years younger than he was, accepting a Nobel Prize in Literature. There he was with Warhol at the Factory. There he was, posed at his massive desk, the famous book jacket photo where his dark-eyed charisma burned off the page, his elbows resting on a pile of his rivals' books, a smoking pipe held lightly in his large hand. With a surge of nostalgia, Ben focused on a photo from ten years ago, the Lion before he had retreated to the Hamptons in the final stages of his illness, when he was aged but still powerful. At the time, Ben was sixteen years old, a sophomore in high school, playing basketball, reading the books his mother gave him, but restless, not seeing a way out for himself. In this photo, and Ben remembered it well because he had been there watching, the Lion posed with some of the other writers at the Bread Loaf Writers' Conference, and the pull of his magnetism tipped everyone toward him.

Every August, when the famous writers and workshop students gathered for two weeks in the mountains of Vermont, there were readings open to the public. Ben's mom, Jeanie, an English teacher at his local high school, and his dad, Doug, a general contractor at Green Mountains Construction, had dropped him off up the hill. (He didn't remember where they went, or why his mom hadn't come too, just that he was thrilled and nervous to be alone with all the writers, who didn't seem to know that he didn't belong there.) He wandered among the soft yellow buildings and green Adirondack chairs, making his way with the flow of people toward a big barn that Middlebury College had converted into a space with high ceilings, a snack bar, and places to read, write, and hang out. He had been on the Bread Loaf campus once before, in the winter, when it was deserted, with a group of older kids, and they had broken into the barn to drink beer, but it was freezing and felt haunted, so they'd left pretty quickly.

It was a different place in the summer, filled with people talking animatedly, laughing, carrying around books. Ben didn't even remember who else was reading their work that night, just that everyone was confident and straightforward when there were stories and poems about sex or violence or just beautiful, vivid ways of seeing the most normal things. It was almost fully dark when the Lion got up to read, and there were strings of white lights twinkling in the barn rafters, and bright stars in the sky Ben could see through the windows. The way the Lion lowered his massive head before he started and the room fell absolutely silent; even the clinking of glasses ceased. The way his voice hypnotized, seduced, held the big space, owned it. Ben couldn't remember exactly what the Lion had read; he had searched for it in every collection afterward. Maybe it had never been published? But he remembered distinctly how the experience had cracked him open, how the story—something about a man, a girl, a horse, a misunderstanding that led to tragedy—made him cry, and all around him in the dark he could hear people sniffling too, and when the last word of the story was uttered, there was a long, heavy pause that seemed to contain everything in the world to Ben, and then there was thunderous applause, people standing, the Lion raising his hand in acknowledgment before stepping into the throngs of admirers and camera flashes.

Ben still didn't know how he got the nerve, but he made his way up to the great man and shook his hand. There was a brief moment when the Lion had really seen him, maybe noticed how young he was—though he was already tall for his age—how enraptured, and he had clasped Ben's shoulder before being pulled away. After that, Ben read everything the Lion wrote, and then every interview, profile piece, every book by adjacent writers, and then branched out even more, read younger writers, all genres. He got a job working summers at the Bread Loaf School of English, hauling kegs to the parties, setting up chairs for the performances, working among the young English teachers and the professors, and then attending the Bread Loaf Writers' Conference at the end of the summer, working as a waiter but encouraged to sit in on workshops and lectures.

It was the summer before his senior year in college, where he was majoring in English and warming the bench for the Division 1 Catamounts basketball team, that he first heard agents and editors and publishers talk about how they worked with writers and thought that was something he could do. But he wasn't done with school yet—he got his master's degree in English lit (hardly setting foot on campus since they had moved all classes online during the pandemic), and his thesis was on the Lion himself, focusing on how his work filtered the autobiographical tradition through the lens of postmodern fiction, with a close look at his most famous novel, *The Coldest War*, a biting satire of marriage. Ben couldn't believe the Lion had died. Sure, he was old; he was sick. It's not that it was unexpected; it was just that the world felt smaller without him in it, as if something Ben would never be a part of had ended for good.

Ben closed out his emails, feeling melancholy. At least he was here, at Hawk Mills (he had tried to get a job at the Lion's longtime publisher, PK—he had heard Maury Kantor speak at Bread Loaf about his relationship with the Lion—but they seemed to be downsizing instead of hiring), and Hawk Mills was committed to publishing the kind of fiction Ben liked best. He was rereading the agent's cover letter for the Google exec's short story collection (cleverly described as a "novel in stories") when Howie pinged him on Blabber.

HOWIE:
hashtag girlboss invited you to stop by kick the tires you know

BEN:
you kick the tires before you buy the car

HOWIE:
never got my license

BEN:
Caro asked you to ask me if I would stop by her office?

HOWIE:
affirmative

BEN:
before or after the meeting?

HOWIE:
. . . .

Ben looked up and caught Howie's eye across the room. He gave Ben two enthusiastic thumbs-up, then disappeared from view. Howie was not making things much easier for Ben. He had met Caro only twice before: once when he was interviewing for the job online, and once during orientation last week when she stopped by the conference room where he and two other "newbies," as the leader kept calling them, were role-playing scenarios to determine conflicts of interest. (It turns out accepting tickets to a Yankees game in exchange for hiring a particular paper vendor was, surprise, a conflict of interest. No issue for Ben, obviously a Red Sox fan.) He had seen Caro briefly last week but hadn't been to her office yet. Ben thought it would be strange to have an office—politically controversial maybe, since there was a clear dividing line in the hierarchy (his sister, Ava, would say the private office dwellers reinforced an oppressive class system), and also it would be a little lonely in an office; the open floor was buzzing and much more interactive. He walked to Caro's half-closed door and knocked. "Hey, good morning, it's Ben. You wanted to see me?"

"Ben—come on in. I wanted to hear how your second week was going. How are you settling in? Is Josh helping you to get squared away?" It took Ben a minute before he remembered that Josh was Howie. He gave Howie a positive review because it seemed like the decent thing to do. Caro didn't ask him to sit down, but he didn't want to loom awkwardly over her, so he took a seat. She was probably about his mom's age, but while his mom was open-faced and affectionate, always wearing a fleece vest and either Birkenstocks or Sorels, Caro was draped in layers of matching beige silks—a top, a top over that top, a scarf, a jacket, flowing pants—and very pointy brown boots. Her face was unreadable, her hair a sleek gray helmet, and her tone clipped. On the wall behind her was a photo of Caro with Toni Morrison and one of her arm in arm with Elizabeth Warren. Ben was startled to see a large coffee mug on her desk emblazoned with the phrase #GIRLBOSS. "I'm glad to have you here at Hawk Mills. I hope you're finding the desk sharing initiative tenable. Did you find orientation helpful?"

"It's all been good," Ben said. "Everyone has been great. I'm already getting submissions, and I'm interested in a linked short story collection."

"I look forward to hearing about it. Short story collections are having a bit of a moment."

"That's what I thought." *Suck it, Howie,* was what Ben actually thought.

"Wonderful. I'll see you at the meeting." Caro had clearly dismissed him, so Ben hauled himself up and headed back to his desk, accepting a freshly brewed cup of tea from Mrs. Singh on the way. He was a tea drinker now.

Ben got to the 11 a.m. meeting early. Caro's assistant was efficiently moving equipment and setting up the huge screen that dominated the entire back wall. Did he have time to scour the kitchen for leftover donuts? Before he could decide, Howie ambled in, offering a bagel slathered with cream cheese. "Dude, I took a guess that you were a sesame man with a schmear. Am I right?"

Ben was a sesame man with peanut butter on the side, but who was he to complain? "Thank you. I really appreciate it."

"Aww, you looked hungry."

"I did?" Ben took the bagel gratefully, but also, did he look hungry?

"You have a hungry look about you. Hungry like the wolf." Howie, Ben noticed, always said at least one thing too many.

"Anyway, thank you," Ben said hastily, before Howie could howl like the wolf. He took big bites to finish it before Caro showed up. Someone who wore that much silk probably did not want cream cheese oozing anywhere near her. Caro's assistant came back in and pushed a button on the pad. It was sweet to be on this side of the big screen after calling in from his apartment for meetings on Monday and Tuesday. People's squares started blinking on, and Caro and a few others he hadn't met or met in passing came in and sat down.

Caro sat at the head of the table, working on her computer until exactly 11 a.m. Then she looked up and got right to it with a brisk welcome. Ben admired her control of the room and her efficient point guard energy. She continued: "I'm sure you've all heard about Edward David Adams's estate. I'd like to talk about the incredible opportunity it presents for Hawk Mills."

Ben had not heard about the Lion's estate except for a mention at the end of the *New York Times* obituary that the Lion didn't have an agent, having conducted all his business "in a gentlemanly agreement" with Maury Kantor.

"We want to go all out to get the whole shebang," Caro continued. "I'm sure Ami Ito at Avenue will have her best people on it, not to mention competition from every other publishing house, but I'm confident Hawk Mills can get there first and bring it in. I'm counting on it."

"We're going to need a robust plan to demonstrate how we can preserve the Lion's legacy while also introducing him to new generations of readers in an appropriate way," said Ty, a senior editor. "Any ideas on that are welcome."

Ben listened intently. If they needed an editor to get in there, he was the obvious choice. Well, okay, not the *obvious* choice, being that he was brand-new to the job and twenty-six years old, but did anyone else here write a thesis on the Lion? Did anyone else here have a life-changing encounter with the man? And, Ben thought triumphantly, did anyone else have the trump card that was Atticus Adams?

"Unmute, Susan, unmute!" Caro snapped with such vehemence that Ben felt badly for poor Susan, who was fumbling at her computer, mouth still moving. It was a mistake anyone could make. On the days he worked from home, Ben called in from the kitchen/dining room area of his apartment, separated from the living/foyer area of his apartment by a few feet and one old couch he had driven down from Vermont in a rented truck with his dog, Butch, and sister, Ava, a junior at NYU. He would continue to keep his camera off, even though he thought it was kind of suspect when other people did it, until he painted the place and hung something on the walls. This weekend he would buy some paint.

After a half-heard point from poor Susan in Sales, and Caro's intriguing comment that there were rumored to be unpublished short stories and definitely some journals and letters involved, Ben interjected quickly. "I'd be really interested in helping. Especially if it's true that he was working on something. Or if there was older work. I know that he was writing every day, even toward the end."

Caro gave him a cool but interested look. "Go on," she said.

"I wrote my thesis on the Lion, and when I was working on it, I reached out to him. He was sick at that point, but I kept writing to him, and I communicated pretty regularly with his son, Atticus, who was really helpful." Ben did not add that the one time he had come to New York City to meet up with Atticus, they stayed out until 4 a.m., having been booted from a bar when Atticus did lines of coke on a framed photo of Muhammad Ali he had knocked down from the wall, and that Ben half carried Atticus to the famous East End town house before walking four miles on mostly deserted streets back to Ava's dorm at NYU.

"Do you think we could leverage your relationship with the Lion's son to give us an advantage? Your connection to Atticus Adams could be the emotional dimension we need to bring in the business. He could be a direct line to Rose Adams, and we should pursue every angle."

"I'm sure that he'll meet with me." Ben was mostly sure. Atticus was a prolific drunk texter and had more than once woken Ben from a deep sleep and engaged him in a late-night back and forth, but he'd texted Atticus after the Lion died and hadn't heard back yet. Ben hastened to add, "Meet with Hawk Mills," because he was a team player. "And I'd really like a chance to look at any new work. It would mean a lot to me." He didn't dare add that he wanted to edit it. But he did. He knew he could edit the fuck out of whatever the Lion had left behind even without the man himself there. He could almost feel that heavy hand on his sixteen-year-old shoulder. It was all coming full circle. And it was only his second week on the job.

Caro and Carlotta from Marketing exchanged a glance but Ben didn't know anyone well enough yet to decode it. "I like your confidence, Ben," Caro said. "Ty and I will contact Rose Adams, and you let me know what you hear from Atticus. Let's keep talking."

After the meeting, Howie followed Ben to the kitchen, where there was not a crumb left of the donuts. "Dude, I like your style!" Howie enthused while Ben refilled his water bottle. "High five! Don't leave me hanging!" Ben slapped Howie's outstretched palm quickly, hoping no one would come in while he was acting more like an assistant basketball coach than the editor of the Lion's posthumous work.

"Yeah, he's the reason I wanted to be an editor." Ben began to tell Howie the story but thought better of it when Howie took three eggs out of the fridge and started to juggle them.

"Your face, man!" Howie laughed. "They're hard-boiled!" One of the eggs fell to the floor and cracked. "Shit," Howie said, not nearly abashed enough. "Two eggs is enough for"—he squinted at the initials that someone had written on the eggs—"P.L. I'm guessing Paul from Production, and that guy should be watching his cholesterol . . ." He was tossing the cracked egg into the sink when Mrs. Singh came into the kitchen.

"Josh, have you compiled all the evaluations from the other interns?"

"Absolutely. Did it this morning when you first mentioned it," Howie answered smoothly. Then he left the kitchen, moving quickly toward his desk.

Ben smiled at Mrs. Singh, tempted to tell her the good news about his big chance to edit the Lion.

"I have lasagna that I am just heating up. Maybe you're hungry?" Mrs. Singh pulled out a half pan of lasagna. There *was* a lot of it.

"If you're sure?" Jesus, did he really look hungry like the wolf?

"Sit, sit!" Mrs. Singh bustled around, spooning the lasagna onto plates and into the microwave. "It's vegan but, shhhhhh, you will not even be able to tell."

"My sister, Ava, was vegan for a while." Ben sat at the little table, his knees bumping against the top. "Then she was vegan-ish but with fish. Seagan? Now I guess she eats what she wants but no meat."

"A very smart young lady," approved Mrs. Singh. They sat to eat the lasagna. It was delicious, and Ben would never, as promised, guess it was vegan. The secret, apparently, was red lentils. "Ben, I am hoping you would consider serving on the Desk Share Cooperative Community Group Committee. It's an important, democratic way to hear feedback and make improvements, and you would meet colleagues."

"I'd be honored," Ben said, really the only thing he could say as he forked in another bite of lasagna.

"I am so pleased!" Mrs. Singh clapped her hands. "I'll email you the information, and you will be able to begin assessing comments, pros and cons. Then I'll schedule a meeting."

By the end of the day, Ben was almost as tired as after a half-court pickup game. He was packing away his water bottle and wiping the desk down with disinfectant wipes (because, again, *he* had read the Clean Desk Policy, which recommended sanitizing *every* night) when he stepped on another chocolate-covered almond that had rolled under his chair. It wedged in the treads of his new boot. "For fuck's sake," he muttered. He patted around under the desk and found another one. The mysterious "**WHAT IS THIS ABOUT?**" Post-it stuck on Rebecca Blume's cactus caught his eye. He pulled it off, crumpled it, and tossed it in the trash, then was immediately filled with remorse. What if it was a reminder about something important? He still wanted to be a good desk partner. Ben opened the drawer and peeled off a neon (?) Post-it. The green wasn't too bad. "*WHAT IS THIS ABOUT?*"

he wrote with a Sharpie that he fished out of his bag and stuck the note back on the cactus. Then, because he wasn't a pushover, he wrote on another Post-it (pink this time) and put it in the corner of his desk under the chocolate-covered almond that was not smashed up in the sole of his boot. Caro liked his confidence. He was going to text Atticus and nail down a meeting to discuss the Lion's estate. He was kicking ass at Hawk Mills. Errant candy, random Post-its, and an unsanctioned cactus wouldn't stand in the way of his success. Rebecca Blume would get that message on Monday, he hoped, loud and clear.

CHAPTER FOUR

WEDNESDAY
HOME, BEN

Coming out of the subway on the Lower East Side, Ben walked the three blocks toward his apartment, breathing in the fresh air of early evening, feeling spring had fully arrived. He had wondered whether he would feel overwhelmed by the move to New York City, but so far, he felt only energized, alive. It was some kind of sign that Caro had brought up the Lion today and had said she liked Ben's confidence; he was going to grab the chance to get involved with the Lion's estate, to continue what he had started in grad school—no, what had started that night at Bread Loaf when he was just sixteen. He would reach out to Atticus again tonight.

Ben slowed down at his corner and was relieved to see the "Help Wanted" sign still up on the propped-open door of Betty Jack's, and when he peered in, there were a few people sitting at the bar, a couple kissing in a red pleather booth, and some men playing pool. Every time he passed by, at any time of day or night, there were people inside, a good sign for a bartender. There was a jukebox, a small TV always turned silently to off-brand sports—darts, billiards, greyhound racing. Ben imagined himself already hired and changing the station to the NBA playoffs. There was an old woman behind the bar moving a bar mop vigorously around the surface. She had a purple-tinged blond beehive and muscular forearms and was wearing a calico housedress and matching apron. Ben stepped into the bar and breathed in deeply to enjoy the familiar sour fermented smell. A Patsy Cline song was playing softly, and he heard the clack and thud of pool balls. He moved forward with his hand outstretched. "Hello? I'm Ben Heath, and I'm interested in bartending on the weekends, maybe once or twice during the week."

The old lady ignored his hand and nodded. "I've seen you walking by. Got your big dog."

"Yes." Ben shifted his messenger bag. "I've worked in bars the past six years or so."

"Can you make a pomegranate cosmopolitan?"

"Sure." Ben looked around and caught the eye of an old man in a dirty white bucket hat slumped over his bottle of Miller Lite. The man revived, gave Ben a surprisingly crisp salute, and shook a near empty bowl of pretzels in the old woman's direction.

"Then you're overqualified," she cackled. "And hired! And your big dog is an emotional support dog."

"Butch? No, he's a rescue from—"

"He's an emotional support dog, and if the Department of Health asks, he waits outside on the patio while you work." She gestured to an open door toward the rear of the bar, where Ben could see a small square of dirt, a few weeds, and a carpet of cigarette butts. "Boris passed last month, and I can't bring myself to get another one. It's good to have a dog in the place. A little backup." She reached behind the bar and drew out a wooden baseball bat, cradling the barrel end in her palm. "You aren't afraid to use this?"

"Is there much need to use it?" Ben's height usually deterred assholes from trying anything, but this was New York City, and he wasn't sure how much good a baseball bat would do against a gun.

"Chases away the junkies. And the grabbers. And the geezers who don't pay their tabs." She shook the bat menacingly toward the old man, who ignored her. "Anything else I got covered elseways." She gave Ben a significant look without explaining the significance. "You like old people?"

"I do." Ben did. Old people in bars talked a lot, and Ben always loved hearing their stories and making them happy by agreeing vaguely to meet their granddaughters or nieces.

"You start Saturday. Be here by three to fill out the paperwork."

"Okay! It was nice to meet you . . . um . . ."

"Call me Betty Jack," Betty Jack said. "See you Saturday, and bring your dog."

His fifth-floor walk-up rental was basically ten flights of climbing, and even though Ben was in basketball shape, he was still sucking air by the third floor. The third floor was home to an old lady in a bathrobe who had her door open every time she heard him coming by: "Well, aren't *you* a tall drink of water?" Fine, no harm done, but then he had to take his pit bull mix, Butch—a rescue who had come all the way from Alabama with that name, and he answered to it, so there was nothing to be done about it (Ben had tried)—down and back up, and there she was: "Well, aren't *you* a tall drink of water?" While Ben was at work, his sister, Ava, walked Butch, and she reported no sign of life whatsoever on the third floor.

Ben took the stairs to his apartment as quickly as he could and was halfway to the fourth floor before the old lady finished her refrain. In terms of working at Betty Jack's, he would have plenty of time to play in the Saturday morning pickup game, shower, and get to the bar. Perfect. He reached his door, panting, and bent over his knees for a minute to catch his breath. As he fumbled with the key, he heard Butch's low, rumbling half bark and the sweet tone Ava used with Butch and Butch only.

"Hey, hey!" He hung his bag on its hook and triple-locked the door behind him. "Nobody get up or anything. You know he's not supposed to be on the couch."

Ava, wearing a semitransparent white slip, brightly flowered kimono, heavy boots, and Ben's socks, was sprawled on the big couch, with all seventy-five pounds of Butch sitting on top of her. "Technically he's not on the couch."

"Seriously. He has his own chair."

"He wanted to snuggle! Butch, Ben's home! Go say hi to your dad." She gave Butch a little push, then a shove. He gave her sad whale eyes, heaved himself off the couch, and lumbered over to Ben. Butch, age and provenance undetermined, was a fine Southern gentleman with a noble block head and a laconic disposition. Ben had been worried about his getting enough exercise in the city, but going up and down the stairs three times a day was more than enough for Butch, who spent most of his time in his chair gazing with calm concentration out the window. "We went to the dog park today but Butch does not give one single fuck about other dogs. And he was misgendered by the lesbians again."

"Well, technically, he is ball-less," Ben pointed out. "I don't think he minded."

"How many times do I have to tell you that biology is not destiny? Jesus."

Ben ignored her as Butch leaned his massive head against him, which was his way of hugging, and Ben pulled gently on his soft black ears. "Why don't you make some friends, Butch?"

"He's above it. He knows there's no dignity in all that sniffing and bounding." Ava roused herself to a seated position and brushed dog hairs from her kimono. "Doug and Jeanie want you to check in."

"Just call them 'Mom and Dad' like a normal person. Guess what? I got a job at Betty Jack's on my way home. Basically because they want Butch to be the muscle."

"That dive? With the fierce old lady? Amazing!"

"And—and this is the big news—today at work we were talking about the Lion's estate, and there's a good possibility Hawk Mills could start publishing him. I might have a chance to see what he left behind—"

"You told them you knew that dick Atticus?"

"Yeah, of course. That might get me in the door, sure. But after that, if the Lion has unpublished work, you know, maybe I could edit it, assemble a collection, just get involved."

Ava gave a theatrical sigh. "The Lion? Come on. That guy is your blind spot, B. I know you had your moment together, but I would love for you to explain to me how he's any better than Bellow, Roth, Updike, Mailer. I know you're not out here championing them. Who's next, Kipling? Bring back Ezra Pound?"

"He's better because his writing is better," Ben said tersely. It was true: he had no strong feelings about letting go of most of them. Philip Roth was a genius but, as Ava said, admittedly problematic. He could live without Roth. The Lion was on another level. It had been a while, but Ben used to copy his favorite passages from the Lion's books just to shape the words himself, and he used to read them out loud just to hear the muscular, crystalline prose.

"Well, good luck with that." Ava rose from the couch and started loading things back into her fringed suede messenger bag: hairbrush, phone, water bottle, clementine, book, journal, pen, baggie of cashews, ticket stubs from the Film Forum, an Altoids tin that Ben knew contained hand-rolled cigarettes, and some matchbooks, all of which had been strewn on the floor. She tied a silk scarf around her long, strawberry blond hair, her "crowning glory," as their mom liked to say. Ben's hair was much darker and his eyes a deeper blue, but both he and Ava were tall enough to draw attention.

"Are you taking a Citi Bike back?" Ben checked out the window, but it was still light. He hated the idea of Ava riding a bike on the city streets in the dark. He had been better off living in ignorant bliss regarding what Ava was up to in New York City, though she, as she pointed out, had been doing just fine before he showed up.

"I'm meeting my TA for a drink."

"Is that even allowed?"

"Oh my god. Dude."

"Is this the bearded Albanian?"

"No, this is the TA from my Reframing the Old Masters seminar. You should audit it. You might learn something. Anyway, they're brilliant. They did this amazing program in Berlin last summer that I might apply to if I can get funding."

"And you don't just meet them for coffee?" Ben was proud of himself for not even tripping over the preferred pronoun. He was still chagrined from an argument he'd had with Ava a few years ago when he'd registered a mild complaint about plural pronouns for a single noun being difficult for people who cared about grammar and had been lacerated (fairly so, he knew) when Ava held up James Joyce, Virginia Woolf, Faulkner, and even "your beloved Cormac McCarthy" as examples of people close to his heart who didn't give a fuck about grammar because language was fluid and always evolving. He got over himself, as Ava furiously advised.

"We're getting a drink, Ben, not sexing." Ava came closer to drape herself over Butch. "Goodbye, Butch Buttercup. What are you having for dinner?"

"Leftover basil beef and pad thai."

"Beef is literally poison."

"Weed is poison." So maybe Ben was a hypocrite, but he wasn't crazy about Ava smoking. "I don't think you know how to use 'literally' correctly."

"My weed is organic and I know the guy who sells it at the farmers market," Ava said haughtily. "He grows it on the banks of the Hudson. *Lit-ture-ally*. So suck it."

"Sure. I can see him now in his suspenders and straw hat. *Banks of the Hudson*, my ass. Hey, do you want to borrow a sweatshirt?"

"Stop policing women's bodies." Ava slung her bag across her chest.

"I just mean you're going to be cold." Who rides a bike in a slip and a kimono?

"Okay, Mom."

"'Okay' you want a sweatshirt?"

"No!" Ava rolled her eyes and snatched her keys off the top of the low bookcase that lined the hallway. "Aside from eating murdered cow, what are your plans for tonight?"

"Just reading some manuscripts in case there's anything worth going after. And I'm on this committee about the desk sharing policy. I'll probably check out some of the feedback to see what people think so far."

Ava raised a clenched fist, showing off the tattoo on her inner forearm, a quote from Patti Smith: **"the people have the power to redeem the work of fools."**

"Yeah, I'll bring the whole thing down from the inside." Ben pulled his computer out of his bag, put it on the small kitchen table.

"You have nothing to lose but your chains."

"Is that going to be your new tattoo?"

"No, but I did get a stick and poke last week. See? A little maple leaf." Ava showed Ben the freshly dark tattoo on the inside of her middle finger.

"That looks like a pot leaf."

"It's a maple leaf! For Vermont."

"Represent. Okay, I'll see you tomorrow? I'll Venmo you."

"I hate taking money for the privilege and pleasure of hanging with Butch," Ava claimed. "Kiss!" She smacked Ben lightly on the side of his head, fondled Butch's ears one more time, and was gone before he could call "Be careful!" after her.

Ben locked the door, then sat down on the couch to take off his new boots and was unpleasantly reminded of the chocolate-covered-almond incident. He rinsed the boot's sole in his tiny sink, heated up the leftover Thai food, and turned on his computer to check emails. As promised, Mrs. Singh had sent him the information about the Cooperative Community Group Committee. Before the first meeting, he wanted to check the Office Life Inbox. Ben's sense was that desk sharing was here to stay, no matter what people thought. Corporate landlords were fucked—rising interest rates, tenants shrinking their footprint, people working from home—Leesen had no choice but to come up with creative ways to keep the business alive. Ben was just glad to be in an actual office twice a week and getting a paycheck, paltry though it was, to do what he loved.

He was about to pull up the Office Life Inbox when his WhatsApp pinged. Birdie, his on-, off-, on-, and now definitely off-again (as she was in India for a year) college girlfriend, was checking in. Ben did the math quickly in his head: Chennai was nine and a half hours ahead of New York City, so it was 5:30 a.m. there. Birdie was working for India Ultimate Frisbee and helping to start a nonprofit that would introduce girls to sports. Ben loved Birdie. She was tall and strong and capable; he loved her when she was laying out to catch a Frisbee or pulling her blond hair up into a ponytail or driving her pickup truck with the radio blasting. After she was accepted to veterinary school at Colorado State (which was harder to get into than med school, Ben liked to brag on her behalf), Birdie deferred and took off to India. Ben was sad, but he kept thinking of what Ava had said when she heard Birdie was leaving. "I love Birdie"—everyone loved Birdie—"but you already have a sister." As usual, Ava put her finger right on the point and pressed. Being with Birdie was safe; being with Birdie was easy.

Sex with Birdie was comfortable sex with a good friend. Ben had read enough literature to know he wanted more. Not drink poison, lose your mind, jump in front of a train, eat each other alive more, but maybe a little eat each other alive? Birdie had done them a favor, he knew. She had told him at their vet school acceptance celebration dinner right before he learned she was moving to India. "We both deserve sparks, Ben. We don't have enough sparks," she had said in her gentle Birdie way, tears dropping onto her grilled salmon. The waiter gave him a look of pure hatred. Even the waiter loved Birdie.

They exchanged friendly WhatsApp messages and then Birdie was off to an early morning scrimmage with the team. Ben opened the Office Life Inbox to scout out the vibe.

OFFICE LIFE INBOX:

AGIRLHASNODESK:

Where do we find the End Cap Shelf Replacement Request Form?

paul:

why all the higher ups have dedicated desk :/

HOT DESK:

"reach for the stars, even if you have to stand on a cactus" —unknown

LoveGrammar:

Serious question: I want to work at home all week yet I'm being forced into the office. Use my desk. I don't want it. Guess that was not really a question.

renedescarteswasadrunkenfart:
first they came for the breakfast burritos
then they came for the box wine

CarlottaLopez:
I just want to shout out to my awesome desk partner, Gabe! 😊

Anon:
this whole situation is trash

AGIRLHASNODESK:
Is there a spreadsheet for vacation schedules?

Anon:
we were guinea pigs now we are lemmings

Paul:
this is Paul from production and I did not post as "paul" repeat: "paul" is not me

Anon:
it's just a matter of time before we work for robot overlords

HawkHarry:
What if I want to schedule a meeting with my desk partner? Can we just arrange that or is there a procedure to follow?

Admin:
Please speak to your direct report. Thanks—Admin

Paul:

If someone from tech is reading this, please reach out to "paul" and tell them to cease and desist. Also this isn't about desk sharing but to the person who ate one of my hard-boiled eggs, I hope you enjoyed it. Sorry you can't read or don't care about private property.

HaileyB:

there is an assigned free desk to the left of the kitchen that no one is using—whose in charge of that?

HaileyB:

who's

Ben got up and retrieved a pint of Cherry Garcia from his tiny freezer. What a clusterfuck. He knew he should be professional but he couldn't help himself. He pulled up the Office Life Inbox on his phone, took a few screenshots, and texted them to Ava.

Ben:

this "cooperative committee" is going to be fun

Ava:

capitalism is death

Ben:

HOT DESK has to be my desk partner right? the cactus quote?

Ava:

does she have a hang in there poster of a kitten

Ben: so rebecca blume is an inspirational quote person and kind of a slob

Ben: is it a message to me? the cactus the stars?

Ben: renedescartes is howie i'm pretty sure did not take him for a monty python fan

Ava: my fave is "paul"

Ben: should i be worried about anon shooting up the office

Ava: not funny

Ben: sorry i know

Ben: he seems really disgruntled

Ava: what do you have on your desk?

Ben: what? nothing

Ava: jesus b that's like serial killer shit

Ben: we have a cactus!

Ben leaned against the sink and ate half the carton of ice cream. He cleaned the spoon, wiped down the table, dropped and did forty push-ups. Butch wandered over to help by sticking his head under Ben's face. It was almost time to take Butch out before bed, but Ben thought he should post on the inbox instead of just lurking. Honestly, Mrs. Singh could probably identify everyone somehow. Maybe she or someone could keep an eye on Anon? He was surprised no one had used the screen name "Bartleby" yet.

And what about Rebecca Blume, her inspirational quotes and her refusal to abide by the Clean Desk Policy? She reminded him of his sixth-grade teacher, the shapeless and unforgivably dull Mrs. Toddle, whose classroom was wall-to-wall motivational posters that said things like "If life gives you lemons, make lemonade" and "Life is a journey, not a destination." Well, Ben could google a stupid quote about a cactus. He cracked his knuckles. "Okay, Butch. Good boy. We'll go out in a minute." Butch pricked up his ears at the sentences containing at least 50 percent of his vocabulary.

OFFICE LIFE INBOX:

KMarx:
"We reap what we sow. We cannot expect apples when we have sown the seed of the cactus."
—Unknown

JANE

NEW YORK CITY
MAY 1981

Jane had walked for what felt like miles in the wrong direction after exiting the subway station; although she had given herself plenty of time, now she was going to be late. Clutching the piece of paper with the magazine office address written on it, she hurried down the quiet street, heading, as instructed by the second doorman she had asked, toward the water. She didn't have enough time to take off her oversize blazer, though she was suddenly sweating under her best shirt, a red velour button-down that Jane regretted as much as her pointy black ankle boots, which pinched with every step. What had seemed chic and professional this morning now felt wrong as she passed the stately buildings and women in fur coats who looked neither overdressed nor too warm. Smoothing the paper out, Jane confirmed the address of an imposing town house that resembled a museum. Beyond its gray stone facade, the street ended in a cobbled cul-de-sac. Over an iron railing, Jane could make out the bright twinkle of the East River.

Professor Marshall had never visited the *East River Review*, but he had assured Jane that his other former student, *East River Review* editor Larry Parker, would welcome a fellow Penn State grad and writer. In fact, Professor Marshall had arranged for a small stipend when Jane was accepted as an unpaid intern, the good news relayed on a phone call from Larry after she had mailed back a thicket of questions and assignments dutifully filled out in black ink, not blue. Larry had made Professor Marshall proud by parlaying his creative writing workshop stories into a well-reviewed collection published last year. Jane knew that the professor expected her to be his next success story. In her Guess purse, recently purchased for this occasion, Jane had the leather-bound notebook she carried with her everywhere. She slipped her hand into the purse and touched the notebook's cover, cool and reassuring. The *East River Review* sign was understated enough that you had to be looking for it. Stone steps to the lower level curved to reveal a deep blue door, cracked open. Jane squared her shoulders and lifted her chin. *You have an appointment,* she told herself firmly. *You are supposed to be here.*

When she pushed the door fully open, Jane could better hear the clacking of typewriters and murmur of voices. She stepped down another few stairs into the almost damp air of the basement office while heads swiveled toward her from desks that lined both sides of a narrow room.

"Hi. I'm looking for Larry Parker?" Jane addressed the space in general. The typing clatter slowed, then resumed as a man in oversize tortoiseshell glasses and a pink short-sleeved shirt leaped out of his chair.

"It's just Parker," he corrected her, holding out his hand and looking her up and down.

"Jane Kinloch." Jane couldn't remember if she had ever seen a man in a pink shirt before. Unlikely in Fishtown, Pennsylvania.

"How's old Don doing?" Parker kept shaking Jane's hand.

It took Jane a moment to identify Don as Professor Marshall, which was what she had always called him and would forever call him. "He's fine," she answered. "I haven't seen him much since I graduated last year." She had met Professor Marshall for one awkward lunch when he had urged her to apply for the *East River Review* internship and once more when she had thanked him for the opportunity. Professor Marshall had been Jane's most influential professor, moving the class to tears while reciting *King Lear* and singling her out for praise, then accepting her into his senior writing workshop and bolstering her confidence. But in the ordinary setting of a restaurant, he was just a man who fussed over his veal piccata and asked about her family. Jane didn't like it. Still, he expected "big things" from her, as he told her more than once.

"I was glad to hear from him," Parker said, finally relinquishing Jane's hand. "He was raving about you."

Jane blushed and shook her head. "He assigned some of your stories in class," she countered.

"I'll have to mail him another signed copy of the collection, now that it's out in paperback," Parker mused. "Well, let me give you the grand tour!"

There were five other people in the small office. Light came in from the open door behind her and a high, barred window over the stairs to outside, but as they moved down the slim aisle between the desks, the room darkened. It was crowded with bookcases and boxes and posters of past magazine covers lining the walls on each side above the desks. "This is our associate editor, Jonathan." Jonathan was on the phone but raised his hand in greeting. He had longish hair and a gray-speckled mustache. "This is our office IBM PC." Parker looked expectantly at Jane, who examined the squat beige machine and murmured a sound that she hoped conveyed awe. "Assistant editor Ellen." Ellen wheeled her chair around to peer at Jane, said a brusque hello, wheeled her chair back in position, and began typing aggressively. "Voilà!" Parker continued. "Our copy machine. It's broken." Taped to the copy machine was a piece of paper on which someone had scrawled, "I PREFER NOT TO."

"You've caught a rare sighting of our art director, Paco." Paco was sorting photographs on a small table near a back room. He bowed showily to Jane. "And the famous Deedle Duffin, poetry editor, of course," Parker announced. Jane had no idea who Deedle Duffin was, but she smiled politely as he stood up and looked her over.

"Well done, Parker," he said. "Truly you have outdone yourself this year."

"Leave her alone, Deedle, you lech," Ellen called out.

"Can't a man admire the view?" Deedle protested. He was squat and beige like the PC. Jane kept her smile steady.

"Here we have one of your cohorts!" Parker gestured to a handsome Asian boy wearing large headphones attached to a tape recorder and writing intently onto a lined yellow pad. "Drew Kim." He tapped Drew, who slipped the headphones off one ear.

"Lee," Drew said patiently.

"Drew Lee," Parker repeated. "One of our three new interns. He's transcribing an interview at Paco's desk and he can show you how to do it later. He's been here for a week already, so he's got the lay of the land, right?"

"Right." Drew put the headphones back on, but not before he gave Jane a quick smile. Grateful, she smiled back.

"We don't have enough desks for everyone to be in the office at once, obviously," Parker continued. "Some people work at home. Some people, like Paco here, come in when they feel like it." With a flourish, Paco tipped an imaginary hat. "You can use any empty desk. Except Jonathan's. Don't sit at Jonathan's. We usually send the interns upstairs." He paused for a reaction, but Jane wasn't sure if "upstairs" meant more than upstairs. "Of course, you'll get to meet EDA. He always makes a point to take the interns out to lunch at least once. He's in London now. London, right?"

"London," Ellen confirmed. One of the phones shrilled and she picked it up. "*East River Review.* Just a second . . ." She leaned back in her desk chair, stretching the phone cord across the aisle to hand the receiver to Deedle. "It's Marion again."

Deedle took the phone impatiently. "I told you to call *my* extension. Three-four-five!" he snapped. "You keep bothering Ellen!" The way back to Parker's desk was effectively blocked as Deedle continued haranguing Marion.

"Wife," Parker explained, rolling his eyes as Marion's tinny voice took its turn. Jane couldn't make out her words, but the tone was clear. Apparently, his wife found Deedle as objectionable as Jane already did.

"Speaking of wife," Parker said, turning to Ellen, "did the great man even let Clara know he was going to London?"

"None of your business!" Ellen didn't look up from her typewriter.

"It *is* my business when she keeps calling to ask where he is," Parker replied.

Jonathan banged the phone down triumphantly. "Just reeled in Toni Morrison! Teddy can go over to Random House and do the interview. She's cutting back editing to focus on writing. It's perfect timing."

"Congratulations!" Parker enthused. He turned to Jane. "Have you read *Tar Baby*?"

Jane had not, although she was about to say she had studied *Song of Solomon* and that *Sula* had been the strange, mesmerizing book that had first made her want to write, but Parker had moved on, showing her what he blithely called the "slush pile." It was a messy stack of manuscripts in a cardboard box, each paper clipped to a cover letter and an envelope. It was obvious that Jane was supposed to know what a slush pile was, especially since Parker was telling her that going through it was her main responsibility as an intern. She looked over at Drew, but he was still wearing headphones. She would ask him later.

"I'm going out to celebrate," Jonathan announced, snatching his corduroy jacket off the back of his chair. "Who's joining me?"

"I have a call with Tennessee Williams about the interview for the fall issue," Ellen said. "It could take a while. Let's go to Elaine's tonight on Teddy's tab. He'll be thrilled about Morrison."

"What time is it in London?" Jonathan picked up the phone again.

"Careful," Ellen warned. "It's over fifty cents a minute for international. Teddy once got billed a hundred and twenty for one call to Paris. I've never heard the end of it."

Deedle, having abruptly ended his hissing conversation with Marion, immediately perked up, alert to Jonathan in his coat. "Where are you headed?"

"York Tavern." Jonathan placed the phone back in its cradle. "I confirmed the Morrison interview."

"Good man! Good man!" Deedle wrapped a red silk scarf around his neck. "This calls for a rare steak and a cold martini!"

"Parker?" Jonathan lingered by his desk with Deedle close behind him.

"I've got Jane's orientation going here," Parker said regretfully.

"It's fine." Jane tried to sound breezy. "I can come back later, or Drew can show me around?" She hated everyone's eyes on her, and she hated being the reason Parker couldn't leave, something he clearly wanted to do. The office reminded her of a noisy family gathering, everyone in a cramped kitchen speaking over each other and jostling for attention. Except this family was talking about Toni Morrison instead of the Phillies winning the World Series.

"Jane is invited!" Deedle twirled the end of his scarf in what Jane assumed he thought was a rakish manner. "And the other one! The girl."

"Just give me a minute. I'll meet you there." Parker motioned to Jane. "I'll show you upstairs, where you'll be reading, especially on days when all the desks are occupied."

Jonathan pulled a corduroy flat cap out of his desk drawer and tugged it on. "Ellen, would you sign for the bike messenger delivery?"

"Not my job," Ellen emphasized with a furious ding of her typewriter.

"Thank you!" Jonathan flashed a peace sign and headed up the front stairs and out the blue door after Deedle.

"Follow me," Parker instructed Jane as he disappeared into the gloom of the back room at the far end of the long, narrow office.

"Just us ladies," Paco said, winking at Jane. She flushed and smiled nervously. She would not be overwhelmed. She could almost take a full breath now that the room was emptier.

Ellen tapped a cigarette out from a pack on her desk and lit it, squinting at Jane. "Where are you from, Jane? It is Jane, right?"

"Yes, Jane. Philadelphia."

"The *city* part?" Ellen asked. She didn't even try to mask her skepticism, Jane thought.

"Did I lose you?" Parker's voice called out.

"Come on, darling, you know the new 'suggestion' about smoking." Paco motioned for Ellen to come outside with him.

"Suggestion, my ass." She handed him a cigarette. "These walls have been grimy since the 1800s." They disappeared up the front stairs and through the blue door, trailing smoke. Jane was alone in the office with Drew, oblivious, bent over the yellow pad, scribbling furiously. She hurried after Parker.

"Somebody has to get this sconce fixed!" Parker was complaining from halfway up a steep set of stairs in the back room. Jane put one hand on the wall, covered with dingy yellowish wallpaper, and looked down at her boots so she wouldn't trip in the dim light. She took the opportunity to flap her blazer and get some air on her sweaty back.

"There's another one of you up here," Parker called over his shoulder.

"I'm sorry?"

"The third intern," he explained as he opened the door at the top of the flight. "Here we are! Upstairs!" Jane blinked in the sudden expanse of a large galley kitchen. "It's not the main kitchen," Parker said. "You can keep your lunch in here if you want—just have to clear it all out for the parties." He kept moving past the glass cabinets, steel basin sinks, and white tile into a hallway that led to an enormous room filled with light. How was it possible that New York City was all of these things: her tiny fourth-floor walk-up apartment with its shrieking radiator and brick wall bedroom view; the magazine's cluttered basement office; the wide, gracious buildings she had passed to get here; and this grand room with its windows reflecting the river's sparkle, its ceiling easily three times the height of any living room she had ever been in before?

"Knock, knock!" Parker barged through the wide French doors. Jane was arrested by the sight of a massive pool table, its green felt pristine, and the gleam of unscuffed balls gathered into the rack, all of it rich with heft and color. For the first time today—actually, for the first time since she arrived in New York City last week—Jane felt a surge of familiarity. Pool she knew. Maybe the tables she ran in Fishtown were in crappy shape, but run them she did. She had practically grown up in her uncle Mike's bar, and if she wasn't reading a book and drinking a ginger ale, she was learning angles and practicing shots until the regulars knew not to accept her challenge, hastily swiping their dollars from the table's edge when she wandered over. True, she hadn't played much lately, what with college and work, but her fingers still itched to center the rack, to handle one of the heavy walnut cues.

"Do you play?" Jane looked up to see a tall, willowy girl unfolding herself from the window seat. "Willowy" was the right word, she thought, and also refined and . . . not beautiful; "beautiful" was too boring to describe her. The bones of her face and her limbs were long and a little sharp; Jane might have said she was too skinny, but there was strength and litheness to her. Her hair was bouncy like a Wella

Balsam shampoo ad. She was wearing green cowboy boots, a long petticoat, a tight white undershirt, a chunky silver necklace, and a cropped black leather blazer.

Jane had taken in all this in the amount of time it took Parker to say, "This is Rose. Rose Bergman, right?"

"No, Larry, it's Bergesen," Rose answered coolly. "Three *e*'s."

Jane hid her smile from Parker, who, flustered, waved generally around the room. "All right, so this is it: here and the kitchen we came through, and, uh, there's a bathroom to the left. Those are the places we're allowed, right? Don't go exploring. Remember, people live here." He gestured to a spiral staircase that Jane could see through the doors. "Never up there, obviously."

"Right." Jane nodded. As if she would wander around. As if. She ran her hand against the side of the pool table.

Parker noticed. "EDA's pride and joy. He's been known to challenge a few of us. Don't ever play him for money!" He laughed a little too loudly and glanced quickly at Rose. Jane knew Rose had the upper hand as girls who looked like her usually did. "Rose can tell you about the rest of it. We're pretty easy here. No punching the clock or anything. Well. Gotta bolt. Later." He flipped up the collar of his shirt and left. They were both quiet until he had disappeared.

"'Gotta bolt. Later,'" Rose said, breaking the silence.

"Larry," Jane added.

They both burst out laughing. Jane couldn't remember the last time she had laughed so hard. Every time she tried to take a breath and get a hold of herself, she collapsed into more laughter. Rose was also hysterical. "Stop, stop," she gasped. "I'm going to pee!"

Jane doubled over, her bag slipping. It wasn't even that funny. Her ribs ached and tears slid down her cheeks. Rose crumpled to the floor. "I can't. I can't . . ." Her laughter pealed like a bell, then suddenly honked.

Jane, who was starting to calm down, instead started up again. "'Later,'" she snorted.

"Larry . . ." Rose buried her face in her hands, a column of silver bangles clanking down her wrist.

Jane went over and sat down on the floor next to Rose. It seemed like the only thing to do. She hiccuped and quieted. She could tell she was bright red. Rose dropped her hands and shuddered. "I'm wrung out," she said weakly. "I love your shirt. I love velvet."

"It's velour," Jane admitted.

"The color is perfect on you," Rose continued. "Crimson. Brings out your eyes, stunning against your black hair. You look like Snow White."

"Snow White if she had crimson skin, you mean," Jane deflected, but she felt a glow spreading in her chest. She had, just this morning, secretly thought to herself that the shirt brought out her eyes. She sneaked a glance at Rose, who was looking at her with frank interest.

"How did you get here?" Rose asked.

"The subway. But also my old college professor. He taught Parker a few years ago and pressured him to give me the internship, I'm sure. How about you?"

"A taxi. But also my dad donates money to the magazine. He was roommates with one of the advisory editors. He's a big patron of the arts." Rose said the last part in a slightly mocking way, and Jane understood that Rose had a complicated relationship with her father.

"Apparently we're both here based on our talent and skill," Jane said.

"They interviewed me in person," Rose added. "So definitely my talent and skill."

"I'm sure famous poet Deedle Deedle found you very talented."

"He immediately composed an ode to my talent."

"I think he's at lunch right now composing a limerick to mine."

"Why sell yourself short?" Rose nudged Jane's shoulder. "Definitely sonnet material."

"How long have you been here?"

"A few weeks. I finished the graduate writing program at NYU and started right away."

"That's so cool. So you're a writer?"

Rose paused before she answered. "Yes? I mean, I wrote a lot of short stories while I was there. I have a whole portfolio of them now. I guess they're pretty good, but I don't know if they're great, you know what I mean?" She reached up to the window seat and pulled down a fringed suede bag. "I got more into photography. Not, like, darkroom photography but Polaroids." She pulled out a boxy black camera.

"Oh, I have one of those at home," Jane said. She thought about the writing workshop with Professor Marshall and her own portfolio of short stories. "Do you ever have readings? I'd love to go." There was one student in her college workshop who had invited Jane to the campus pub after class to read each other's stories. But Jane had to go to work, and the woman had never asked her again. One of her best memories was of the reading Professor Marshall had organized for the graduating seniors. Usually Jane was shy about sharing her work, but that night her voice was strong and she found the power of her words as the audience stilled, then applauded, then rushed up to her afterward with praise. It wasn't like her to take the lead, but if there was a chance to recapture that feeling . . . and Rose, as tall and striking as she was, made her feel comfortable, not intimidated.

"I mean, not really readings, but I'd love to show them to you! Honestly, my workshops were filled with wannabe Kerouacs and one deluded boy who worshipped Tolkien. As in he handed out a ten-page addendum with made-up vocabulary so we could follow along. I love to edit, but it was rough going. Are you a writer?"

A litany of possible answers—hedging, noncommittal, self-deprecating—ran through Jane's head. She thought again of the reading, of her stories coming alive in the expectant hush. Rose was waiting, her clear eyes fixed on Jane. "Yes," Jane said simply. She felt a thrill surge through her as the affirmative lingered in the air. How easy it was to say it! Why had she been so afraid? So knotted up? She thought of the leather notebook in her new bag and the pen already staining its lining. She lived in New York City now. She worked at the *East River Review*.

"I'd love to read yours! Short stories? Let me guess: You're working on a novel, right? Something sharp and observant like Joan Didion?"

Jane felt a flutter of familiar doubt. "Nothing like Didion," she protested. "I mean, I only took a few creative writing classes in college."

Rose cocked her head. "It sounds like your professor must have thought you were pretty good, though."

"He did, I guess," Jane admitted. "I do have some short stories." Why was she acting like this now? She knew she was better than anyone in any of her workshops. But that wasn't the same as a master's program at NYU.

"We'll have a reading party! Like, get some wine and bake a Brie or something," Rose suggested. "Bring our red pens!"

"I'd love that." Jane pushed down a hint of panic at the thought of showing Rose her writing. But at the same time she wanted to pull out her notebook and read it all to her right now, every word.

"It's a plan!" Rose enthused. "Now, what do you need to know about being an *East River Review* intern? I've been here almost three weeks, so I'm kind of an expert."

"Okay, don't laugh. I mean, really, please don't start laughing again, but what exactly is a slush pile?"

Rose smiled. "Ha! I had no idea either! Parker kept saying it, and I kept imagining one of those sno-cones you get at Coney Island. Like an electric blue one that gives you a cold headache?"

"I thought about Broad Street after it snows and all that gorgeous white turned ash gray in piles, icy and wet and dirty."

"We are obviously super-talented writers," Rose joked. "Okay, so the slush pile is where they dump all the unsolicited manuscripts that come in. All the people who don't have agents or who are unpublished or whose dads didn't room with an advisory editor, when they mail their writing here it gets sorted into the slush pile for the interns. If we find something good that we think one of the real editors should read, we have to write up a description and recommendation. Then we give it to one of them, and they reject it. I mean, it's like a unicorn. Ellen told me that a few years ago, one of the interns pulled T. C. Boyle out of the slush pile. That intern was Parker. I can't believe he hasn't mentioned it to you yet."

"Ellen was taking a call from Tennessee Williams. *Streetcar Named Desire* Tennessee Williams." Jane knew she was probably being uncool, but she couldn't help it. She had never heard of T. C. Boyle, but she had read Tennessee Williams's plays in high school.

"I know! It's amazing! I'm transcribing an interview with Nadine Gordimer."

"Seriously?" Jane paused. "I'm not sure who that is?" Should she have pretended to know? *There goes the evening of sharing our writing*, she thought.

"Oh, she's not that well known in the States! She's a white South African who writes about how terrible apartheid is. I think you'd like her. Maybe we can have a book club too?" Rose looked at Jane warmly. "Don't worry, I promise I won't monopolize all of your time."

"I'm not worried," Jane said. She stopped herself from adding that she would be happy to spend all her time with Rose. "Have you met EDA yet?" She changed the subject so she wouldn't linger in the emotional impact of Rose's easy kindness. Except for one "I made it here without being murdered and none of my belongings were stolen" call to her mother from the graffiti-splashed phone booth outside her apartment on the Lower East Side, Jane hadn't spoken to a single person in more than a transactional way since she arrived. The next day the phone had been ripped out of the booth, a development that Jane tried not to take personally. She could deal with meanness or neglect; they only hardened her will. But kindness had the capacity to undo her. When she bought her *New York Times* from the kiosk yesterday morning and the old woman working there slipped her a blueberry muffin, Jane had swallowed a sudden, embarrassing lump in her throat and escaped down to the subway, barely suppressing tears.

"Yes! Drew and I met him quickly last week. He's been traveling a lot. I almost asked him to sign my copy of the collected stories, but I didn't want to be too much of a groupie and freak him out."

"And?" Jane tipped her head. Edward David Adams was famous for his writing, yes. But he was also famous for other things.

Rose laughed. "Okay, he's a stone-cold fox!"

"Details?" Jane demanded. She thought of the photo on the book jacket of the collected stories and EDA's novels. Adams, somewhere water-adjacent, windswept, his broad shoulders bare, eyes intense. She and every other English major she knew had spent plenty of time gazing longingly at it.

"Hmmmm . . ." Rose tapped her long, slender fingers against her chin. "I would say tall, magnetic, and overwhelming, but I can do better than that. He's a huge presence, like he takes up all the space. But you *want* him to take it all up, you know what I mean? Physically and more. He makes the rest of them seem small. And his voice . . ." Rose trailed off. She pressed her hand against her chest. "You feel it everywhere."

"Do you think he'll take us out for lunch? Just the three of us?" Jane remembered what Parker had said.

"He mentioned it after we met him! I think he will."

"I can't believe how lucky I am," Jane blurted.

"How lucky *we* are! Do you think he'd ever look at our writing?"

Jane shook her head. She was having enough trouble imagining showing her work to Rose. "I could never ask."

"Fine," Rose said airily, "I'll ask 'Teddy' and you ask Deedle."

Jane burst out laughing again.

"Oh, hey, excuse me?" They turned to see Drew in the doorway looking curiously at them. Without the headphones on, his hair sprang up in a fashionable swoop. He was tall and graceful, and he was wearing a thin gold chain over a black T-shirt. Jane remembered that they were sprawled on the floor and scrambled to her feet. She reached down for Rose and hauled her up as well. Rose gave Jane's hand a little squeeze and let go.

"Ellen is asking for you downstairs," Drew continued. "We're going to learn how to call the copy machine repairman." He raised one dark eyebrow in a quizzical expression, and with that, Jane knew they were all going to be real friends.

"Wait, Drew, will you take a photo of us? Jane's first day!" Rose went to hand Drew the Polaroid and came back to lean against Jane, her arm draped casually over her shoulders. She was almost a head taller. Jane's cheek brushed the smooth leather of her blazer.

Drew flipped the flash up, held the camera to his face, and started with demands. "Give me Gia! Give me Jerry Hall! Give me Rose 'Three-*E*'s' Bergesen!"

There was a burst of white light and the photo whirred its way out. Drew shook it by a corner tip. "Well?" Rose reached out impatiently. "Let us have it!"

"Absolute babes," Drew confirmed. He handed the blurry photo to Rose, who held it so the three of them could see.

"We are very talented," Rose confirmed.

"Very skilled," Jane added. Her heart swelled, and instead of a lump in her throat she felt almost giddy.

"Oh, we are going to have a killer time here," Drew promised. "Best interns ever!"

Heads bent over the Polaroid, they watched as the colors deepened and it all came into focus.

CHAPTER FIVE

TUESDAY
WORK, REBECCA

Ami sent Rebecca to the East End town house in an Uber Black. She had spent most of the last week refamiliarizing herself with the Lion's body of work (and was surprised to find herself caught up in reading rather than skimming sections of *The Coldest War*), trolling for photos of Rose Adams (at first, many glamorous society shots, then a slow fade into intermittent charity galas and award ceremonies with the Lion), and reviewing ideas for keeping the Lion relevant: a collection of essays by and about him that would "speak to each other"; a reprinting of the novels with introductions and commentary by a who's who of diverse young women writers and critics; an HBO miniseries based on *The Coldest War* that Rebecca had secretly cast with Alexander Skarsgård.

Stuck in midmorning traffic, Rebecca sent a quick text to Max.

Rebecca:

see you tonight at stella's dinner!

hope you forgive me for the mead hall

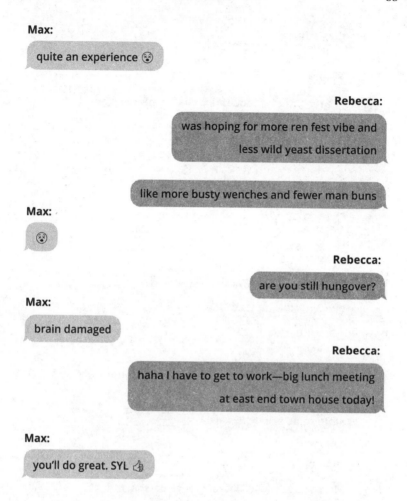

Rebecca wasn't sure if Max understood what a big deal it was that she was going (by herself!) to meet with Rose Adams. Of course he knew who the Lion was, but his reading taste ran more toward biographies of power brokers. He had been reading the same book about Churchill for the entire duration of their relationship. In his defense, it was about ten thousand pages long. Speaking of boring, Rebecca suddenly remembered that Mrs. Singh had reminded her about next week's Desk Share meeting. She pulled up the Office Life Inbox on her phone reluctantly while the Uber driver leaned on his horn.

OFFICE LIFE INBOX:

KMarx:

"We reap what we sow. We cannot expect apples when we have sown the seed of the cactus."
—Unknown

Bartleby:

i prefer not to

Anon:

did you ever think every time we swipe our cards they are tracking us

HaileyB:

no one seems to know anything about the free desk? admin? if no one is using it, i'd like to store some belongings in it?

Admin:

Please use assigned lockers for all personal belongings —Admin

AGIRLHASNODESK:

We don't have an H-shaped bookcase under our desk, but I see that other desks do. Is there a requisition form to fill out for that? It might be helpful to have all the forms in one easily accessible place

paul:

tbh you have to break eggs to make omelet ¯_(ツ)_/¯

JANICESTRONG:

> How dp I mute notices ob Blabber

> How do I mute notices ob Blabber?

> OB

> ON ON ON ON ON ON ON ON

Rebecca stopped reading Janice's breakdown-in-real-time and scrolled back up to KMarx. It was 100 percent not a coincidence that there was another cactus quote, was it? Could KMarx be Ben Heath? Was Ben following up on his annoying message from yesterday, a hot-pink Post-it with her own words—"*WHAT IS THIS ABOUT?*"—under a chocolate-covered almond? She had eaten the almond and pondered her next move. And now this apple quote? If anyone had sown the seed of the cactus, it was him! (It was he?) Was he a socialist making commentary on desk sharing? Wouldn't a socialist *prefer* desk sharing? Or, Rebecca mused, was he using his screen name as a cover for his true reactionary nature as a redheaded blue blood who pretended to flee the monarchy but was so steeped in its culture he was still one of them? She had gone with "Reach for the stars," but he was going with "We reap what we sow." Was he getting a dig in at her for expecting apples? Fine! She expected apples, not a fucking cactus.

KMarx:

> "We reap what we sow. We cannot expect apples when we have sown the seed of the cactus."
> —Unknown

HOT DESK:

 "the revolution is not an apple that falls when it is ripe. you have to make it fall." —che guevara

Rebecca closed out of the Office Life Inbox with a satisfied smile. She had real work to do.

The East End town house was an impressive six-story gray limestone building with ornate balconies. There was a small sign in the distinctive *East River Review* font above stone steps leading down to a separate entrance, its deep-blue door the only clue that the literary magazine was alive and well and churning out issues from the basement level. Deposited by the Uber, Rebecca halted, sweating in the afternoon sun, unsure if she was supposed to meet Mrs. Adams at the magazine office or in her home. She refused to call Ami this early in the assignment. Just this morning, Ami had given her marching orders to feel out Mrs. Adams regarding her position on the Lion's relevance to young women today. Ami had smiled in a quick, tense way and revealed they would need to strategize on how best to introduce him to this new audience. No pressure! Had Rebecca gone into publishing to make the Lion relevant? Ugh. And her mother? Jane had been absolutely ghosting her. "Planning a party for the boys"? Seriously, so busy scouting bouncy castles that she couldn't be bothered to check in with her daughter? For someone who had called her at work every morning, Jane had been suspiciously absent ever since their unsatisfactory phone call about the internship. As soon as she was through with all her very important work responsibilities, Rebecca was going to get a straight answer.

At that moment, two people came clattering out of the iron gate under the *East River Review* sign, an older man wearing a fedora who looked vaguely familiar and a young woman toting a satchel stuffed with papers.

"I can't eat at York Tavern again," the woman was saying. "They swear it's oat but it's always dairy."

"It's your lucky day, then." The man held the gate open for her. "Taco truck Tuesday!"

"Excuse me," Rebecca said. "I have a meeting with Mrs. Adams. What's the best way to find her?"

The two stopped and looked Rebecca up and down. "I don't know if Rose is in the city today," the man said finally. "She lives in the Hamptons."

"I have an appointment," Rebecca said. *I'll bet you're completely bald under that fedora*, she thought uncharitably.

"You can just ring the front bell," the young woman said. Was she being helpful or snide? Rebecca squinted nervously at the enormous entranceway, guarded by two potted trees. *I'm supposed to be here*, she reminded herself.

"Great. Thanks!" She turned away, resisting the urge to look back and catch them gawking at her. On the heavy door was (of course) a lion's head door knocker, a doorbell, and a big brass doorknob in the middle of it all. Rebecca lifted the heavy lion and let it drop with a bang. She pressed the doorbell for good measure. Eventually a beautiful older woman—not the *Downton Abbey* butler Rebecca half expected—opened the door and ushered Rebecca into a cool, marbled foyer dominated by a curving staircase and museum-size sculptures of naked women. Mrs. Adams—Rebecca recognized her from internet sleuthing—was tall and elegant in a gray fluted skirt, high heels, and white silk blouse. There was a huge arrangement of white hydrangea and pink peonies on an imposing round table.

"You must be Rebecca Blume," Rose Adams said. "May I take your coat?"

A group FaceTime effort with Stella and Gabe last night had Rebecca dressed in dark, wide-leg, high-waisted trousers, chunky-heeled shiny black boots, a new blouse with shirred cuffs, and a cropped green blazer Stella had found on Poshmark that was "Chanel adjacent" and delivered in the nick of time. "No, thank you!" Rebecca, though desperate to shed the Chanel-adjacent jacket, remembered Gabe's instructions that it was an essential part of her outfit and would not be tricked out of it. "Thank you, though. It's so nice to meet you." Rebecca offered her hot hand to be clasped in Mrs. Adams's chilled, firm grip.

"Please, call me Rose." Rose led Rebecca up the graceful stairway and through the arched French doors until they were both standing in a palatial room lined with huge windows looking out onto the East River. There were a number of separate seating areas, including window seats lining the far wall. In the center of the room was a massive pool table where someone had spread papers and left a coffee mug. On every side table there were neat piles of books.

"Let me get a good look at you, Rebecca Blume. Come over by the light." They moved to the bank of windows and Rebecca looked down at the wide river, where barges and sailboats floated serenely by and all traffic noise was muffled by the insulated glass. Rebecca could see the string of bridges farther downtown. She pulled her attention from the expanse of river and met Rose's intense gaze. "Your jacket is a lovely color; it brings out the green of your eyes." Rebecca, flustered and pleased, had just that morning thought the same as she twirled for Gabe over yet another FaceTime consultation. Rose had thick silver hair streaked with light brown and the erect carriage and long limbs of a former model. Rebecca knew that Rose was sixty-five years old but she looked younger, her angular face pale and smooth, her eyes bright with interest as they examined Rebecca. How was Rose so unruffled and cool in her silk blouse while Rebecca's short-lived victory in hanging on to her jacket had resulted in trapping heat beneath it?

"Thank you. What a beautiful view," Rebecca said, looking away from Rose, who was still appraising her.

"It is. The house was built in 1869, and Teddy's parents bought it in the early 1900s."

Rebecca did some calculations, including one that identified Teddy as the Lion. "How long has the magazine been in the building?"

"Oh, Teddy founded it not long after he graduated. We celebrate its sixtieth this year."

"That's right," Rebecca said. "I read that in the obituary." She winced. "I'm sorry. Sorry for your loss." Ugh. Could she be more insensitive? And generic? "Sorry for your loss"? She was off to a great start: sweaty, bumbling, clearly wilting under Rose's continued (not entirely professional?) scrutiny.

"Thank you." Rose touched Rebecca briefly on her arm. "He was sick for many years, but of course it's still a bit of a shock. Teddy was always such a . . . presence. I appreciate your coming here, Rebecca. Beginning the process of finding a new home for Teddy's work, handling his estate, meeting you . . . it gives my days shape and purpose. Thank you."

"I'm happy to be here, of course." Rebecca highly doubted that her showing up at the town house had given shape to Rose's days, but somehow Rose had managed to put her at ease. And thankfully Rose's gaze had landed elsewhere as she picked up the coffee mug from the pool table.

"The magazine staff often work up here. They always have." Rose gave the mug a little shake. "Teddy called them the 'kids.' No liquid anywhere near the pool table was one of his rules."

"What a great place to work." Rebecca imagined herself curled up on the window seat, paisley pillow on her lap, reading, watching the boats go by. No desk sharing for the spoiled staff of the *East River Review*! For the first time since their unsatisfactory phone call, Rebecca thought about her mother in this very building. She wondered if Jane had ever been upstairs.

"They come and go using the rear stairway," Rose explained. "The stairs connect the back room in the office to the second kitchen over there. Former house staff quarters." She gestured through one of the arched doors. "I found it difficult sometimes, living here. One of the reasons I moved out to Southampton: for privacy."

Would Rebecca mind if magazine staff sprawled all over her living room? Not if she could have two kitchens, she decided.

"Lorraine!" Rose called unexpectedly, and an old woman in a linen smock came into the room. "Would you be so kind as to bring us our lunch? I have everything ready in the refrigerator. Except the cheese: that's coming to room temperature on the board. Please bring the trays so we can eat in here."

Lorraine nodded and gave Rebecca a sympathetic glance. "Unseasonably warm for May today," she announced. Had she noticed Rebecca's flushed face? Rebecca would not be sidetracked into a conversation about the weather. She had business to conduct!

"So Ami Ito, the editorial director at Avenue, my boss—I think you spoke to her?" After a tight smile to acknowledge Lorraine, Rebecca launched into her pitch, determined to take control of this meeting. "She has a list of innovative ideas to introduce Edward"—she could not bring herself to call him "Teddy"—"to a new generation of readers. We were thinking, in particular, of young women."

"Are you a fan of my husband's work, Rebecca?" Rose asked, while motioning her to sit.

Rebecca sank into the wide, cloudlike couch with the too-late realization that she would need a crane to haul her back up. Rose took a seat on a higher, straight-backed chair opposite Rebecca, who tried to lean forward but was held back by both her high-waisted pants and the width of the seat. There were two choices: surrender to the enveloping down cushions or perch unsteadily on the very edge, waistband cutting off her circulation and elbows resting uncomfortably on her knees. Because this was a business meeting, Rebecca heaved herself forward. "He's a great writer of sentences," she answered honestly. "And scenes. And endings. I loved *The Coldest War*. I know everyone says that, but it's my favorite. His short stories. The early ones, especially. Brilliant."

"And do you think it's possible his work could reach a new audience? As you mentioned, a younger female one? The culture has changed, I'm well aware." Rose tapped her long, slender fingers against her chin. "Mercifully. And not nearly enough, of course. Though I wonder if the present landscape will be hospitable to Teddy's particular brand of, shall we say, male energy?"

"That's exactly the dilemma," Rebecca said excitedly. "His writing, at its foundation—at the sentence level, as I said—it's powerful, sinewy. There's a kind of violence in the language that's punctuated with moments of almost delicate sensuality, right? I'm thinking of that part in *Hoydenish* when the girl is poking at the dead deer with the stick and the butterflies explode in this cloud around her. And in *The Coldest War*, how the domestic scenes are both evocative of myth and almost painfully naturalistic. But you just can't escape the way the women are portrayed. So many of his female characters are presented as perfect objects to be won or reduced to castrating nags. And their own cluelessness about privilege echoes his . . ." Rebecca snapped her mouth shut. What was her problem? Ami had certainly not mentioned critiquing the Lion in her meeting prep. But Rose was nodding encouragingly, so Rebecca tried again. "What I mean is that we don't have to throw out the baby with the bathwater . . ." What in the ever-loving fuckety fuck was she saying? Baby? Bathwater? She took a deep breath. "I truly believe that the writing is persuasive enough to overcome . . . And there has to be a way to reconcile . . . not reconcile, to reframe . . . not reframe . . . to engage—yes—to *engage* with him, to engage with the work in all its flaws and brilliance. To appreciate the brilliance and to call out the flaws. To kind of reclaim it, if you know what I mean?" Rebecca could feel her face reddening, as it always did when she was passionate or when she exerted herself in any kind of physical activity.

"Oh, I do. I know exactly what you mean." Rose laughed tartly. "'Appreciate the brilliance' and 'call out the flaws' . . . Sounds like my marriage. With perhaps less appreciation and not enough . . . what did you say? 'Reclaiming'? Teddy was a complicated man, of course. Complicated because he was a genius. I don't use that word lightly, Rebecca. A man without his gifts might not be called complicated or . . . what do you say these days? 'Problematic'? No, he would merely be a handsome asshole."

Fortunately, so that Rebecca didn't have to respond as the word "asshole" hung in the air, Lorraine came in with two folding trays tucked under her arm and a cheese board that she deposited on Rose's lap. "May I get you something to drink?" she asked Rebecca meaningfully. "You must be parched."

Rebecca *was*, suddenly, parched. "Yes, please. Water?" Her tongue was dry and sweat tickled her back. Lorraine left and Rose offered the cheese board to Rebecca, holding it between them. There was a gorgeous, oozing wedge of Camembert, peppered crackers, a bunch of green grapes, and a wooden-handled cheese knife that matched the board. Gabe had taught Rebecca, after an unfortunate faux pas during cocktails with a Parisienne author, that one never cuts the nose off the cheese wedge. Balancing awkwardly, Rebecca sliced a piece along the side of the Camembert like a French countess, smeared it on a cracker, and opted for putting the whole thing in her mouth rather than chance any cheese landing on the couch or her shirt.

"Did your mother tell you that we worked here, at the *East River Review*, together?" Rose asked suddenly.

Rebecca, still chewing what was, in retrospect, too large a mouthful, shook her head violently. Unthinking, she slid the cheese knife into the slot in the front of the cheese board where it belonged. Where it belonged when it was clean and NOT when it was covered in Camembert, she realized. Her face flamed. Also, WTF, Mom! Rebecca coughed a little, kept her mouth shut to avoid flying crumbs, choked, turned even redder if possible. Why hadn't Jane told her this VERY RELEVANT information? Hadn't Rebecca asked her point-blank? And didn't Jane know that Rebecca would be meeting with Rose here today? Why lie? Or omit the crucial truth, which was pretty much the same as lying? Lorraine appeared with a glass of water that she handed silently but maybe judgmentally to Rebecca.

"I'm sorry to have startled you," Rose said gently. Lorraine returned with a large bowl of greens and two plates of chicken salad and set them out on the trays. "I'm not surprised that she never mentioned it."

Rebecca swallowed, took a sip of water, and cleared her throat. "I knew that she worked here a long time ago, but she never said anything about you or . . . him . . . and she knew I was meeting with you." She took a plate from Rose and balanced it carefully on her knees, as the couch was too far away from the tray for safety. This mansion had two kitchens and who knew how many dining rooms. Was there not a table to eat on like a normal person? With another flush of shame, she watched Rose inspect the cheese board, its tucked-away cheese-smeared knife, and politely put it to the side. "I guess this is why I'm here? How did you know I was her daughter? Have you been in touch with each other?"

"I do understand how to use the internet, Rebecca. And, no, I haven't spoken to Jane in"—Rose paused—"almost forty years."

"I see," Rebecca said. She did not see. "You worked together? Forty years ago?" Following Rose's lead, she took a few bites of chicken salad but avoided the unwieldy greens.

"I was a writer. Like your mom. I had just received my master's degree at NYU, where my thesis adviser was another 'genius.'" Rose didn't have to use finger quotes for Rebecca to get the subtext. "One of the most coveted jobs in the city, or anywhere people cared about these things, I suppose, was at the *East River Review*. Teddy was founder, editor in chief, lord of the manor if you will. He was such a charismatic, larger-than-life figure. All entwined, you know, with the writing, the power of his genius, the parties, the famous people, the beautiful women, the drinking. We had softball games in the park against the *Hudson Review*. One time Salman Rushdie knocked Updike over and claimed it was an accident. It was not." She smiled, stood up, and walked to the windows, her back to Rebecca, who took advantage of this moment out of Rose's gaze to launch herself clumsily from the couch. "And Teddy presiding over it. The most talented of all of them."

"And my mom?" Rebecca hastily readjusted her jacket, flapping it for a moment to get some air onto her sweaty back. Had Rose said that her mom was a *writer*?

"Jane was an intern with me. And the most fabulous writer. So talented in a way that I wasn't, even though I had more training. We read the slush pile looking for the next Joan Didion. Your mother was the only one of us who ever pulled anything that got published. Did she ever tell you she found Sandra Cisneros? Jeanette Winterson? I mean before their first books were published."

It was strange and disorienting to think of her mother as a person who had had a life so different from the one she lived in front of Rebecca. She had always been interested in Rebecca's English essays, come to think of it, though by the time she got to college, Rebecca had stopped allowing Jane to read anything before she handed it in. And after Rebecca left for college, her mother had a part-time job at Germantown Friends in the publications department, and she volunteered at the town library. But that didn't add up to a woman who hung out with Salman Rushdie and discovered Sandra Cisneros. "But you didn't stay in touch? Why did you ask for me to come over here? Is it really to do with the estate?"

Rose kept her back to Rebecca and looked fixedly out the window. "I did try a few times, but your mother didn't want to be contacted. Not by me. Teddy was quite sick for the last six years. We mostly stayed in Southampton, where I took care of him. It's true that he was still writing, in longhand on yellow legal pads, as he always did. There are some new short stories that he was excited about. After he died, I had to sort through all his papers, which he had always insisted on keeping to himself. Now it's my responsibility to gather information for the lawyers, for our financial adviser. In his desk here I found a novel he had written but never spoke to me about—and I had read and edited everything he wrote after we married." Rose paused again, her shoulders stiff. "Hundreds of yellow pages. Unpublished and, as far as I know, unseen by anyone but me. There's only one handwritten copy. I don't know when he wrote it exactly, but it seemed he had been working on it for years."

Rebecca thought immediately of Ami, Avenue, and Frank French. An entire unpublished novel by the Lion. Coming on the heels of the publicity after his death—the glowing obits, the tortured think pieces, the magazine articles—a new novel would be one of the biggest publishing stories of the past twenty years. Like Harper Lee's found manuscript, published posthumously to unprecedented fanfare. And sales. Okay, so maybe they should have edited out the parts about Atticus Finch being an actual racist.

"Is it something you want Avenue to publish?" Rebecca asked. "I know we could do it justice."

"What I want is for Jane to read it." Rose turned away from the windows and faced Rebecca. There were tears in her eyes and she let them fall without wiping them. "She was my best friend."

CHAPTER SIX

TUESDAY
HOME, REBECCA

Rebecca splurged and took a cab home from the office. Her debriefing with Ami had gone as well as could be expected. She had left three messages for her mom, who was clearly still ghosting her. She kept thinking about Rose and Jane, the discovery of the unpublished novel, and, most importantly, how her mom (a writer?!) was a piece of the puzzle. Jane's interest in and—let's face it—her sometimes unrealistic expectations for Rebecca's career had always seemed centered on Rebecca, but clearly there was something else going on. Ami had barely restrained her excitement at the possibility of Avenue's landing the Lion's estate. Rose had asked Rebecca not to say anything to anyone about the novel, so Rebecca played up the unpublished stories instead. As the cab lurched up Central Park West, she texted Gabe.

Rebecca:
SO MUCH TO TELL

Gabe:
ami told me WHAT. THE. FUCK. jane!

Rebecca:
of course mom MIA now totally ducking me

Gabe:
we know where she lives

Rebecca:
but her secret life

Gabe:
housewife spins web of lies to camouflage glam misspent youth

housewife in shocking celebrity throuple

housewife ID'd as elena ferrante

Max:
Hey, Rebecca

Rebecca:
hold on max texting me

Gabe:
👌😂🍆

Rebecca:
rude

just a sec

Max:

> Hey Rebecca, I'm not going to make it to dinner tonight. I've been thinking about this and I feel I only want to be dating in a more serious way right now and I don't think I'm in a place where I am ready to do that with you right now I know that isn't how I've been treating this and I apologize for giving you the wrong impression. You are a lot and great but maybe too much for me right now. Although I have had a lot of fun with you the past few months; hoping things went well for you today. Have a good time tonight. Again I am sorry to be dramatic. I wish you all the best

Rebecca's thumb hovered over her phone. Furious and hurt tears sprang up, and she rubbed her eyes with all the vigor she had been holding back the entire day. Suddenly, Max was composing a text novel? He was ditching her tonight and blowing her off forever and he couldn't bring himself to call? To break it off in person? She was "a lot"?? A lot of what?? He wanted to be dating in a more serious way? But not with her? The semicolon was tragic. HAD HE LEARNED NOTHING? Rebecca knew she couldn't text Stella, who would be muddling mint for the rhubarb spritzers and baking the shortcakes. She would have to stiff-upper-lip-it through dinner because it was Stella's night and Rebecca could not make it all about herself, even though objectively she did have a few major reasons for needing attention.

Gabe:

> hellllooo? jane called: admitted she and marlowe wrote all of shakespeare's plays. not merchant tho

Rebecca forwarded Max's text to Gabe.

Gabe:
oh honey

I'm so sorry what a dick

so many questions

did you respond

Rebecca:
fuck no

Gabe:
please in the name of all that is holy delete and block

DELETE AND BLOCK

Rebecca:
i know

Gabe:
WAIT SCREENSHOT TEXT

Rebecca:
obviously

Gabe:
cool shower wear that black dress with the pockets and i will come early

Rebecca:
thank you ♥

ugh

Gabe:
tonight we drink 1000 rhubarb spritzers

Rebecca:
"again i am sorry to be dramatic" ???????????

Gabe:
max! who knew she had all that drama in her

hang in there, kitten

Rebecca:
ok see you soon

When Rebecca got home, there was enough happy mayhem that she was able to follow Gabe's instructions without even laying eyes on Stella or Mimi. Only Scout, Stella's assistant, who was meticulously winding tiny white lights down the center of the dining table, looked up as Rebecca called out that she was heading to the shower. Once she was clean and cool and had collapsed on the bed in her black dress, Rebecca was finally able to breathe. She knew she should go help, but she needed to find a calm, neutral expression so that Stella wouldn't know something was amiss. Was her mom never going to call her back? Fine. She would show up at her nephews' birthday party in Philadelphia this weekend and confront Jane face-to-face. Now she had to go convince Stella and Mimi that she was fine, it was fine, she was perfectly fine. *You are a lot and great*, she thought. That's right, motherfucker, she was. Boosting herself up off the bed, Rebecca took a quick look in the mirror, tamped her hair down, patted gently under her eyes, squared her shoulders, practiced a giant grin. Perfect.

"Hey, baby! Grab a drink and slice the asparagus on the bias— like, one-inch pieces?" Stella was a whirl of brown curls, freckles, silver nails, a thrifted blue taffeta dress under one of Mimi's splattered aprons, colorful tattoos up and down each arm: bouquets of carrots and radishes, oysters, pomegranates, peaches, one spectacular artichoke, a gleaming chef's knife, and the one that matched

Rebecca's—a silver olive branch with green leaves and black olives encircling her upper arm.

"Sure!" Rebecca grinned.

"What's wrong? What happened? *Are you okay?*" Stella wiped her hands on the dish towel slung over her shoulder and threw herself at Rebecca in a crushing hug. She smelled of mint and shrimp. Rebecca remembered moving into her first-year dorm room at Barnard and her new roommate Stella's welcome hug. Stella's dad, Stanley Miller (Dr. Stan), had dropped Stella's suitcases to the floor. Her mom, Lissa Marino, an artist whose medium was entirely wire hangers, followed close behind, entrusted with Stella's French press. Stella had gone immediately to Rebecca's mouse pad with its Julia Child quote, "People who love to eat are always the best people," and hugged her again, saying, "Oh, thank god! We're going to be best friends!" Stella Marino-Miller was right, Rebecca thought. As the daughter of a Black man from Georgia and an Italian mom from Rome, Stella had grown up in LA and now found herself in New York City. She had inherited a passion for food and cooking that followed no rules but that Rebecca knew from the beginning would lead to fame and fortune.

"I'm okay." Rebecca gave Stella a squeeze. "But you need to give me the waitlist: I can start making calls for a last-minute place at the table. Max isn't coming."

"You finally ended things?!" Stella said gleefully, then caught herself and tried unsuccessfully to arrange her face more seriously.

"Well, let's put it this way: things are ended . . ."

"*Whaaat?!* That loser dumped *you?*"

"Sounds comforting when you put it that way." Stella saw Mimi in the kitchen snipping basil. "Also, keep it down. Give me the waitlist; we can discuss later."

"Okay, but *only* because I have to poach the shrimp." Stella snapped the dish towel in Rebecca's direction. "Gabe's coming, right? Miles is still doing that residency in New Haven." Rebecca had met Miles at her first and last frat party at Columbia, where they'd huddled miserably together until she'd suggested they go meet up with her roommate Stella. "Here, start with the starred names." Stella handed Rebecca her phone.

"Holy shit, Stella, there are, like, fifty names on this!" Rebecca scrolled down. "Ever since that article . . . I think it's time to find a pop-up opportunity. You're ready for an underground supper club of more than twelve. You're growing out of this place. The people have spoken!"

"You think so?" Stella poured a drink from one of Mimi's silver pitchers and garnished it with a sprig of mint. She handed it to Rebecca. "I'm in! But I can't do it without you, you know." Rebecca was already managing Stella's social media. In fact, she found that she was often working on expanding Stella's reach when she should have been editing.

"Obviously." Rebecca lifted the tiny glass. "To your future career as a foodie influencer, viral recipe maven, supper club hostess extraordinaire, cookbook writer, and person eating clams on the Amalfi coast for money!"

"I'll drink to that!" Stella lifted an imaginary glass. "Eating clams with my newly single smokin'-hot best friend! Sponsored by *Gastronomica* and Pucci."

Rebecca knew better than to bring up her encounter with Rose Adams, since Stella had her hands full with guests arriving in less than an hour. She finished her drink (refreshingly tart!) and headed into the kitchen to say hello to Mimi. By the time Gabe showed, Max's seat had been snatched up by a grateful stranger, the asparagus had been sliced on the bias, Mimi had admitted to never thinking Max was good enough for Rebecca—Mimi believed this to have been top secret information—and Rebecca had downed five rhubarb spritzers and been gently redirected by Stella to the wine in the back of the fridge. Gabe had spirited her away into her bedroom and presented a thorough editing of Max's text that cheered her immensely:

> Hey Rebecca *(Too informal for the occasion)*, I'm not going to make it tonight. *(Rude!)* I've been thinking about this *(vague)* and I feel *(cut)* I only want to be dating in a more serious way right now *(More serious than meeting Grandma, you dick?)* and I don't think I'm in a place where I am ready to do that with you right now *(repetitive)*. I know that isn't how I've been treating this *(comma)* and I apologize for giving you the wrong impression *(You apologize for wasting her time or for living a lie? Be specific)*. You are a lot *(a lot of what? Brains, beauty, and body, you milquetoast bore?)* and great *(obviously)* but maybe *(100%)* too much for me right now *(repetitive and obvious)*. Although I have had a lot of fun with you *(you don't know what fun is)* the past few months; *(This is an incorrect use of a semicolon in which you have jammed together an incomplete sentence with a gerund phrase even though you were recently taught that semicolons must join two complete and RELATED sentences. Did you actually graduate from Swarthmore? I am truly sorry for your clients and may all judges hold you in as much contempt as I do)* hoping things went well for you today. *(You made sure that they would not)* Have a good time tonight. *(Seriously?)* Again I am sorry to be dramatic. *(Girl, please)* I wish you all the best *(Where is the final period in your Hallmark sign-off? Are you James fucking Joyce?)*

Rebecca gave Gabe a grateful hug. "I could never be with a guy who was incapable of absorbing my semicolon lesson."

"Here, drink this water." Gabe gave her a glass and smoothed her hair behind her ears. "And I never want to hear any bullshit about how you're 'too much' or 'a lot' or anything like that. If you weren't too much for him, *that* would be the tragedy. Now let's go eat some poached shrimp with pickled ramps."

As always, the dining room had been transformed with little white lights, candles, mismatched glasses, and Mimi's blue-and-white wedding china. Stella kept popping in from the kitchen to uncover dishes, while Scout made herself invaluable clearing and cleaning. It was Rebecca's job to keep the conversation flowing and to take photos to upload later while Mimi presided over the table, in her element. Gabe sat between a delighted Swedish tourist and a well-dressed couple who were repeat diners. Rebecca entertained a food writer she had been working to entice to the dinner for the past few months and three giddy roommates from Gowanus who had been trying to get seats at the table for over a year. People talked about the food they were served, food in general, and whatever Rebecca steered them toward. She noticed the conversations had split into separate exchanges and decided to conduct the room back into one harmonious whole before Stella served dessert. "Henry James said the two most beautiful words in the English language are 'summer afternoon,'" she announced, continuing a well-trod and infinite discussion she and Stella had begun in a first-year writing seminar. "Agree? Disagree? Submissions?"

"Lace doily," Mimi started, having already played this game. "Crimson velvet."

"Did the summer streets of Washington Square smell of urine and desperation when Henry James lived here?" opined the obviously literary last-minute guest, a portly man with dreadlocks wearing a wildly flowered shirt and blindingly white sneakers.

"'Urine and desperation' are three words," said one of the Gowanus roommates.

"*Ciao, bella!*" the Swede called out enthusiastically, which wasn't, Rebecca noted, technically the English language but still a melodious pairing.

"Pickled ramps," Gabe said loyally as Stella came into the dining room with trays of strawberry shortcakes laden with whipped cream and garnished with lemon zest and mint. Rebecca rolled her eyes at him, having heard him answer both "erect cock" and "cowboy sashay" in the past.

"Passed hors d'oeuvres!" Stella cried, as she always did, even though, one: basically four words, and two: mostly French.

"Artichoke heart," the food critic murmured. "Silvery elixir."

Rebecca laid her hand lovingly on the food critic's forearm. "Exactly," she whispered loudly. She retrieved her phone and snapped a few photos of the strawberry shortcake, the table with its dripping candles, the relaxed and laughing guests, Mimi and Stella clinking shots of Amaro. She tried to imagine Max here among her people. Honestly, his two most beautiful words might have been "Apple watch." Or "pickleball league." She knew he wasn't right for her, and after the clarifying insight of many rhubarb spritzers and glasses of wine, she knew he had done her a favor, and in the unexplored recesses of her mind—where it would stay unexplored, if she could help it—she even knew that his stupid text, flawed as it was, was an attempt to explain himself without completely ghosting her. If only she had done it first. But now, as decreed by Stella's highly curated playlist, it was Erykah Badu time.

Later, finally in bed, Rebecca texted Jane again, imagining she would be asleep but wanting to let her know that she had some explaining to do.

Rebecca:

mom i really wish you would tell me what's going on

why did you let me walk in there knowing nothing

rose seems really nice

Jane:

Does she?

Rebecca:

mom! wtf??? where have you been?

Jane:

This is a lot to process, sweetheart. I'm sorry I haven't been completely candid with you.

Rebecca:

i would say not candid at all like the opposite of candid

Jane:

It's such a long time ago. Water under the bridge.

Rebecca:

water under the bridge?? MOM

MOOOMMMMMMMMM

Jane:

How was Rose?

Rebecca:

beautiful. mysterious. sad.

Jane:

Her husband just died.

Rebecca:

honestly not so sad about that imo more sad about YOU

are you going to tell me what's going on?

i have to go back and see her again

she wants you to come

Rebecca watched the three dots come and go, signifying her mother's typing and erasing, typing and erasing.

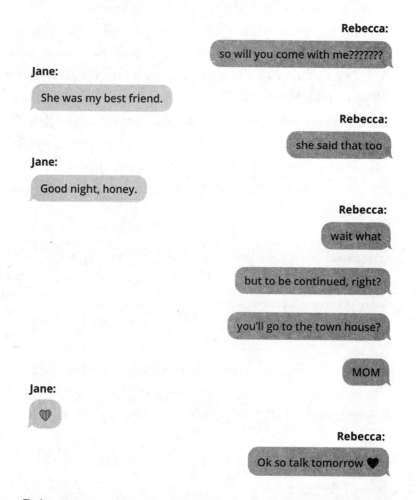

Rebecca spent the next twenty minutes googling the masthead for the *East River Review* and found her mother, listed as Jane Kinloch, and Rose, listed as Rose Bergesen, both interns in the early 1980s. After that, Rose was listed as an assistant editor. After a few years her name disappeared. The Lion was founder, editor, then eventually editor emeritus. The list of advisory editors was an impressive collection of well-known writers, including the present associate editor, a mildly successful novelist whom Rebecca recognized as the man in the fedora. Rebecca's deep dive also uncovered a few of Rose's short stories in *The New Yorker* in the mid-'80s that she was a little too drunk to read. She found an article in last week's *New York Times* about the *East River Review*'s sixtieth anniversary and speculation about what would happen to the East End town house and the magazine office now that the Lion had died.

There was only one place to learn the real gossip, however. Rebecca pulled up Instagram and checked BLURB, the anonymous account that was a mix of clever memes, complaints about publishing, rumors, and the many moods of Ben Affleck. Rebecca was chagrined to read the most recent posts:

BLURB more layoffs announced at harpercollins—deets please

Anon, please can confirm. jobs not being replaced but consolidated

BLURB [meme of two girls reading books by the pool in *White Lotus* juxtaposed with Connie Britton and a giant glass of wine] Me when I loved reading books vs Me after working in publishing

BLURB mid-level avenue editor swoops in on EDA widow— deets please

Anon, please can confirm. [meme of fat baby clenching fist]

juleswolf0910 eyes on atticus adams

BLURB [meme of sad Ben Affleck on the beach] Me when I realize publishing execs don't believe cost of living increase is a thing

Rebecca reread the pertinent post. Was she, in this scenario, the fat baby clenching his fist? Really? "Mid-level" sounded, somehow, more insulting than low-level. It had to have been Fedora or more likely Satchel Girl snitching on her. Did they have nothing better to do? Rebecca did a quick search for Atticus Adams. Very handsome, sort of dissolute, always in a suit with gorgeous women draped over him. Had recently "parted ways" with an investment banking job according to Page Six, the gossip page of the *Post*. He was tangentially involved in some sort of vague scandal involving a tech start-up. Rebecca was caught by one photo of Atticus as a child wearing what looked like a sailor suit, gazing up at his father, whose admittedly leonine head was turned away. Whether the photographer was Atticus's young mother or paparazzi stalking them, it was impossible to tell. It was strange to think of the Lion (Teddy!) as a real man with a wife (a few wives) and a child. How much could Atticus complicate things? Rose hadn't even mentioned him.

Sleepily, Rebecca checked her email one last time. Mrs. Singh had sent another reminder for the first Cooperative Committee Group Meeting about desk sharing on Monday. Positively Orwellian. *Note to self,* Rebecca thought as she turned her phone to do not disturb: *cactus, apples, someone unmask Office Life Anon, fedora, UGH MAX, rhubarb spritzer, sailor suit, Jane and Rose, Rose and Jane, sad Ben Affleck, Ben with cactus, cactus* . . . She was fast asleep.

JANE

NEW YORK CITY
OCTOBER 1981

Jane sat at Paco's desk, on a call with the New York Public Library. When had Elizabeth Bishop lived in Brazil? What was the exact spelling of Penobscot Bay? The librarian at the information desk had put the phone down, and Jane could hear her heels clacking as she walked away. How or where they found the answers, Jane had no idea, but the librarians of the information desk never expressed annoyance or impatience; they never scoffed at a question, no matter how seemingly unimportant or strange. Most importantly, in the five months she had been at the *East River Review*, Jane had never asked a question they couldn't answer. She fiddled with the phone cord, twisting it around her finger. A flash of white caught her eye, and she looked up to see Drew posing behind the bars of the window up near the blue door. Ever since they had watched Blondie's "Rapture" video, first on *Solid Gold*, then on MTV's launch in August, Drew always did a little dance like the man from Mars before entering the *East River Review* office. Jane and Rose found it hilarious every single time.

"What is that boy doing?" Deedle asked, the ash from his cigarette trembling over his typewriter. He caught it in his palm, then looked around for a place to dump it, eventually choosing a sad cactus on Ellen's desk that she used for the same purpose. The phone shrilled, and Deedle wheeled back to his desk to pick it up. Jane ignored Deedle as she usually did; she and Rose had gotten adept at dodging his plump hands and pretending not to hear his steady stream of obnoxious comments. When he was drunk, as he often was after lunch and always at parties, he affected an Irish accent and leered even more aggressively than usual. His slim volume of poetry was Dylan Thomas–esque only in the sense that Deedle also frequented Chumley's and the White Horse Tavern, the West Village establishments that Jane had never heard of before a crash literary pub crawl that Parker insisted on leading. There had been a minor upheaval last month when one of the young poets championed by Deedle had come crying to the office and Jonathan had hastily ushered her upstairs. She hadn't been heard from since. The next day, Deedle's wife, Marion, until then only a scolding voice on the phone, had arrived in person, much to everyone's delighted surprise, and delivered in public what Jonathan later referred to as "a proper tongue-lashing" that left Deedle chastened for at least two full days.

Drew came down the narrow aisle between desks, humming "Rapture" as Jane contained her laughter. He gave the Rolodex on Jonathan's desk a spin, something he dared to do only because Jonathan was out preparing for the fall issue party tomorrow night. "Be careful!" Parker spluttered. He had given all the interns the same very serious instructions a number of times: Don't sit at Jonathan's desk. Don't touch Jonathan's Rolodex. Don't even *look* at Jonathan's Rolodex. If J. D. Salinger's phone number got out, there would be hell to pay! Of course, the minute Jane, Rose, and Drew were alone in the office, they examined Jonathan's Rolodex with the clandestine attention one might give an uncle's *Playboy* magazine stash. Typed, written in Jonathan's cramped script, or in EDA's distinctive block handwriting, the Rolodex cards contained enough informational treasure to stun them: Kurt Vonnegut's nearby address, Jackie Onassis's phone number, Picasso's name crossed out, the secret number to call for the best table at the Rainbow Room.

"Going upstairs?" Drew asked.

"In a minute," Jane answered. "I'm fact-checking the Bishop interview."

Drew started sorting through art portfolios on the table, and Deedle hung up the phone on Marion. "Never get married!" he announced to the room. Turning to Jane, he kept talking, even though she was clearly occupied. "Busy little bee! You and Rose have really improved the atmosphere in the office." He winked suggestively. "In fact, we're thinking of moving Paco upstairs and commemorating a permanent desk for you two." Jane said nothing, noting that Deedle had misbuttoned his shirt, exposing an unfortunate glimpse of pale belly. "The hot desk." He made a sizzling noise, like bacon cooking. "Because you're both hot," Deedle continued unnecessarily. If Jane thought about his miserable marriage and sloppy shirt, she could almost feel sorry for him.

"Jane!" Ellen came out of the back room brandishing a manuscript. Jane hung up the phone on the librarian of the information desk. She would call back later. "I like this. I like it." Ellen sat heavily in her chair and scooted over next to Jane. She smelled of smoke, perspiration, and damp wool. It was a warm day for October, and the noisy fan Ellen insisted on had been blowing both fetid air and papers around until Parker snapped it off. "The slush you pulled? That story by the Mexican girl from Chicago?"

"Sandra Cisneros?" Jane's pulse quickened. She had read the story to Rose only last night and put it on Ellen's desk this morning after staying up late to write an impassioned plea for it. Ellen was notoriously difficult to impress, and her taste ran to dense excerpts of novels in translation or indecipherable prose poems. She had ignored all of Jane's previous slush pile pulls, which was better than facing her withering judgment.

Jane had been sleeping most nights at Rose's father's co-op on East Eighty-Eighth Street; he commuted to Wall Street from Connecticut and almost never used the apartment where Rose was living. The first time Rose had visited Jane's apartment in the East Village, one of the pimps had grabbed her breast while she was waiting for Jane to drop a sock with the key in it from the fourth-floor window. "It's fine," Rose had said. "It's basically what Deedle tried last week!" But she had been shaken, and Jane had despaired. After she admitted to Rose that the same guy had taken to stalking up and down in front of her building, Rose insisted that Jane stay uptown with her. Jane was paying a hundred dollars a month in rent but making at least two hundred in tips over her $2.13 hourly wage working one night a week as a hostess at the Apple on Madison Avenue. It was walking distance to the co-op and the office, and once the Upper East Side ladies who lunched cleared out, the uncomfortable wicker chairs filled with businessmen eager to impress their clients. Men with expense accounts were happy to press cash on Jane, and she learned to smile flirtatiously while pocketing phone numbers that she later crumpled into the trash.

Rose referred to her father's co-op as a "soulless box" with parquet floors, hospital-white walls, and vertical blinds that kept breaking, but at least the bathtub wasn't in the kitchen, and there was an elevator. Rose wanted her to move in officially, but Jane didn't enjoy her occasional run-ins with Rose's handsome, creepy father. Anders Bergesen worked at an investment bank that Jane had just very recently learned was called "Salomon Brothers" and not "Salmon Brothers," but her mental image of him in his double-breasted suit, barking out orders at the Fulton Fish Market—which she knew was all wrong but still amusing—had persisted. Jane preferred Deedle's obvious, lecherous jollity to Anders's chilly scrutiny and habit of opening closed doors without knocking, once catching Jane half-dressed in Rose's bedroom, once standing in the bathroom doorway while Jane turned off the shower and called out "Who's there?" until he finally left without saying a word. But Anders, between commuting and traveling, didn't spend that much time in the apartment, so Rose and Jane had it mostly to themselves.

Both of them loved the frenetic energy of downtown much more than what Jane thought of as the mausoleum chill of the Upper East Side. They wanted to spend every minute together, and after work most of that time was below Fourteenth Street. Then they would take the subway back up to the co-op, or Rose would insist on a taxi if it was really late. Once, they used Rose's father's town car account to pick them up from the Pyramid Club even though they were almost next door to Jane's apartment. That night Drew, who often joined them, also slept over, since the 7 train to Flushing was out of service again.

"I'm going to run this story by Teddy when he's back from Southampton tomorrow," Ellen was saying. "Good eye, Jane."

"*She has Bette Davis eyes*," Parker sang off-key. Parker, intimidated by Rose, spent a lot of time explaining things to Jane, such as how to pronounce Basquiat. (Jane squirmed at the memory of saying "Base-quee-at" instead of "Baa-skee-aat" in front of all of them.)

Behind Parker, Drew mouthed the word "douche," drawing out the syllable and finishing with an audible "shaa."

"I'm so glad you liked the story!" Jane said quickly to Ellen, turning away from Drew so she wouldn't laugh. "Publishing her would be amazing! She's only twenty-seven years old."

"Well, settle down," Ellen groused—already, Jane knew, regretting her slip in praising anyone or anything. "Teddy might not go for it. Might be too urban for him." She relented when she saw Jane's face.

"But I'll see what I can do," she added grudgingly. "Go find another needle in the haystack."

"Another pearl in the oyster," Deedle said. "Which reminds me, one of you kids needs to go pick up the order at Citarella for the party tomorrow night."

"And make sure there's nothing in the refrigerator upstairs," Parker added. "Also, Drew, would you call Jo to confirm that Clara is still across the pond?" He and EDA's assistant in London spent hours determining who was where so as to prepare for any awkward encounters between EDA and his wife.

None of the interns had yet laid eyes on Clara, and Jane sometimes wondered if she even existed. Everyone dropped their voices when they spoke of her, and when she, Rose, and Drew compared notes, it seemed clear that Clara and EDA were living separate lives. Deedle referred to her as a "twat" more than once, and Parker screened her calls, often lying to her about EDA's whereabouts. When he hung up, everyone pretended they hadn't been listening.

EDA himself wasn't around as much as Jane had hoped since she arrived at the *East River Review*. It had something to do with his failing marriage, a new apartment in London, an excursion to Morocco. When he burst into the office, always exuberantly, he took up all the space, as Rose had described. The rest of them fluttered around him adoringly, Parker particularly sycophantic, while even gruff Ellen cooed and touched his sleeve. He had hardly glanced at Jane, only once clapped her shoulder with a heavy hand and urged everyone to find him "the best words in the best order!"—which was, Drew told her later, a quote from the poet Samuel Taylor Coleridge. EDA's latest novel, *The Coldest War*, was already garnering rapturous advance praise even though it wasn't being published until early next year. There were rumors that he was to be photographed by Annie Leibovitz for an article titled "The Celebrity Writer" in *Rolling Stone* magazine. The interns hadn't been invited to the summer issue party in Southampton, but tomorrow night's soiree was at the town house, and it was all Drew, Jane, and Rose could do not to talk about it every second of every day. All three of them were officially Edward David Adams fans, as much for his magnetic good looks and commanding presence as for his writing, though they could each quote passages from his books. Jane hadn't yet gotten used to the daily interaction—on the phone, in unpublished work, even in the occasional office drop-by—with literary stars she had only studied and read, and she was learning all the time about those she had never heard of before. Towering above all of them was EDA, whose talent, success, and charisma were the subject of much exaggerated swooning among them.

"Lord, I need a coffee," Ellen groaned. "Jane, cull the slush dollars for me."

Most of the unsolicited manuscripts arrived as required with self-addressed stamped envelopes to carry the firmly worded rejection letters or the slightly more encouraging rejection letters back to the hopeful writers. Some people clipped dollar bills to their envelopes, and those people never saw their precious work again. The editors often rifled through the slush box to snatch up the money, sometimes even the loose stamps, and although Jane was at first chagrined, she had become more cavalier, though she could not yet bring herself to pocket any of it. She found a few dollars, handed them over to Ellen, and plucked a stack of slush to bring upstairs.

"Don't go far," Parker warned. "We need you on call today." Parker was wearing bright green corduroy pants and a canvas belt covered in little whales. Rose was convinced he used the *Official Preppy Handbook* as his bible; Jane, who knew Parker came from a small town just outside Pittsburgh, recognized and empathized with his desire to remake himself, though she could do without the lectures and the whales.

"I'll just be upstairs." Jane and Rose had arrived together, as they did most mornings. Rose had already disappeared, and Jane was eager to join her on the window seat. Jane had had plenty of friends when she was younger, and her Fishtown neighborhood was still filled with girls she had known growing up. But with each passing month she felt the distance grow between herself and everything that had come before New York.

There was no one like Rose, and already Jane couldn't imagine her life without her. Most nights they went out, dancing at Danceteria, table hopping at the Odeon, gawking at Warhol at the Mudd Club. Even better were the nights they stayed in, ordering Chinese dumplings, perusing the *Village Voice* missed connections ("you: blue bag, blue eyes on the C train at dusk; me: black coat, Hemingway paperback, let you slip away at 96th"), and reading to each other. Jane basked in the glow of Rose's enthusiasm for her writing; she carried her notebook everywhere and filled it with observations, lines, ideas. Rose's stories were fully formed, neat, with subtle metaphors and devastating little turns. Jane loved them. She loved Rose's fearlessness, her intelligence, her radiance. Rose wasn't particularly passionate about her work; she got more pleasure out of tacking up her Polaroids or going over Jane's stories with a painstaking precision that overwhelmed Jane with gratitude. With Rose's encouragement, Jane wrote every day; she kept all her drained pens and counted them with satisfaction every time she had to buy a new one. She measured each story she plucked from the slush pile against her own stories. Hers were usually better, she and Rose agreed. But the gulf between her work and what the *East River Review* published still seemed wide. She and Rose kept a list of quotes from the author interviews that they transcribed, writing out their favorites and taping them to the wall above Rose's bed. Jane hurried up the steep back stairs.

Rose was in her usual spot on the window seat, long legs tucked up under her. "I don't even know how we're supposed to get any work done," she announced. "People have been in and out all day with their preparations."

"Forget work," Jane said. "Parker wants us at his beck and call."

"Is Drew coming up?"

"He has to make some calls. Guess what? Ellen actually likes the Cisneros story. She's showing it to EDA tomorrow."

"Jane! You rock star!" Rose leaped up and gave Jane a hug, her joy immediate, genuine. "Last week Ellen told me I was 'unpleasantly optimistic and naively undiscerning,' so . . . anyway, now we can celebrate when we're getting ready for the party! I have a surprise for you."

"I'm not going to wear your jacket with the shoulder pads," Jane warned. "I look like a football player."

"That's from the Norma Kamali show, I'll have you know," Rose scolded. "Trust me, you'll be wearing shoulder pads to the office next year. But that blazer is for work! This is a party—you'll see."

The next night, as she and Rose waited for Drew, Jane learned the surprise was the brand-new Betsey Johnson dress that she had tried on a few weeks ago but didn't buy. "I can't!" she protested, but even as she said the words, she was slipping off her clothes to put it on.

"Jane, you're sexy! You have to show it off! Lean over and pull your boobs into the bodice, like this . . ." Rose made a scooping motion. "If I had any boobs at all, I would totally wear this."

Jane obediently maneuvered herself into the top and let the rest of the short dress flounce down. She spun in front of the mirrored closet doors. "I'm practically naked," she complained, but she was dazzled by her appearance.

"Your bangs look perfect, and you can wear your black ankle

boots. You can borrow my leather jacket. I'll do your eye makeup and you'll look just like Chrissie Hynde." They had been listening to the Pretenders nonstop.

"Chrissie's boobs wouldn't be all—you know—like this," Jane pointed out.

"Right," Rose agreed. "She wishes!"

"Fine. What are you wearing? Still the puffy sleeves?"

"Yes, with the skinny belt and the chunky heels."

"You're going to be ten feet tall!" Jane flopped onto the bed, clean and cool.

"All the better to see eye to eye with Teddy." Rose tapped her chin. "But I'll still only be up to his shoulders. His broad shoulders."

The buzzer interrupted their back-and-forth, and Rose ran into the other room to tell the doorman to let Drew up. Jane brought their empty glasses into the kitchen to refill them with wine and to pour a glass for Drew.

"Are you ready?" Drew asked when he came in, his hair taller and more gelled than usual. "I brought supplies." He reached into his blazer pocket and pulled out a mixtape and a bindle of cocaine. Rose popped the tape into her dad's stereo. Donna Summer. Drew took a framed photo of a horse off the wall. "I'll cut some lines on Secretariat here."

"That horse is named Betsy!" Rose corrected him. "My dad loves her more than he loves me."

"Impossible!" Drew assured her, moving the white powder around niftily with a razor blade that he kept in his wallet.

"Is that from Paco again?" Jane didn't know how she felt about Drew's partying with the magazine's art director, Paco, though their adventures did make for entertaining stories about Badlands on Christopher Street or Rawhide in the city's gay neighborhood, Chelsea. Drew wanted Jane and Rose to come with them to a drag show, but

Jane wasn't sure she wanted to hang out with Paco outside of work. With his assertive artistic eye and confidently feminine mannerisms, Paco was like no one Jane had ever met before. Of the entire *East River Review* staff, he intimidated her the most: when he turned his coolly appraising gaze on her, it was as if he could see into her uncultured past and tiny closet of uninspiring clothes. She always felt as though he were one minute away from saying something so cutting that she would die.

It had been a lightning-quick education for Jane, who flushed as she remembered asking Rose if she thought Drew liked her. "Of course he likes me," Rose had answered, looking at Jane quizzically. "Wait. Oh, Jane! You know that Drew likes boys, right?" As soon as Jane heard Rose's revelation, it was blindingly clear. Once that got sorted, Jane thought about how Rose hadn't teased her or made her feel stupid; she had given her the information she needed in a kind way and moved on. Now Drew sang, *"Jane's lookin' like hot stuff, baby, tonight,"* and he offered Rose a line. He patted his own chest. "Nice!"

"She does look hot, doesn't she?" Rose quickly and efficiently snorted the coke through a ten-dollar bill, licked her finger, and rubbed the rest on her gums. Jane was impressed and annoyed by the rigmarole of cocaine, all its elaborate procedures and codes. The first and only time she had done it was last month with Drew in the tiny bathroom of the Blue & Gold Tavern on Seventh Street, right near her apartment. It had left a bitter taste in the back of her throat but had fueled her running the pool table for hours until Rose and Drew begged her to step away. Jane still hadn't dared to play pool upstairs at the East End town house.

"Let me do your eyes too." Rose hovered over Drew with an eye pencil, holding the mascara like a cigarette in her mouth.

"Make me look like Grace Jones." Drew passed the framed photo of Betsy to Jane, who hesitated, then did the line. She shivered and sat up, her head suddenly clear.

"Truth or dare?" Rose asked around the mascara, tipping Drew's head this way and that.

"Truth," Jane answered, taking a long swallow of white wine to mask the taste of the coke dripping into her throat.

"What do you want most?" Drew jumped in, seamlessly continuing the game they often played.

Jane thought for a moment. "To publish a book," she surprised herself by saying. It was a leap from her rapidly filling notebooks to an actual book, she knew, but she was getting better about saying aloud the things she hadn't even fully articulated to herself. Her answer was a truth *and* a dare, she thought. Rose and Drew strode through the New York City streets drawing attention and second glances; when Jane was with them, she basked in their confidence and beauty, and when they bent toward her, she felt herself grow wittier, more assured. Bartenders showered her with free drinks, the handsome (married) chef at the Apple clutched his heart whenever she ducked into the kitchen, and, most gratifying of all, Rose and Drew seemed to believe that Jane was a real writer, that she would find success, that one day she would be featured in *The New York Times* with a bestselling novel and a killer outfit.

"No taking it back." Rose smiled at her. "I know you'll do it."

"Truth or dare?" Jane asked Drew, a little flushed from the headiness of the truth she had told. She caught a glimpse of herself in the mirror again and thought briefly of her mother, whose strict rules about modest clothing, modest thoughts, and modest ambitions had dominated her childhood. Jane smiled at her own image. *Hot stuff.*

"Truth." Drew did his line of coke, then submitted again to Rose's ministrations.

"Tell us a secret," Rose ordered.

Drew was quiet. "Okay," he said finally. "My name is Joon-woo."

Rose and Jane looked at each other over the top of his head. "Can we call you Joon-woo?" Rose asked.

"No," Drew said firmly. "Joon-woo is my Flushing name. Drew is my Manhattan name."

"Why Drew?" Jane filled everyone's glasses with the last of the wine.

"I guess my parents thought Andrew sounded American? I lobbied for Elvis, of course."

"Elvis would have worked." Rose stepped back and admired her handiwork.

"Truth or dare, Rose?" Jane asked.

"Dare, obviously."

"Tonight," Drew said. "At the party. I dare you to tell EDA that you'd love to edit his work sometime."

"What?" Rose laughed. "That would be crazy!"

"And," Drew continued, "I dare you to call him 'Teddy' to his face."

"That's two dares!" Rose protested.

"Fine! Just the first one, then."

"He'd be lucky if you did edit his work," Jane said. She watched Rose carefully. All of them professed to adore EDA, with Drew leading the way; he had even mocked up a fake *Interview* magazine cover featuring himself as EDA's "favorite girl." Interns infatuated with the country's most well-known writer was funny precisely because reciprocity was so far-fetched. But Rose had actually been speaking to him; she had breathlessly reported a chat about the delights of sushi and a longer discussion about what they were reading (Rose: Octavia E. Butler's *Kindred*; EDA: an unpublished manuscript in Italian by Umberto Ecco). Jane, whose faith and pride in Rose's ability to charm anyone, still knew that EDA—older, married, famous—was out of reach. Even though they lounged around in his living room and held their breath when he careened into the office, he was from another world. Though tonight, she remembered, they would all three be entering that world officially.

"I'm sure he'll be too drunk to remember anyway." Drew stood up and gazed at himself in the mirror. His eyes met Jane's. "You know what they say about an *East River Review* party . . ."

"I'll do it," Rose stated firmly. "You know I will." She pulled the Polaroid out of her bag. "Smile, beauties," she said.

To stay like this forever was what she could have answered earlier, Jane thought, as they stepped into the foyer of the town house, the whole place ablaze with lights and chatter and shrieks of laughter. It was the first time any of them had entered the town house through the front door. Deedle's red scarf was wound around the slender neck of a marble statue, and Rose whispered, "Oh my god, Joan Didion!" and Jane saw the frail writer ahead of them. Drew plucked a white tulip from the hundreds in a vase on the round entrance table and tucked it behind his ear. Rose reached for her hand and together they started to climb the wide, curving staircase.

CHAPTER SEVEN

WEDNESDAY
WORK, BEN

Ben put his messenger bag down and looked at his desk. Cactus and apple. Rebecca Blume's stuff was multiplying. The apple was probably from the basket of fruit someone had left in the kitchen last week, where it unfortunately seemed to have replaced the afternoon cheese-and-salami platter. There was a pink Post-it under the apple: **MAKE IT FALL**. This was clearly in reference to the HOT DESK posting that quoted Che Guevara, which had Ben questioning his previous vision of Rebecca Blume as akin to Mrs. Toddle, who never had a poster of anyone more political than Garfield the cat. There was a new Post-it on the cactus, too, a veritable avalanche of communication from someone who still hadn't managed to follow the rules and reach out to him officially. **I'M 90% DRY**. What the hell? Was she writing in the voice of the cactus? Was he the cactus keeper now?

Ben opened the desk drawer for a Post-it and knocked over a half-empty, luckily capped bottle of kombucha. Seriously? Not only a violation of the Clean Desk Policy but also, couldn't kombucha explode if it was in a dark, warm place and someone unwittingly jostled it? He couldn't in good conscience put it in the recycling bin unemptied like a bomb, could he? Ben pulled a Bill Russell bobblehead doll and a photo of the Lion at Bread Loaf out of his bag, the only personal desk effects he could come up with to get Ava off his back. He would not have a serial killer vibe at his new job. He was a professional committed to his workspace. Maybe next week he would bring in some favorite books? A mug for tea so that he didn't have to keep borrowing Mrs. Singh's "Crazy Vegan Lady" cup? Ben felt a little glow of satisfaction at how well he was settling in at Hawk Mills. He leaned the photo against the monitor and was positioning Bill Russell when Howie suddenly appeared in his red sweater.

"Dude! Is that LeBron?"

"No. Bill Russell." Ben gritted his teeth.

"Just fucking with you! I'm a Wilt the Stilt man myself, if we're going old-school."

"Russell was better in the playoffs, better under pressure," Ben said.

"I'm just looking at the stats." Howie shrugged his shoulders. "I'm just looking at the math. I think you need to water your cactus."

"It's not my cactus."

"Ready for the acquisitions meeting?"

"Definitely." Ben took stock of his newly personalized desk space. He was on track to pursue a collection of short stories, he had Caro's confidence, he was certainly going to hear back from Atticus anytime now, and Howie had revealed an unexpected knowledge of basketball. The cactus *was* a little dry, though. No, he reminded himself, watering it was not his job!

"So I was thinking," Howie said casually. "I know a guy performing at Howl&Yawp this weekend? You know, the underground performance art collective in Bushwick? Maybe you want to go check it out?"

That sounded like a nightmare to Ben. But he was new to New York. He was hanging out with his sister and—if you could call playing absurdly competitive pickup basketball "hanging out"—with a few guys at the West Fourth Street court. Not exactly crushing it socially. Between reading for work and bartending, Ben hadn't had time to explore the city. And, honestly, he didn't want to reject Howie, who was looking at him with a hopeful expression. "Sure," he said.

"Seriously?" Howie did a double take. He pumped his fist and hissed, "*Yassss*," under his breath. "You won't regret it!"

Ben was already regretting it. "Just text me the details."

"I thought we could head over together. Maybe grab some Korean fried chicken first?"

Before Ben could answer, Howie dropped his voice. "Incoming."

"What?"

"See you around!" Howie backed away as Caro came up behind Ben.

"Hey, good morning." Ben moved the apple and bottle of kombucha to the side of his desk. Caro was wearing a brown silk dress, a brown silk jacket, and complicated red shoes.

Caro barely nodded a morning acknowledgment. "Have you set up a meeting with Atticus Adams?" Ben appreciated her directness but would have appreciated it more if Atticus hadn't responded to his texts with only a string of champagne and oyster emojis at 2 a.m. on Saturday.

"We're in contact. I should have something firmed up today."

"By the end of the day, Ben," Caro said sternly. "I'm concerned that Avenue has the jump on us. Ami is making some surprising moves, if I'm to believe the scuttlebutt. Rose Adams has been impossible to reach, and, believe me, I've tried. Ty's tried. I'm starting to think that you and the son are our best way in, at least until I can get a formal meeting set up for us with Mrs. Adams."

Ben noticed she didn't look too thrilled with that conclusion. He wondered if Howie, who often lurked around Caro's office, was the scuttlebutt. "I'll make it happen," he promised, more confidently now that he knew Atticus was at least alive.

"Please do," Caro replied pleasantly, though Ben sensed how restrained she was being, and he really didn't want to disappoint her. He turned on his computer and immediately pulled up Blabber.

BEN:
what do you know about avenue and the lion?

HOWIE:
i heard his widow met with one of their "mid-level" editors like she went over there by herself for hours

BEN:
heard from where?

HOWIE:
BLURB

BEN:
?

HOWIE:
you on IG right?

BEN:
not really

HOWIE:
facebook?

BEN:
srsly? no

HOWIE:
but hinge, right?

BEN:
can you tell me how you heard about avenue?

HOWIE:

just trying to decode your online presence

if looks could kill haha

fine i'll be over in a sec

Ben watched as Howie trotted across the office and arrived at Ben's desk, waving his battered phone. "So BLURB is the Instagram account for the publishing world. Like forty thousand followers, even though execs don't admit to stalking it." Howie leaned over Ben, reeking, as always, of smoke.

"Who runs it?"

"Top secret!" Howie put his finger to his lips. "Probably some kind of socialist bookworm? English major at Brown is my guess. Hired for paltry wages at an entry-level job; thought it was their big break. Disillusioned. Holding management to account. Pro-union and lots of Ben Affleck memes."

"Okay, show me." Ben waited while Howie navigated his cracked and smeared screen. He pulled up the BLURB account and handed Ben his phone. Ben resisted the urge to scrub it down with a sterilizing wipe.

BLURB mid-level avenue editor swoops in on EDA widow— deets please ♡

Anon, please can confirm. [meme of fat baby clenching fist] ♡

juleswolf0910 eyes on atticus adams ♡

HOT DESK

MBeeWrites scramble to scoop lion's estate is a joke: the 80s called and want their old white guy back

skyelovesbooks would not edit that sexist POS if they paid me. which they barely would anyway LOL

Anon, please rose adams going to sell town house out from under ERR

jfoxgoldner boohoo they've been squatting rent free for years

MargaretTate battle shaping up between avenue and hawk— caro trying to get in there all week

Anon, please atticus going to fuck some shit up

suburbangirl everyone getting laid off in the industry— can you imagine the $$$ lion's estate rakes in

skyelovesbooks atticus also sexist 🐶

HarveyWark.author saw AI at the grill with frank french plotting no doubt—caro must be freaking

suburbangirl riddle: how many hours do i have to work to afford a $55 cobb salad?

BLURB who is rebecca blume?

bookguy2130 [meme of Michael Jackson eating popcorn]

MargaretTate this is a HAWK V AVENUE brawl

Anon, please 6% of published authors are black but by all means let's resurrect 🦁

BLURB [meme of DiCaprio as Gatsby holding a martini glass juxtaposed with Gatsby floating face down in pool] Me when I loved reading books vs Me after working in publishing

Ben handed Howie back his phone. Even though he knew there was no chance Atticus was awake yet, he texted him again. "That your bootch?" Howie picked up the kombucha.

"No. That has been living in my desk drawer for I don't know how long," Ben warned him. "What do you think about the Avenue rumors?"

"Waste not, want not." Howie unscrewed the cap and Ben flinched, but there was no fizz, let alone explosion. "Who am I?" Howie stuck his lip out in a disturbing manner. "Fat baby clenching its fist!"

"Howie." Ben didn't know how it had gotten to this point, but he needed Howie. Ben was a scrupulous editor. He was a thoughtful reader. He was pretty fucking good at basketball and old people in bars loved him. He might even pull off getting Caro access to the Lion's estate. But this BLURB shit was unsettling. Ben was in over his head with the gossip, the memes, the innuendo. He was all for socialism, especially when he saw what was left of his paycheck after rent and bills, but how did anyone have time for so much drama? Also, he didn't need his reading acumen to sense hostility toward both the Lion and Atticus. For the first time since moving to New York, he felt a little lost, more so than the time he took the F train to Coney Island by mistake.

"Ha ha, dude, your face!" Howie took a long swig of kombucha, let out a prim burp, and clapped Ben on the back. "I will look into this. Fear not."

"Why would Rebecca Blume be mentioned? And who is AI?"

"Ami Ito is the Caro of Avenue. She and Hashtag Girlboss have a friendly rivalry. And by 'friendly' I mean they would shank each other with a shiv."

Again Ben thought it didn't seem quite right for Howie to talk about Caro and, by extension, Ami, in this way. He filed it away for the sit-down he hoped was forthcoming, but for now he needed Howie to figure out some shit for him. "Okay, I have to prep for the acquisition meeting. Can you let me know if you find out anything?"

Howie finished the kombucha and clanked it into the recycling bin. "Will do, chief."

Ben worked steadily until it was time to head over to the meeting. It was teatime. He knew this because Mrs. Singh was brewing a fresh pot. "Greetings, Ben! I think you will enjoy this oolong!" She carefully placed a saucer on top of his "Crazy Vegan Lady" mug in order to let it steep for exactly four minutes. During this time, they made plans to meet in the kitchen later so that Ben could give his opinion on Mrs. Singh's leftover vegan lemon cake and sign the card for someone named Janice's baby shower. Ben took his tea and headed to the meeting, glancing at his phone on the way.

If Atticus didn't text him back, Ben was going to have to figure out plan B. He walked past the conference room where he'd had all his meetings so far. There were a few people he hadn't seen before, and Paul from Production. As Ben peered into the space, a young woman's face filled the entire screen against the back wall. Ben stopped so suddenly that hot tea slopped onto his wrist. Fuck! She was gorgeous. Seriously. His breath caught. A ton of brown wavy hair, big green eyes rimmed in dark lashes, her skin flushed pink. She was wearing a green shirt with a low V-neck and a chunky silver necklace. Her mouth was perfect.

Howie jogged up next to him and Ben sloshed the tea again. "Shit! Ow! Hey, who is that?"

Howie looked into the conference room. "I dunno. The queen of England?"

The vision was gone and in her place was an old lady wearing a pink hat and many strands of pearls. *Was* it the queen of England? The old lady adjusted a pair of red reading glasses and frowned peevishly. Ben watched for a moment more before following Howie to the meeting, the image of the green-eyed woman imprinted in his mind.

As Caro called everyone to order, Ben tried to bring his focus back to the Hawk Mills agenda and a review of last week's notes. They had decided not to bid on a TikTok therapist's proposal, *I'm OK, You're a Toxic Jerk*, despite her three million followers and successfully acquired a literary memoir about a competitive coed crew team from South Korea (*The Boys in the Boat* meets *Crying in H Mart*). It was time to move on to new projects.

Ben was glad when Caro started with Harry, seated to his left, since he knew they would move clockwise around the room, and he would be the last to present. Even in the short time he had worked in publishing, his ideas of passionately debating literature had been pretty much dashed. Publishing seemed to be all about competition, publicity potential, and author connections. But still, this was a meeting where he could wax at least a little poetic. When his turn finally came, he took a breath.

"*Our Ghostly Machines* is a novel in stories that examines the potential for AI to change our subjectivity, to radically alter how we relate to one another and ourselves. A cross between Jennifer Egan and

George Saunders, Marc Cooker is a fresh new voice, one that takes a topic usually reserved for genre fiction and brings it into the literary world." Caro was watching him—encouragingly, he hoped. "I think we would get excellent review coverage for this, and since Cooker is a Google exec, I can see getting off-the-book-page coverage. Maybe public radio? Definitely some tech podcasts." Ben sat back in his chair. He was especially pleased with his use of "genre fiction" and "off-the-book-page," terms he had originally thought of as "science fiction" and "multimedia." First, a homey desk setup, now facility with publishing jargon. Next, if this meeting went well, his first real editor-author relationship with Marc Cooker. Then, just maybe, he would be masterfully editing the Lion, but humbly behind the scenes. He loved his new job.

"Does this Cooker guy know Mike Zuckerberg?" demanded an older editor who had never been introduced to Ben.

"Mark Zuckerberg?" Ben asked. "Of Facebook?"

"Zuckerberg is Meta," chided Harry.

The older editor continued undeterred. "My wife took a lot of quizzes on Facebook, and let me tell you, it was a scam! She was hacked!"

"They're developing AI now that'll write the next Great American Novel," someone from marketing announced glumly. "But it will be the Russians. Does the book address that?"

"Well, the Russians write pretty good novels," someone else pointed out before Ben could answer. "What I want to know is: Can AI foster a relationship with an author? That's what keeps *me* up at night. How long before we're replaced by chatbots?"

Ben made a note to self: Find out from Howie who everyone was so he could make some educated guesses at which one was Anon from the Office Life Inbox.

"A novel in stories, you say?" asked Carlotta from Marketing. "How connected are they? Could they be published separately?"

"Definitely linked," Ben assured her. "But also perfect for *The New Yorker*."

"I mean," the older editor soldiered on, "they tried to get her mother's maiden name. These scams are an epidemic. She's a Carrie from *Sex and the City* and a Rachel from *Friends*, by the way."

"I'm 100 percent a Samantha," Ty interjected.

Caro wrested back control of the meeting. "Can we get your profit and loss statement up on the screen, Ben?" In the end, Caro agreed to let Ben make a modest offer, with instructions to come back to her if things escalated.

After the meeting ended, Ben hurried out in order to check the conference room, but the room was empty, the screen blank. He went back to his desk, sat down, and tossed the apple from hand to hand. One, he had to call the agent and make his offer. Two, Atticus. Three, figure out who that woman was on the screen. Four, lunch and Mrs. Singh's lemon cake. Five, Rebecca Blume's stupid cactus. Should he water it? It was *her* cactus! Wasn't it pretty much impossible to kill a cactus? Still, what if it died on his watch? Six, Atticus. Ben had been working on a pitch for the Lion's estate and, sure, Atticus was his "in," but could plan B be his approaching Rose Adams directly? He thought she of all people would appreciate his ideas about reissuing the Lion's work in conjunction with essays on what the Lion had meant to younger writers. It would be cool to have independent bookstores feature readings of the Lion's work by new authors.

It wasn't until late afternoon that Ben allowed himself to check his phone. A photo from Ava, of Butch looking handsome, and, finally, a text from Atticus.

Atticus:

> chill chill chill i got you

Ben:

sorry for all the texts but hoping we can meet up sooner rather than later

Atticus:

you know you're the man

Ben:

can you come by hawk mills office? Or do you want to meet up somewhere this afternoon?

Atticus:

IV drip therapy at two

Ben:

...

Atticus:

then some shit to do but how about tonight

Ben:

i'm working until 11 but could sneak out for a minute or meet you at 5?

Atticus:

damn they get their money's worth

Ben:

i'm bartending at betty jack's

Atticus:

respect

Ben:

so 5?

Atticus:

nah

you got my word about tonight tho i'll come by BJ

Ben:

ok

Atticus:

> no sweat man i will be there 🦁

Ben:

> see you tonight

Ben didn't love the plan such as it was, but at least he had something to report to Caro. Once he got face-to-face with Atticus, he knew he could make headway. He googled Rose Adams and ended up reading two of her stories published in *The New Yorker* in the mid '80s. He hadn't known she was a writer too. The stories were neatly formed, meticulously observed, wise about being a young woman moving through the fashion world in Paris and London. Ben searched, but aside from society photos of her and the Lion, snippets about her work with HIV-AIDS and education charities, and a long piece in *Vanity Fair* in which Rose was described as "flowing gracefully into the room" and "alighting attentively at her husband's side" but not quoted, he found no more trace of her work. One thing he was sure of was that tea alone was not going to get him through a night with Atticus. He needed to hydrate and caffeinate. Also, carbo-load.

"I'm open!" Ben looked up and Howie was slow jogging toward his desk, hands up as if to catch a football. "Hit me!"

Ben tossed the apple to Howie, who promptly fumbled, caught it on the toe of his grubby Converse, and dribbled it back toward Ben, who was sorely regretting his actions. Ben scooped up the apple and looked around to make sure Caro was shut in her office. "Did you get any intel from Avenue?"

"All the interns have a group text," Howie explained. "And I sent out a Bat-Signal."

How was Howie both such a New York City trust fund Ivy League kid *and* a giant nerd? Ben wondered.

"There's a super-hot assistant at Avenue who told one of the interns that Ami Ito thinks it's pretty much a done deal with the Lion's estate."

"What does she look like?" asked Ben, suddenly alert. The woman he had seen on the screen must work at Avenue, right?

"Ami Ito?"

"No, the assistant."

"Buttercream blonde, wears a lot of plaid, smells like flowers," Howie said wistfully. "The interns and assistants have happy hour every Friday. I'm sure I could wrangle you an invite if you want in."

"I'm good, thanks." Ben leaned back in his chair, absentmindedly trying to spin the apple on his finger like a basketball, attempting to focus. "Did they say why they think they have the estate?"

"The widow asked for one of their editors specifically. So word is she's the Lion's secret love child, and the widow wants to see if she's contesting the will. Or the widow is using her to get back at Maury Kantor because he enabled the Lion's bad behavior. *Or*—and this is my hunch—the Lion and Maury were secret lovers but it ended badly and this editor has photos."

"Seriously, how is any of that helpful?"

"Just sayin' you better get on it with Atticus."

"Thank you. I know that. I'm meeting him tonight."

Howie snapped his fingers like the audience at a poetry slam and gave Ben a meaningful look. Jesus, was Howie going to be wearing a beret or, worse, a wool beanie and smoking clove cigarettes at Howl&Yawp? Ben grabbed his water bottle to refill and headed to Caro's office, ready to spin his hope that Atticus would show up and that the night would somehow result in snatching the Lion's estate back from Avenue. He knocked on her door, took a deep breath, and thought, in the words of Larry Bird: *When you step on the court, you play to win.*

CHAPTER EIGHT

WEDNESDAY
HOME, BEN

Ava sipped her soda water with its generous handful of maraschino cherries and a few sliced limes. Ben couldn't in good conscience, his second week on the job, accept her dubiously doctored fake ID. Butch lolled at her feet, enjoying the attentions of Belinda and Shoney, two of the regulars. Ben had already learned which one (Belinda) took vodka in a water glass and which one (Shoney) took water in a martini glass. He had solved the mystery of the subpar TV sports when he tried switching to the NBA playoffs and a previously silent old man in the corner wearing a tweed cap had revealed a strong British accent and an enraged preference for cricket. Ben placated him with a pint and a packet of corn nuts.

"So what's your plan again? Charm that sociopath into giving you all his daddy's work? How do you know he has any juice at all? What about Rose Adams?" Ava was shredding paper napkins and picking at candle wax, making little piles that Ben had to sweep away.

"I'll find out tonight." Ben juiced lemons and kept an eye on the customers. It was still pretty early. "I mean, it's just the two of them left, so if I can get Atticus to introduce me to Mrs. Adams or if he knows exactly what the Lion was working on before he died, that could be good information for Caro, right?"

"I hope you know what you're doing." Ava dropped a pretzel for Butch. "This plan is basically a wing and a prayer. Livin' on a prayer, that's you. Whoa-oh."

"Remind me not to give you any quarters for the jukebox."

"I don't think that's how jukeboxes work anymore. Like, I'm sure there's an app."

Ben tossed a series of squeezed lemons into the trash. "Nice follow-through," Ava said. "But keep your elbow up."

"Thanks, Coach."

"Wanna work on a Hinge profile?"

"I do not."

"Seriously, you need to get back out there. When's the last time you even had dinner in a restaurant?"

"I'll have you know I have a date with Howie this weekend," Ben said huffily.

"Do you even hear yourself?" Ava shook her head. "Come on, it will be fun."

"Nope. And I thought you disapproved of the heteronormative paradigm?"

"Obviously. But tragically you are hopelessly, boringly straight, and all I can do is teach you not to center your privilege." Ava dug around in her bag and pulled out her phone. "Okay, I'm going to lead with 'Tradwife is a big turn-on. Green flags include Milkmaid chic.' That should pull the ladies for you."

"*Milkmaid chic?*"

"Calico, very long braids? Relax! Don't look so stricken—I'm kidding! Okay, here's a brilliant Hinge prompt: 'Facts About Me That Surprise People.' How about: 'I can hold two opposing ideas in my mind at the same time because I contain multitudes.'"

"I think you just did a mash-up of F. Scott Fitzgerald and Walt Whitman."

"Fuck off. You'll meet the milkmaid of your dreams if you just cooperate." Ava scrolled through her phone. "How can you millennials stand this? But also, you need a more robust social media presence."

"I'm actually also Gen Z, as you well know. And I thought social media was the opiate of the masses."

"Oh, so you do listen to me!"

"So you're single?" Shoney (water) leaned against the bar and looked Ben up and down.

"A big hunk like you?" Belinda (vodka) chimed in. "Those deep blue eyes! A gal could swim in them is what I'm saying."

"I know! Can you believe it?" Ava put her elbows on the bar and rested her chin on her hands.

"My grandniece Martha is a paralegal," Shoney bragged. "Smart as a whip and a real pretty girl. She lives in Jersey, but I'm going to have her come take a look at you."

"My grandbaby Britt's got a good government job with benefits," Belinda chimed in. Ben nodded, impressed. He was sure Britt made more than he did, even combining both of his paychecks.

"She lives in Phoenix," Shoney shouted. "And she's married!"

"Sunny dry weather," Belinda continued, unfazed. "And nobody likes Joey. Especially Britt." She patted Ben's biceps. "She could use a big, strong man around the house."

"Martha can be here in forty-five minutes on the train," Shoney threatened.

"What about my Olga?" Betty Jack interrupted. "She was an alternate for the 2014 Olympic biathlon team."

"She lives in Belarus!" Shoney snitched.

"She can travel," Betty Jack snapped. "And she's divorced."

"I'd love to meet her one day," Ben promised. Who wouldn't want to date a Belarian (Belarusian?) biathloner (biathlete?) instead of a milkmaid? Although he would clearly have to get his terms straight before he could impress Olga. Betty Jack nodded, placated, and the other two accepted defeat for now, but Ben knew he hadn't heard the last of Martha and Britt. Ava was right. He should get out there. He felt a warm, anticipatory thrill. Why? Then he remembered the gorgeous woman he had seen on Zoom at work. He had stored the image away; it wouldn't be too hard to track her down.

"Who did you say you shared a desk with?" Ava asked suddenly, still scrolling through her phone. "Rebecca Blume, right? You share custody of a cactus?"

"It's her cactus. Why?"

"There's a Rebecca Blume tagged in all these posts on an account I follow, *salute!*? Very cool supper club; I get on the waitlist every month but it's impossible to get a reservation. Stella Marino-Miller? Let me guess, you haven't heard of her."

"Let me see." Ben took Ava's phone and examined a series of photos that managed to be both casual and artsy, not trying too hard but giving a good sense of the food—the strawberry shortcake looked amazing—and the people lit by candles and surrounded by half-empty plates and wineglasses. There was a flurry of tags that Ava had investigated, including "rebeccablume." Ben tapped on her name to see what clues he could find on her account. It was private and the profile photo was half of a face in large sunglasses mostly hidden by a cone piled high with soft ice cream. Ben peered closer, but it was hopeless. He did a quick search of who she followed and saw enough author and publisher names among the restaurants and chefs that it had to be her. How many Rebecca Blumes could there be following Avenue Publishing? All he could say with confidence was that she was much younger than he had thought, and the whole thing reminded him that he was hungry and needed more protein in preparation for when Atticus showed up. *If* Atticus showed up. "It's private. I can't see anything."

"Okay, request to follow," Ava suggested.

"No! She's the worst, honestly. I'm not going to give her the satisfaction."

"'The worst'?" Ava cocked her head at Ben, who regretted his overreaction. It was never a good idea to allow Ava to get a whiff of any strong feelings on his part or he would spend the next year fielding questions from her. "Let's google her!"

"Absolutely not. Forget it." Ben made himself busy opening beers and mixing gin and tonics. He had no interest in pursuing anything to do with Rebecca Blume. The last thing he needed was Ava getting involved. Luckily, she was distracted by a man with mirrored sunglasses perched on top of his head who was trying to hit on her. Ben kept one eye on them, but he had full confidence that Ava could handle herself; soon enough, the man had put on his sunglasses and slunk away. The bar was starting to fill up.

"Okay, it's getting too crowded for Butch," Ava called to Ben. "And I'm meeting some people at a gallery opening in Greenpoint."

Ben gave her a quick thumbs-up and looked over the bar to tell Butch he was a good boy. He didn't stop moving for a few hours, but the rhythm was second nature to him, and the tips were good. After a while, the crowds dispersed, and Betty Jack's returned to the small, already familiar group of regulars still in their spots. It was past 10 p.m., and Ben was setting glasses to air dry and wiping down taps when Atticus showed up.

"Benjamin, my man!" He was dressed the same way Ben remembered from last time, in a fitted gray suit, a white shirt unbuttoned at the neck, black dress boots, and a signet ring on his pinkie. Everything about Atticus was good-looking and understated, and Ben understood (as it had been explained to him by Ava) that the simpler the outfit, the more it cost. Atticus's skin was shiny and a little puffy up close, but maybe as a result of IV therapy? Whatever that was. He reached across the bar and Atticus gave him a bone-crushing handshake. Firm was good, but Ben was always wary of guys who tried to bring him to his knees like some kind of annoying uncle.

"Thanks for coming down here." Ben pulled out two shot glasses. "What can I get you? I'm almost finished up."

"Woodford Reserve?"

"Nope."

"Rittenhouse?"

"Nope."

"Okay, I'm guessing you don't serve Pappy Van Winkle? Just hit me with whatever you've got." Atticus pushed his hair back and took out a money clip monogrammed with a lion's head.

Ben poured two shots of the house bourbon. "It's on me." He pushed the glass to Atticus, who lifted it and clinked Ben's glass. "To the Lion," Ben said.

"To the Lion." Atticus downed his shot and motioned for another.

Ben threw back his second quickly, pretended not to notice Atticus's signal to go again, put away the bottle, wiped down the bar, and tried to avoid Betty Jack's aggressive mopping. "I was thinking we could go somewhere and talk. Maybe get something to eat?"

"Absolutely, absolutely. Just need to stop at a place nearby where a friend is working, then a quick appearance at a little get-together, and if we can make it to the Octopus Lounge, they don't stop serving until four a.m. Their crudo is flown in from Sicily every morning."

Fuck coffee. Ben was going to need a Red Bull or a Celsius. Maybe both? And a few bagels to line his stomach. He said goodbye to Betty

Jack, helped Shoney and Belinda off their stools and out the door, ran into the deli for supplies, then followed Atticus into the back of a black car that had been idling outside the bar.

Their first stop was a burlesque club on Rivington, where the bass player turned out to be the friend who "had something" for Atticus, so they sat through the show, which wasn't the same as being at a strip club, was it? Ben hoped not. He could bide his time until he raised the matter of the estate with Atticus. All was going pretty well until a dancer almost strangled him with her feather boa and let loose a handful of glitter in his face. It had been too loud and sparkly to talk much in the burlesque club, so Ben grabbed the precious minutes of quiet in the black car after they left but before Atticus could consume whatever he now had in his pocket, courtesy of the bass player.

"Do you know what your dad was working on? Are there unpublished stories?" Ben accepted a swig of something smooth and delicious from a silver flask Atticus offered him and politely refused a bump of the powder Atticus had scooped out of a small vial with a key.

"Yeah, man." Atticus sniffed with the skill of a habitual user, then put his head back on the leather seat. "Good stuff. Good stuff."

Ben wasn't sure if he meant the stories or the drugs. "Have you read anything? Did he talk about it with you?"

"Listen," Atticus said. "This is why I wanted to see you." If Atticus had wanted to see him, he had a pretty funny way of showing it. Ben had been chasing him for a week. Atticus continued, "There's a book. A whole fucking book. Rose has no idea I know about it. I just happened to be looking around, you know, after they read us the will. I have my lawyers on it now. The will, the estate. Rose hasn't said anything to me about the book. Not one fucking word."

A book! An entire unpublished manuscript by the Lion. "Seriously? That's incredible! What do you mean about the will? Do you not get along with her?" Ben's emails to the Lion were written into the void, care of PK Publishing. He hadn't known if the Lion was reading them, but one day he got an email from Atticus about the Lion's health, his writing, and what seemed to be direct responses from the Lion. Atticus was more like a disreputable uncle or prodigal older brother than a friend, honestly. But if Atticus was feuding with Rose, that was going to make it hard for Ben to be of any use to Caro and Hawk Mills. He hadn't heard anything from anyone about an actual book, though, so he was pretty sure they didn't have that information.

Atticus looked out the dark tinted windows of the car, but all Ben could see were muted lights. The car rolled along silently, flattening the city's din. It was like being in one of those modern LA homes high above the city, Ben thought. Not that he had ever been in one.

"We're not that close, no." Atticus kept his face turned to the window. "I never saw her much before my mother died. And then they shipped me off to boarding school in eighth grade. We coexist when she's in town. She's disappointed in me." He let out a bitter laugh and did another key bump. "I mean, get in line, right? I guess we were doing all right until all this bullshit with the will. Apparently, I have to jump through hoops before I get my share. And Rose not telling me about the novel she found. You'd think she'd be thrilled, right? She's the executor of the estate—thanks, *Dad*—but anything that makes money goes into my pocket too. And anything by the Lion should be out in the world. I know you agree with me on that point, Benjamin, my man."

Why was Rose separating the book from the rest of the estate? Ben knew that someone at Avenue had already met with her. Did Avenue know about the book? He needed Atticus to introduce him to Rose too. "Do you know how many publishers she's met with so far? I mean, for the estate? Has she met with any agents?"

"Fuck no. The Lion never wanted to give up that 15 percent commission to anyone."

"I know there are a lot of people really interested in making money off the Lion. Like, I know there's a lot of money there, and I'd be lying if I said that wasn't motivation for Hawk Mills too." Ben took another sip from the flask. "But I promise you that I'm not in it for that. Your father and his work shaped my life. You know that. He really means something to me."

"It's not just about the money. I've got plenty of money," Atticus said. "It's about legacy. To legacy." He raised the key and toasted Ben, took a quick snort, shook his head wildly, then put Ben in a headlock. "Just bullshitting you! Fuck yeah, I care about the money! I've got expensive habits!" Ben patiently allowed Atticus to rough up his hair, then extricated himself. "Don't be sad," Atticus said. "It's also about legacy. But can legacy foot my bills? I think it can. And that's where you come in. I need someone who's got my back."

"Can you set up a meeting for me with Rose?" Ben asked.

"Are you running the place over there at Eagle Eye yet?"

"Hawk Mills. And not exactly," Ben admitted. "But I have the go-ahead to take a meeting about the estate."

"Look, whatever stick Rose has up her ass about this book, I trust you can help me convince her that it's worth its weight in Colombian blow. I don't need to read it to know that. I'll see what I can do about a meeting. Enough business now, *capisce*?" He rapped on the closed window shielding the driver. "Central Park Tower, Leon." He turned up the music. "Whaddaya think of this?"

Ben thought the pounding EDM was just short of unlistenable. "It's loud? What is it?"

"Just some brostep I've been working on with Skrillex. Yeah, I got in the studio with him, and I'm looking to get a gig in Ibiza." Atticus went hard on the Spanish pronunciation: *I-bee-tha*. "I'm taking some time off from the bank to follow my passion."

"DJing is your passion?" Ben had to raise his voice over the throbbing music. Wasn't Atticus too old for this shit?

"I don't fucking know," Atticus said, locating a bottle of tequila that had been rolling around on the floor. "Say *hola* to my dear friend Don Julio."

By the time they left the rooftop party on the Upper West Side, where Ben was treated to a sprawling view of Central Park, dark and calm, surrounded by the grid of apartment building lights, and the sight of twelve coked-up finance bros (at least two in suits and one in a tux) and five seemingly naked women in a ten-person hot tub, Ben was, he had to admit, a little drunk and a little high. The entire scene was being recorded by a trio of influencers in vinyl jumpsuits whose phone flashes were blinding and who were trying to convince everyone to try detox tea. Then it was a long ride down to the lobby in a mirrored elevator with Atticus attempting to persuade a bored woman to join them for dinner. (Someone had whispered to Ben that she was starring in a scandalous HBO show, but Ben had not retained any of the pertinent information.) It was 2 a.m.

"They fly the crudo in from Sicily every morning," Atticus was saying, and if Ben was not mistaken, he was sliding very slowly down the mirrored wall as the floors ticked by. The woman yawned.

"I like your tiny bag." Why had Ben said that out loud? It was, in truth, the tiniest bag he had ever seen. It could hold, max, one container of Tic Tacs.

The woman looked at her bag and then at Ben. Atticus was definitely sliding lower. "I like your glitter," she said. "Brave for a normie like you." Ben looked past her at his reflection. Apparently he had partied all night with glitter stuck in his eyebrows and all over his stubble. "Do you have a ciggie?" she asked.

"No."

"I do!" Atticus, perched in a kind of wall squat, halted his downward progression and began pulling things out of his inner suit pocket. ChapStick. Money clip. A receipt for more tequila and a pizza. Matches from the burlesque club. An empty vial. A hundred-dollar bill. Two stray cigarettes, slightly bent, and a fat joint. "Lookie, lookie!" he crowed, still balancing in a crouch. More quad strength than Ben would have guessed.

"Cheers." She plucked both cigarettes from Atticus, tucked one behind her ear, and put the other one in her lipsticked mouth. The elevator dinged as the doors slid open to reveal the enormous lobby. The woman clicked on high heels all the way across a sea of gray-and-white marble and disappeared with her tiny bag through the door held open by a uniformed guard.

"You win some, you lose some," Atticus was saying. "Nice ass, though. Am I right?" Ben, annoyed, hauled him roughly to standing. "At least she left us this." He waggled the joint obliviously at Ben.

Atticus was becoming more of a jackass as the night progressed. At least he hadn't said anything offensive *in front of* the woman. But it was close, and Ben didn't feel like standing around waiting for Atticus to be a real dick. He had new and very valuable information that the Lion had left a book behind, and he had confirmation that Atticus could set up a meeting for him with Rose Adams. He was in the running. Other elevators were lighting up and coming down, and who knew how many wet models would be disembarking. If they left now, he could avoid any confrontation if/when Atticus got out of hand. "Let's go." Ben straightened Atticus up and marched him out the door. "I'm going to head home. I can grab the subway at Columbus Circle. We can follow up tomorrow."

"My man! The night is young! The Octopus Lounge is open till four a.m.! They fly crudo in from Sicily every morning."

"Yeah, so you've said." Much as Ben loved raw fish, he knew it would never fill him up, and though Atticus had generously paid for drinks and pizza earlier, Ben didn't want to assume he would keep paying. And even with his pockets stuffed with tips, he knew that crudo flown in from Sicily would cost more than his monthly paycheck. "I'm going to pass, though. I have to get up in a few hours."

Atticus fumbled to light the joint and examined the line of black cars in front of the building. "Which one?" he muttered, dropping matches. He finally, impressively, got the joint fired up and passed it to Ben, who took a hit. "You need to chill, Benjamin. Look, let me treat you to a fat steak at Cafe Lulubell. They close soon, but I know the owners. And they make Belgian fries—you know, the ones that get fried twice. *Twice*, Benjamin. Two times the frying. That's the secret."

As tempted as he was by Belgian fries, he needed to get home. "Next time. I've got my dog to deal with." That was technically true, though Butch was fast asleep and would be fine until morning. But he served as a decent excuse when Ben wanted to get to bed.

"Listen, just listen." Atticus's shirt had come undone a few more buttons and his handsome face was even puffier and shinier. "Look. Forget those fries. Those crispy fucking fries. How about we go back to the town house and get a drink there? And I can show you the book."

Better than the mythical crudo; better than the Belgian fries; better than anything Ben had dared hope for tonight, this offer almost knocked the breath out of him. "Let's do it." He maneuvered Atticus toward the black car and Leon. "You're sure you can get your hands on it?"

"Hunnred percent," Atticus slurred. Ben felt a rush of affection for him, fueled by what he had ingested this evening, Atticus's touching need to keep hanging out, and, most of all, by the very real chance he had to read the Lion's unpublished book.

Thirty minutes later, Atticus handed Ben a manuscript of yellow legal paper bound with a rubber band and left him on a window seat overlooking the East River while he went to "rustle up" some food. He had sloppily poured overfull glasses of what he assured Ben was a glorious natural wine with a barnyard funk and left them on the pool table hulking in the middle of the room. The lights in the big room were off, but the lights from the river and outside cast enough of a glow for Ben to read the Lion's handwriting. "*Making the Sun Run* by Edward David Adams." Ben traced the Lion's words. He couldn't help himself. With the exaggerated precision of someone who had been drinking and smoking weed all night, Ben slid the rubber band down. He wanted to take his time. Even Atticus hadn't read any of it yet. Had Rose Adams? Was it possible he would be the first person to read it? His hands were shaking a little, and he took a deep breath. Out the window, Ben saw a barge floating serenely by, its wake white in the dark water.

Suddenly, the lights in the room snapped on, and Ben could see his reflection, clear as in a mirror, blinking back at him. Behind him, in the window, he saw a woman wearing a white bathrobe, looking like a beautiful ghost. He turned around and carefully laid the manuscript down next to him, raising his hands in the air to signal he meant no harm and also please don't call the cops. "I'm here with Atticus," he said. "My good friend Atticus." Where the hell was Atticus?

"Atticus is sleeping on the kitchen floor," said the woman, who must, Ben thought dazedly, be Rose Adams.

"Oh, I'm so sorry." Ben knew he should get up, apologize some more, and leave. He stayed rooted to the spot, where he hoped he was less intimidating than if he stood. "I'm so sorry we woke you. I didn't know anyone else was here." He made an effort to enunciate.

"I assume Atticus gave you the manuscript." Mrs. Adams was leaning against the doorway, hands in her bathrobe pockets. Was she going to shoot him? "And that you didn't pluck it from inside the desk on your own. Are you an agent?"

"No!" Ben put his hand over his heart as if to pledge allegiance. He was not an agent! "I'm not. I didn't! And I'm not just somebody. I mean, not just anyone. Wait. What I mean is that I love your husband. I love his writing. I'm a fan. But not a stalker fan! I'm an editor. I work at Hawk Mills. I . . . I can show you if you want?" Ben thought better of reaching for his phone in case Mrs. Adams felt threatened and pulled out a handgun. "I'm reading out of love." *"Reading out of love"? Pull yourself together, man*, he chastised himself.

Mrs. Adams looked amused. At least Ben hoped she looked amused. His hand was still pressed to his heart, so he slowly put it back in the air. "But you're also reading it as an editor, is that correct?" she asked, her head cocked.

"Well, yes, but first and foremost as a lover of the Lion. Not a literal lover! A lover of the work!" *Jesus, Ben, just zip it*, he implored himself. "My name is Ben Heath. I wrote a lot to the Lion, and then Atticus and I were in contact, and now we're friends, and I was writing my thesis on him, on the Lion, and then when he died . . ." Ben paused. "I'm so sorry for your loss. The world's loss! My loss. But of course," he added hastily, "mostly your loss."

"Ben Heath." Mrs. Adams took her hands out of her pockets. "You can return the manuscript to me now. Atticus had no right to give it to you. I'm very sorry that he got his hands on it in the first place. It hasn't been transcribed, and this is the only copy. I'm going to ask that you not mention its existence to anyone. I'm going to have to trust you. Do you understand?"

Ben picked up the manuscript, the precious only copy, and slowly rose to his full height. "Okay," he said solemnly. "I'm walking over to you." He took a few steps, steadied himself, and handed it to Mrs. Adams.

"I'll go now," he said. "And I'm so sorry." He looked in the direction where Atticus had disappeared, but it was just dark room and hallway and more dark rooms. "Do you need any help? Do you want me to get him into bed?"

"Oh, he usually prefers to sleep it off without my involvement." She looked at the manuscript. "Did you read any of it?"

"Not a word," Ben promised. "But if you ever saw fit, I mean, I know it's three in the morning and I'm in your living room and it's true that I'm a little bit drunk and that we woke you up, and none of that is very good. I know. But maybe if I could just read it? Sometime? Not even as an editor. Though, honestly, I think I would be a really good editor for it. But, no, I mean just as a person. A person who cares."

"You understand what I'm asking you?" Mrs. Adams said. "Not to say anything about it? I know it's my mistake that Atticus found it, and I'm going to have to deal with the consequences. But you're in the business."

"I understand," Ben assured her. "Do you mind my asking, though: Are there stories?"

"There are stories," Mrs. Adams confirmed. If Ben couldn't say anything about a book yet, he could at least offer Caro the promise of unpublished stories. "It's late. I'll show you out." Ben followed her white figure down the wide, curving staircase, past the statues, the flowers, and to the front door. The light from the streetlamps pooled on the floor and lit Mrs. Adam's face. "I know who you are," she said unexpectedly. "I recognize your name from the emails. He appreciated them. He did get a lot of mail. Atticus and I helped him with all of it in the past years. Many young men, especially. But yours did mean something to him. You should know that."

Ben's voice caught in his throat. "Thank you."

Mrs. Adams opened the heavy door and stood aside. "Good night, Ben Heath," she said, and closed the door firmly after him. Ben stood for a minute listening to the locks turning and the alarm setting. Exhausted but exhilarated, he rubbed his eyes, then reached out and touched the lion door knocker. When he pulled his hand away, the brass was streaked with glitter.

JANE

NEW YORK CITY
JANUARY 1982

It was winter before EDA took the interns out to lunch. Jane had bought a Russian hat with earflaps from a thrift store on Astor Place—Rose insisted it was real fur—and had taken to wearing it everywhere in the bitter cold. She was wearing it now as she waited for Drew and Rose to meet her at York Tavern, stomping her freezing feet but reluctant to go inside in case EDA was already there. The idea of being alone with him was both terrifying and intriguing. Mostly terrifying, though, so Jane stayed outside until she spotted Rose in her puffy white parka and high shearling boots, followed closely by Drew, who looked miserable, shoulders hunched, and hands stuffed deep in the pockets of his beloved red plaid jacket.

"Jane!" Rose gave Jane a hug even though they had seen each other an hour earlier. "Why are you out here?" With a sharp-eyed look, she answered her own question: "He's not worse than freezing your ass off!"

"My hat keeps me warm," Jane answered, looking pointedly at Drew, who refused to tamp down his self-described "fabulous" hair.

"We'll see who has hat head during lunch." He brushed by her, teeth chattering.

The York Tavern, with its always-crowded wooden bar up front, was also a fancier restaurant in the back, with long banquettes of cracked green leather situated under antiqued mirrors and brass chandeliers. Despite its mediocre food and nonchalant service, the York Tavern had been the lunch destination of choice for *East River Review* staff since 1960, as both magazine and restaurant were established at the same time and had grown comfortably tolerant of each other's shortcomings. Jane had frozen for nothing, as EDA was nowhere to be seen. The brusque hostess led them back to "Teddy's booth," where they were ignored.

"Let's go to the Film Forum tonight." Rose took the Arts and Leisure section of *The New York Times* out of her bag and found the movie information. "I really want to see *La Piscine*. It's a sexy French thriller from 1969."

"Is it in subtitles? Because my French isn't perfect yet." Jane's French was nonexistent, though Rose, who had spent a year modeling in Paris after high school and even now was occasionally persuaded by her agency to walk in fashion shows, had been drilling her on the basics: *le fromage, le vin, le pain, le chocolat chaud.*

"Can't tonight." Drew tried to get the waiter's attention but was unsuccessful. "Though I love Jane Birkin."

Jane took the plunge and removed her hat. In the artfully tarnished mirror and in Drew's expression, she could see that her hair was both flattened *and* static. "Don't gloat," she admonished him.

"I'm just sorry that Teddy has to see you this way," he teased. "Jane should make her hair more like Jane Birkin's, trust me." Drew licked his fingers and tried to tamp down Jane's hair. She batted his hand away.

"Why can't you come with us? It's been so long since you hung out!" Rose complained.

"First of all, we were just at that art opening concert thing at

Club 57. And three nights ago you made us listen to the Joan Jett album a thousand times."

"She's so badass! It's just that we miss you, Drew."

"Anyway, Paco's been pretty depressed lately, and I think I cheer him up, you know? His boyfriend Jermaine is sick and they don't know what's wrong with him."

"I'm so sorry." Rose squeezed his arm. "You're excused from the movie, then. But just for tonight. Oh, now I have ink all over my fingers." She stuffed the newspaper back into her bag. "I'm going to go wash my hands." As Rose was heading to the bathroom, the hostess was leading EDA to their table. They could hear Rose say hello as they stopped to exchange a few more words. EDA turned to watch her as she walked away. Then he was upon them, shedding his heavy leather coat, cashmere scarf, and a Cossack hat similar to Jane's but without the flaps and definitely made of real fur. He flung everything on the seat while the hostess clucked, then gathered it all to hang up.

"Interns!" he proclaimed cheerfully, waving over a suddenly attentive waiter. "Sir! We need something to warm us up, eh? How about a nice full-bodied cab? Find us a '58 or a '68, would you? How does that sound?" EDA rubbed his big hands together and settled into the booth.

"Sounds good," Drew answered, though it was not clear, Jane thought, that EDA expected a response.

"Thank you," she added, but EDA was examining Drew's coat, which he hadn't removed, since, Jane knew, he was still cold.

"Charming!" he exclaimed. "A real Holden Caulfield!" Suddenly he jumped to his feet, almost upsetting a basket of bread that had just appeared on the table. "Please." He ushered Rose, back from the bathroom, into the booth. His glance swept over the three of them and he rumbled, "So it's true! The best-damn-looking crop of interns in quite some time—dare I say, ever?"

Before any of them could speak—not that Jane thought any of them would—EDA was ordering for everyone. "Steak frites all around and some Caesar salads if the girls prefer." He nodded at Drew. "Medium rare?"

"Of course." Drew didn't look at Jane and Rose.

"Now that's settled." EDA leaned back against the booth, his legs spread so that his corduroy-clad knee pressed against Jane's outer thigh. Slowly, slowly, she moved her leg away, fussing with her napkin, but he was oblivious, and she was sure someone his size couldn't help but take up more than his own space. "Tell me your dreams, interns! Let's begin with Rose. How is Anders, my dear?"

Of course EDA would know Rose's father. Jane saw a tiny ripple pass over Rose's face, but she recovered quickly. "Doing very well," she answered, her voice betraying no discomfort, only mannerly calm. "I'm sure he says hello."

"I'll be seeing him at the board meeting next month. We appreciate his generosity." EDA slathered butter on a roll and nodded encouragingly. "I seem to recall you offering your editing services to me at the fall issue party. Is that a path you'd like to take? Will your internship be a stepping stone to a career in publishing?"

Drew kicked Jane under the table. Unlike Jane, who blushed at the slightest provocation, Rose met EDA's gaze with poise. "Absolutely," she said evenly. "I'd love to work in publishing." Jane knew that Rose had carried out her dare that night, but none of them expected EDA to remember, much less to bring it up. All Jane recalled was how alluring she felt in that dress and meeting up with Rose in the bathroom to marvel at the sense of ownership they felt over the town house: there, on the window seat where Allen Ginsberg had climbed up to declaim a poem, was where they read manuscripts; there, where her NYU thesis adviser tried to stick his hand up Rose's skirt, was where Jane had eaten pesto pasta salad for the first time; there, where Paco, in gold hoop earrings, had danced with Yoko Ono, was where they had each met with Parker to receive and mostly ignore "feedback and evaluation."

EDA laughed, a low chuckle that put them at ease. "You Vassar girls are always confident minxes!" He paused to admire the bottle of wine and examine the cork the waiter handed him. "Splendid! Now, Rose, I would be honored if you would take a look at my latest work. I've been tinkering around with an idea for a new novel, but I'm a little stuck. Perhaps you could take your red pen to it?"

Rose paled, a sign, Jane knew, of her excitement. "I would love to," she said, clenching Jane's hand quickly.

"That's the spirit!" EDA took the bottle from the waiter and poured it himself, handing Rose and Jane the first glasses. "And what about you, Holden Caulfield? What are your plans for the future?"

"Well, sir . . ." Drew began, uncharacteristically formal.

"Call me Teddy! None of this 'sir' nonsense! Wasn't that long ago that I was sitting where you three are, plotting the birth of the *East River Review*."

"I'm interested in the art side of it," Drew said. Jane could tell he was trying not to say "sir" again but couldn't bring himself to say "Teddy."

"Ah! And Paco has taken you under his wing, has he?"

"Yes, he's been really helpful. I'm learning so much."

Jane and Rose exchanged quick smiles. Yes, Drew was learning about cover design, but the image of Paco taking Drew under his wing evoked wild nights at the Saint more than commissioning print series.

"Maybe you'd be interested in visiting Keith Haring's studio? He's a friend of the magazine's and of mine, and I know he would make the time to show you around. If you'd like that?"

"Of-of course!" Drew stuttered. "Really? I would love that! I . . . I saw his first solo show last year."

"Wonderful! I'll make that happen. We'll get a silk screen out of him for the cover one of these days." EDA turned the high beam of his attention on Jane. This was the closest she had ever been to him. He was the most attractive man Jane had ever seen, yes, but the book jacket photo she had mooned over didn't do justice to the force of his presence. And it wasn't just his size, Jane thought; it was a particular charisma, one that layered an absolute confidence over the magnetism of talent and a whiff of danger. Jane couldn't have said what the danger was, but she felt it when his leg pressed against hers and when he held her pinned under his focus. "Ellen tells me we have you to thank for the Cisneros story. A very keen eye! It's not unusual that interns who show a knack for that sort of thing stay on, get added to the payroll. Ellen thinks you might be a good candidate to follow in Parker's footsteps. What do you say?"

Jane was speechless. Staying on, getting paid, becoming an assistant editor at the *East River Review*—she and Rose had spent many nights planning exactly how it would go.

"Jane's also a great writer," Rose enthused before Jane could answer.

"Is that so?" EDA poured each of them more wine, finishing the bottle. "The most rewarding part of my job is discovering new voices. At the very least, I hope I'm good for some valuable feedback. Oh, my dear, you're blushing! What I'm trying to say is that I would be willing to read a few poems or a story or whatever you have to offer. If you are so inclined!"

Jane finally mustered the words: "I am." The heat rose off her cheeks, and she pressed the back of her hand to one side and then the other to cool them. "I would love that. Thank you!"

"Splendid!" EDA said again. Jane was unsure if he was speaking to her or to the waiter who was delivering plates of food. Both? "Now, interns"—his dark eyes sparkled as he lifted a steak knife—"ask me anything!" As the lunch unfolded and another bottle of wine was poured, Jane relaxed. EDA—no, *Teddy*, as he insisted again—commanded the conversation, but he drew them out, pinpointing their interests and casually expounding on the exact well-known artist or writer that dovetailed with their enthusiasm. Jane saw each of them blossoming under his consideration, presenting for his approval their brightest laughter, best ideas, most eager selves.

Teddy insisted that they order the carrot cake for dessert, but before it arrived, he looked at his watch and announced that he had a meeting. Clad once again in his outerwear, he shook hands with Drew, patted Jane warmly on the shoulder, and kissed Rose's cheek. They watched as he steamed ahead through the dining room, stopping to greet those he knew and those who introduced themselves. The hostess trotted behind him with his satchel. The carrot cake arrived and was disappointingly dry. Jane felt the three of them struggling to recalibrate, to fill the sudden emptiness they had never before experienced when they were together. The glow of his stories, the warmth of his bulk next to her, existed alongside his sudden absence. The contradiction of it was something they would usually parse; instead, they were quiet, a little dizzy from the wine. Jane was sure they were thinking, as she was, about all the promises Teddy had made.

Later, after the movie, Rose leaned against her bed, on the floor with her knees up, while Jane lay on the bed on her stomach, head near Rose's. "Everyone was so tan!" Rose moaned. "I'm like a ghost! I'll never be invited to a villa on the Côte d'Azur."

"Everyone was so beautiful, it was distracting," Jane added. "Was the movie even good? All I can remember is gorgeous limbs, gorgeous clothes, gorgeous pool."

"Jane Birkin is stunning! Do you know that she's eighteen years younger than Serge Gainsbourg?" They were listening to "Je t'aime . . . moi non plus" on repeat, with Rose getting up to lift the record needle every time the song ended.

"And so?" Jane was editing one of Rose's stories, and Rose was editing one of Jane's.

"And so I'm just saying . . ." Rose tapped her pencil on Jane's notebook. "Your story is perfect, by the way."

"I don't think it's really done! What am I going to show him?" Jane fretted. Since lunch, which had left all of them awed and headachy, she had been trying to think of something finished enough to present to Teddy. "Yours are all so polished!"

"Polished doesn't mean great," Rose assured her. "You have to help me toughen up this motorcycle story, please. I hear you have a very keen eye . . ."

"I thought you'd never ask." Jane tugged Rose's hair gently.

"Just promise me you won't chicken out," Rose demanded. "You need to show him 'Tomboy.' It's your best one. It's like a punch in the stomach. But in a good way."

"You can write all my flap copy," Jane laughed. She knew "Tomboy" was her best story, but Rose's confirmation made it official. She had written most of it in Professor Marshall's class but had started it years earlier when she had found a photo of herself as a ten-year-old, hands on her hips, her sturdy legs planted firmly apart, her steady gaze challenging. It was the year before her father had died and her mother had started going to church every day. Jane recalled exactly the moment and the feeling: she was pretending to be Peter Pan, and his fearless insouciance had become her own. "Tomboy" wasn't a pretty story—it wasn't even finished to her liking—but Jane loved the powerful little girl at the center of it.

Rose was right: she would hand it to Teddy and see what he thought. She would not chicken out. With a little shiver, Jane rewound: *she would hand it to Teddy and see what he thought* . . . just casually giving her own work to Edward David Adams, who had asked her—sincerely, warmly—to do so. Jane had turned his generous offer over and over in her head ever since lunch. Teddy had been a real-life fairy godfather (as Drew declared), and they marveled at how he had granted each one of them a fondest wish. *For me, two wishes*, she thought. *Staying at the East River Review and reading my story*. Jane was incredulous, yes, but there was something stronger than disbelief at her luck that thrummed below the surface: a wave of confidence, of craving. Everything was falling into place.

"Okay." She smoothed out Rose's manuscript on her lap. "I have ideas about your motorcycle story. Are you ready?"

"Wait!" Rose got up and started the song over again.

"Here's what I think," said Jane. "She's a little wild, right? But nothing really bad. Then when he takes her on the motorcycle at night, it's reckless: it puts her life in danger. I would play that up. Some way to show she's changed. Okay, remember you had that stray cat in the first draft? Bring him back! But this time he's not friendly. Maybe he bites her?"

"Yes!" Rose gnawed at her pencil. "Or he scratches her? Like a big, mean swipe. But she kind of likes it?"

"Exactly." Jane made cat claws and hissed at Rose. "She licks her wound. Literally!"

"You're a genius!" Rose exclaimed.

"*You're* a genius! *And* you're going to be *editing a genius* any day now."

"I'm editing one right now," Rose said. "Except you don't really give me much to do. I can't wait to hear what Teddy thinks of your tomboy!"

"So how many years is it?" Jane asked.

Rose didn't even pretend not to know what Jane was talking about. "Nineteen," she said immediately.

"He *is* better looking than Serge Gainsbourg," Jane allowed.

"Serge is pretty sexy, though." Rose smiled. She got up to attend to the record player.

"Not again, I beg you," Jane said. "Put on Joan Jett. Anything else!"

Rose was starting to argue when the buzzer blared. The girls looked at each other, startled. "What time is it?" Rose asked.

Jane rolled over so she could read the big clock radio on the bedside table. "It's after one. Could it be your dad?"

"No—he's in Geneva. Also, he has a key. Also, if he didn't, Joe would just let him up, right?"

"Did we get stoned and order Chinese?"

"That was last night." Rose went into the other room, where Jane could hear her garbled conversation with Joe the doorman.

"It's Drew," Rose called out.

"That's weird." Jane sat up. Drew had only spent the night with them at Rose's a few times. "Maybe the train wasn't running?"

Rose opened the apartment door to wait for the elevator. Jane heard a ding and then Drew's footsteps. Rose gave a little cry. Jane scrambled off the bed and stopped cold in the doorway. Drew's face was swollen below his eye, and there was blood under his nose. The sleeve of his red plaid jacket hung off his shoulder where it had been ripped.

"What happened?" Before Drew could answer her, Rose opened her arms and hugged him.

"I was walking to the subway"—Drew's voice was muffled by Rose's hair—"and I got jumped."

"What do you mean?" Jane asked. "Why?" She knew the wording was wrong as soon as it came out of her mouth.

Drew pulled away from Rose and wiped a hand across his bloody face. "Because, Jane, I'm a queer," he said sharply.

Jane had wanted to go to him, to hug him too, but she stayed rooted in the doorway, flushed. Everything was bunched up painfully inside her. *I know that*, she thought, and *I'm sorry*, and *It's not fair*, and *We couldn't protect you*. But she didn't say anything.

"Come on." Rose led Drew gently toward her father's room. "Let's get you cleaned up. You can sleep in here." Jane forced herself to move forward, and as Drew passed, she grabbed his hand. "It's okay," she whispered. She knew it wasn't, but she was grateful when Drew squeezed her hand before letting go. His kindness in the face of her awkwardness, even when he was the one who had been hurt, struck Jane's heart. Tears sprang to her eyes.

She went into Rose's room and gently shut the door. The walls were thin, and she could hear Drew crying and Rose murmuring. In not following them, Jane knew she had opened a tiny fissure. Drew and Rose were already more sophisticated than she was, and they had an easy shared language of growing up in New York City. Jane hadn't even understood that Drew liked boys. Paco was the first openly, outwardly gay person she had ever known. More than that, Rose was the caretaker who knew what to say, how to comfort. There was a small, hard place in Jane formed by her fear of doing the wrong thing, of jeopardizing the incredible good fortune she had found this past year.

She sat down and gathered up Rose's necklace from the bedside table. It was cool and heavy. She slid it from hand to hand until it warmed. She put it against her throat and looked at the mirrored closet. Rose had been wearing the necklace when they first met. Tomorrow, Jane would make it right with Drew. She would give Teddy her story. The necklace dropped from her hand into her lap. She picked up her notebook and began to write.

CHAPTER NINE

MONDAY
WORK, REBECCA

Rebecca was not in the mood for desk shenanigans. Ben hadn't watered his cactus even though she had politely encouraged it. In fact, he had stuck his own Post-it over hers that read "**MAKE IT RAIN**," which, if she was not mistaken, referred to showering dancers with money at a strip club. Rebecca was tempted to report him to Mrs. Singh, but it was possible that her funny joke with the apple (**MAKE IT FALL**), which was a visual reference to her clever Che Guevara posting as HOT DESK, might come under some scrutiny. More vexing was the fact that Ben had left a photo propped up on the monitor. Most vexing of all was that the photo was of the Lion. Rebecca snatched it up and examined it. No doubt: it was the Lion with the Bread Loaf sign behind him, a lineup of men on either side of him. (She thought she recognized a much younger version of Fedora, and, yes, he was already balding.) Was it a taunt? Did Ben not think she could land the estate? What had he heard? What game was he playing?

"How was the City of Brotherly Love?" Gabe handed Rebecca an oat milk latte with cinnamon powder. "I know Mondays are grueling after a visit to Philly, especially when one attends a party of preschoolers, so I picked this up for you."

"I adore you. Thank you!" Rebecca drank the coffee gratefully.

"The good news is Jane came into the city with you, right?"

"I know; I can't believe it. But she still won't tell me *anything* about *anything*! She was supervising the boys' party like a wedding planner, then reading an apparently *riveting* book on the train. I'm not even sure when she changed her mind: one minute she's literally hanging up on me; now she's headed over to the town house? All she would say was that she needed to see Rose. I think she's on her way over there soon. Why so fucking mysterious? I ask you."

"May I remind you that patience is a virtue, though clearly not one of yours," Gabe answered. "And you're having dinner with Rose and Jane tonight. Amazing."

"All shall be revealed." Rebecca tapped her forefingers together.

"I still think I should be there. Jane loves me."

"Jane does love you! But there can be no distractions. And you are distractingly handsome, obviously."

"'Tis a blessing and a curse," Gabe admitted. "I have some very interesting news for you too. Tor received an emergency call this weekend about the *East River Review* party. Apparently, now that the Lion is no longer with us, they want the party to be both a celebration of the magazine's sixty years *and* a celebration of his life. Their budget quadrupled and Rose Adams agreed to host the whole thing at the Southampton estate. Since it's supposed to be happening next week, the original party planners panicked and had to call in Tor. He's been working all night; this morning when I left he was on the phone making Hampton Jitney an offer they couldn't refuse."

"Holy shit! The party of the century!"

"Right? They already had all these writers lined up, but now it's going to be huge. Tor is out of his mind with the change in venue and last-minute brainstorming."

"I think what you're saying is: How do we get invited?" Rebecca finished her coffee with a flourish. "Tell Tor that the all-white party—and I mean all-white in more ways than one—is dead in the water!"

"He does so appreciate your input," Gabe commented dryly. "And I can make myself useful as Tor's plus one. Wrangle your own invite. Serendipitously, you *are* dining with the hostess tonight."

"True, true." Rebecca picked up the Lion photo. "What do you make of this?"

"It's an all-white-man party?" Gabe took a closer look. "The Lion and the usual suspects. I wonder if that was the magical bonding summer of the Lion and Frank French. Obviously not, or he would have shouldered his way into this photo."

"Ben, my obnoxious deskmate, left it there. I think he's trolling me."

"So the ginger has some snap!"

"Seriously? Gabe, focus! What could this mean? Doesn't it seem suspicious to you? Like a pointed barb? Wait, is that redundant?"

"Yes. Barbs are by their nature pointed. Barbara Bush the elder, for example. I've heard that this Ben person is not fully a ginger. Just a hint of ginger. A drop of ginger. Dark ginger! And freakishly big. And here's something else interesting: my source is quite taken with him."

"For fuck's sake! Mrs. Singh loves everyone! Why wouldn't she love a ginger giant?" Rebecca waved the photo at Gabe. "He's a monster! He's trying to get in my head!"

Gabe carefully extricated the photo from her hand and propped it back against the monitor. "I forgot I should have gotten you a decaf. That's on me." He pulled his phone from his back pocket. "Should we google Ben? Find out what Sahila is talking about?"

"Absolutely not!" Rebecca had no interest in learning anything more about Ben Heath. She wanted to forget he even existed.

"Hmmm . . ." Gabe scrolled through his phone. "High school basketball hero? No photo for Hawk Mills yet. A disappointingly meager social media presence, I must say. What?"

Rebecca groaned. "It's exhausting having to watch my back at my own place of work. It's bad enough that everyone's second-guessing me as a 'mid-level editor,' and, honestly, I'd have no business handling this on my own even if I *were* the Lion's love child. And how is my mom all up in my work life? I don't even have MY OWN DESK! Or at least a lovely person like Carlotta to share one with. She left you cookies!"

"Snickerdoodles," Gabe confirmed. "Not the obvious choice."

"I'm just saying that I *hate* him!" Rebecca flicked the photo until it slid down the monitor. "I hate you, giant ginger Ben, and your fucking cactus!"

Gabe stroked Rebecca's shoulder as if he were calming a spooked horse. "I'm going to recommend hydrating. Things will be clearer after dinner tonight, right? And remember that last week there was no chance in hell that either of us would be partying in the Hamptons with the cream of the literati, while this week it is a distinct possibility."

"That does help," Rebecca admitted.

"You going to be okay? Thanks to your brilliant idea, I have a call with Liberty regarding a jaunty neck scarf for a certain Lady we love."

"Go, go." Rebecca waved weakly. "I have to prepare for a meeting with Alice Gottlieb to discuss her new idea for the trilogy follow-up. She wants to go in a different direction. A sci-fi direction."

"I'm sure you will be able to steer her gently back to the land of her bread and butter: quiet tales of poignant family drama and menopausal woes."

"Watch your mouth! We won the National Book Critics Circle Award!"

"Settle down, kitten. See you later." Gabe handed Rebecca her water bottle. "Flush that caffeine out. And call me the *minute* you hear from Jane!"

Rebecca went by Chloe's desk to drop off some books for UPS.

Chloe was wearing over-the-knee white patent leather boots, a tiny plaid skirt, and a top that appeared to be made entirely of dental floss. Rebecca could not stop herself from thinking, in the exact voice of her mother, *How on earth is that comfortable?* "How was your weekend?" she asked Chloe.

"So fun! My roommates and I went to a twink rave in Williamsburg. What did you do?"

Rebecca thought rapid-fire of all the possible answers she could give, but in the end, coffee aside, she didn't have enough energy to lie. "I went to a party with a bouncy castle, a cake in the shape of a basketball, and a clown."

"That place in Times Square? So fun!"

Rebecca hated to dampen Chloe's enthusiasm. Well, usually she didn't mind dampening it a little bit, but in this case she looked so excited about Times Square that Rebecca didn't have the heart to expose herself as not the so-lame-it's-cool partier but the actual so-lame-twenty-eight-year-old-attending-a-children's-birthday-party-in-the-suburbs-of-Philadelphia. "Kind of," she said. "But much farther south."

"Sweet!" Chloe stacked the books into neat piles. "Don't forget to stop by Ami's: she wants to prep you with negotiating tactics for your meeting with Rose Adams."

If by "meeting" Ami meant lots of red wine and probably tears and maybe shouting (Rebecca didn't know *what* to expect) at the neighborhood Italian place near Mimi's, then by all means Rebecca would take notes on negotiating tactics. But somehow she didn't think tonight was the time or the place. There were still too many unanswered questions about the relationship between Jane, Rose, and the Lion's unpublished work. In fact, *all* her questions were still unanswered! What was happening *right now* at the town house? Across the room, she saw Mrs. Singh spritzing her plants and most likely trying to eavesdrop.

"Looking forward to the meeting, Rebecca?" Mrs. Singh called over. How did Mrs. Singh know about her dinner? What kind of sorcery did she practice? Rebecca gave her a thumbs-up.

"Oh my god, did you know that Mrs. Singh's mother-in-law is *famous*?" Chloe asked breathlessly.

"What do you mean?" Rebecca turned her back in case Mrs. Singh was lip-reading.

"Yeah, her mother-in-law has, like, millions of followers on TikTok. She makes Indian comfort food."

Rebecca knew that TikTok could sell books and make her feel uncoordinated when she watched viral dances. But an old lady with millions of followers? "Does she have a hook? What's her thing?"

"Just making the food. CookTok is all about sassy old ladies in the kitchen right now. Let me show you TikTok Nani." Chloe pulled out her sparkly phone and found Mrs. Singh's mother-in-law, a.k.a. #nanicooks #indiangranny #tiktokgranny and #indiancooking, who was wearing an apron over her sari and flipping chapatis. Nani wasn't even particularly sassy, Rebecca thought. She already had over twenty-five thousand views and rising as Rebecca watched.

"This is insane!" If Nani, why not Mimi? Mimi and Stella together—they were kicking ass on Instagram; why not the next frontier? Rebecca was wary of TikTok, mostly because as a person whose job was reading and who actually loved reading, she had more than a few times found herself innocently checking out a hilarious snippet of stand-up and coming to, disheveled and wild-eyed, hours later, her respectable novel untouched next to her. But what if, instead of becoming ensnared in the web of TikTok, she made the platform work for her? She would do research and figure out how to get Mimi and Stella TikTok famous and then actual famous.

"Alice Gottlieb wants to meet you at that coffee place next to the subway? The nitro cold brew place?" Chloe, a matcha tea drinker who traveled with her own frother like a tiny pool cue, wrinkled her adorable nose.

"Ugh, that place. I don't think they even serve food there. And everyone seems so mean!"

"Well, I hear they're really committed to sustainability." Chloe found the bright side, as always.

"Fine. Will you let her know I'll be there by noon? I'm going to see Ami first, and then I have a quick check-in with Lady Paulette and Gabe."

"Of course!" Chloe attached her headset and got to work.

Ami had assured Rebecca that she had confidence in her ability to manage Rose Adams, and that Rebecca should certainly mention that Ami would love to get on a call with everyone, and that it would be great to start talking about the possible deal. Then Lady Paulette complained that Liberty's Meow Organic pattern in goldenrod made her look sallow, and Rebecca could only marvel at how Gabe, invoking Princess Margaret, Posh Spice, and Anna Wintour, convinced Lady Paulette that Meow Organic lit her from within. It was a relief to grab her bag and arrive early to the meeting with Alice Gottlieb.

Rebecca spread her things on an empty two-top and waited for Alice, quickly texting Alice's agent, Trixie Carter, her favorite in the business and a good friend.

Rebecca:
alice wants to "think outside the box" and "is not feeling beholden to the marketplace" for next book

Trixie:
i know WTF

Rebecca:

we are in agreement that she should feel beholden to the marketplace right?

Trixie:

love her but she should be absolutely beholden to the marketplace yes

Rebecca:

the marketplace does not want her sci fi does it?

Trixie:

get her talking about her great aunt flora—think there is a story there

Rebecca:

just want to confirm we are on the same page

Trixie:

next book should be a slam dunk

Rebecca:

unless it takes place on mars

Trixie:

exactly

Rebecca:

kk will see what i can do and you do the same on your end

Trixie:

project keep alice inside the box!!

drinks soon 🍷

Rebecca hearted the last text as one of the very serious employees cleared the table next to her in obvious annoyance. "Excuse me, but you need to order something if you're going to sit there."

"Oh, of course. I will as soon as the person I'm meeting arrives. I'm just a little early."

The employee wore a large button that said "Ask Me About Nitrogen Infusion." Rebecca would never dare. "Yeah, you need to order if you're at a table."

"Okay, no problem. Can I have a decaf oat milk latte with cinnamon?"

"No."

"Excuse me?" Rebecca felt her face flush.

"We don't serve decaf." The employee gestured to a large sign above the cash register.

"I'll take a regular?"

"You have to order at the register."

Flustered, Rebecca ordered the smallest possible size, was denied oat milk, given a short lecture on "nitro cascade," and paid out eight dollars for the privilege. By the time Alice arrived, Rebecca's heart was jittering.

Alice was short and round, with severe bangs and a whinnying laugh that made Rebecca smile. She had spent untold hours soothing Alice's anxiety, pumping up her ego, drawing from her sentence after elegant sentence with patience and respect, if she did say so herself. Every July, she made the trek to Alice's summer bungalow on the Jersey Shore where they ate corn on the cob and strolled the boardwalk with Alice's wheezy bulldog. Years of success, and now Alice wanted to "switch gears" and "push the envelope." For someone whose books resisted cliché, Alice did love her platitudes.

"Rebecca! Thank you for meeting me here: I'm resetting my metabolism." Alice ordered a large cup and plunked down. "I drink coffee for breakfast and lunch, then an enormous green smoothie for dinner. I've never felt more clearheaded and my skin is luminous. Look!" Alice's skin was indeed luminous. "It's been two whole days, and I will never go back."

"What? Never go back to solid food?"

"Never go back to the tyranny of appetite!"

"My appetite is a benevolent dictator," Rebecca reflected. "Now, tell me about your new book. Have you written anything, or is it just in the planning stages? I'm looking forward to reading it." Rebecca didn't add: *unless it's science fucking fiction.*

After twenty minutes of interjecting neutrally while Alice professed her belief that change was growth, Rebecca decided that she was going to have to let Trixie handle Alice. Would anyone who had enjoyed a trilogy of "quiet tales of poignant family drama and menopausal woes," as Gabe had so aptly put it, rush out to purchase a book described by Alice as "a royal Anna Karenina meets underwater Iron Man in a doomed interplanetary romantasy"? Also, Rebecca's phone had buzzed about a hundred times, actually moving her bag on the table in its insistence.

"I'm so sorry, Alice, I have to check this; it might be work." Rebecca fished her phone out of her bag at the same time as her shaking hands knocked the last of her cold brew down the front of her white shirt. Rebecca gasped. It was cold and wet and at least three dollars' worth of dark stain. Alice handed her a wad of environmentally friendly napkins that disintegrated as Rebecca used them to blot ineffectually at her chest. Her phone buzzed again. Rebecca swiped up to discover about a hundred texts from Mrs. Singh and Chloe. Skimming, she realized that she was missing the Cooperative Community Group Committee meeting on desk sharing that she had been volunteered to attend. Fuckety fuck! Apparently Frank French was "dropping by" the meeting. Rebecca didn't have time to get back to the office and would have to Zoom on her cell phone. From the coffee shop. Without turning on her camera. Now. "Oh, Alice, I have to take an urgent call from work."

"I hope everything is all right!" Alice looked concerned. Rebecca didn't blame her. Who knew what was happening in publishing? Maybe Frank French was announcing a *Hunger Games* situation wherein Rebecca would have to fight Ben for the desk. He was a giant! She had no skills but her wits and, frankly, even those were a little scattered these days. She could use his cactus as a weapon against him! Rebecca tried to still her caffeine-addled brain. Frank French was neither calling his divisions to war nor was he closing up shop. He was just checking in to see how desk sharing was going. *Calm the fuck down*, she hissed silently to herself. "I'm sorry, what?" Alice was looking at her strangely.

"Did I say something?" Had she said that out loud? Why did she ever drink coffee? What if she had a heart attack at the nitro cold brew place? She would die having disappointed Mrs. Singh and surrounded by disdainful coffee snobs. "It's fine! Everything's fine! I just need to hop on this call!"

"No problem at all: I have some shopping to do before I head home. I'm buying parsley in bulk. I'll send you the completed draft tonight. I wrote the entire thing in three weeks. I can't thank you enough for your support."

Trixie was going to kill her. Rebecca gave Alice an arm's-length hug so as not to press her cold, wet chest against her. Frantically swiping and tapping, Rebecca finally got the meeting pulled up on her phone, jammed in her headphones, and hoped to attract no notice as the dark screen emblazoned with her name popped up. If only she had an up-to-date professional-looking headshot to upload but it was too late for that now. *Please, god, just let me lurk and be counted present*, she thought.

"Excuse me? You'll need to order a coffee if you're sitting there." It was a different employee, a louder one.

"Are you kidding? I have coffee all over me!" Rebecca gesticulated at her wet shirt and shook the empty cup with such vehemence that the employee backed away warily.

"Welcome, Rebecca! Now we are all accounted for! A reminder to mute yourself unless you want to speak, and of course, we welcome all speakers." Mrs. Singh's kindly face filled Rebecca's phone and Rebecca read its unspoken message: MUTE YOURSELF.

A private chat from Chloe popped up:

Chloe To Me (Privately)

everyone heard you ordering coffee LOL

Rebecca felt lightheaded from the caffeine. She posted a quick message to all fifteen participants.

Me To **Everyone**

sorry i'm late—had an author meeting that couldn't be postponed. so glad to be here!

Harry To **Everyone**

Welcome, Rebecca!

Carlotta To **Everyone**

She toggled over to private chat with Chloe.

Me To **Chloe** (Privately)

did i miss anything? FF?

> **Chloe** To Me (Privately)
> everyone had to go around and say their favorite thing about desk sharing

> **Me** To **Chloe** (Privately)
> good thing i missed that

Mrs. Singh's face looked directly at Rebecca. "Why don't you tell us your favorite thing about desk sharing, Rebecca?"

"So many things?" Rebecca said.

"You'll need to unmute now, dear," Mrs. Singh reminded her patiently. Sweet Jesus, had Rebecca become SUSAN?

Chloe popped up again in private chat:

> **Chloe** To Me (Privately)
> you should turn on your camera?

> **Me** To **Chloe** (Privately)
> trust me NO

Rebecca hit "unmute," but before she could open her mouth, Frank French's face filled her phone screen, his prized mustache never a more welcome sight.

"Just stopping by to let everyone know how much we appreciate your dedication to facilitating this desk sharing project as we utilize our workspace effectively and foster collaborative colleague communication." As always, Frank French preferred the royal "we" and as much toothless jargon as could be crammed into every sentence. He smoothed his mustache down on either side. "Leesen has hit the ground running in the world of dynamic seating, and that is due in large part to the efforts of Mrs. Singh to get all hands on deck. I'm going to turn this meeting back over to her. Again, hot desking, in all its forms, is a key focus for us, and we urge all of you to open the kimono so we can make it as successful as possible."

"'*Open the kimono*'? *What?!*" Rebecca made a face, reveling in the anonymity of her turned-off camera. Who the fuck says "open the kimono"? Was that an actual thing that people said?

> **Chloe To Me (Privately)**
> MUTE

Rebecca startled and muted.

> **Me To Everyone**
> wait did i just say that out loud
>
> and can we admit "open the kimono" is wildly inappropriate?
>
> chloe what did you hear? i'm supposed to be a black hole of silence on this call!!!

> **Harry To Everyone**
> I for one didn't hear anything but Frank French

> **Susan To Everyone**
> I find it more professional to stay muted until I want to speak

> **Richard To Everyone**
> Rebecca you are texting the whole group so stop being cheeky

Rebecca's face flamed. She private-chatted Chloe.

> **Me To Chloe (Privately)**
>
> CAN FRANK FRENCH SEE GROUP CHAT???? DID HE HEAR ME??

> **Chloe To Me (Privately)**
>
> don't worry he's gone now
>
> fwiw i agree about kimono

> **Me To Chloe (Privately)**
>
> OH MY GOD it's the phone it's because I'm using my phone now i'm going to get fired also TOO MUCH COFFEEEEE

Rebecca hoped against hope that Mrs. Singh could later be persuaded to destroy all evidence of the group chat.

"Let's pull up the Office Life Inbox, shall we?" Mrs. Singh resumed. "There are some pressing and not-so-pressing concerns raised here that we can examine. I'll share my screen." Rebecca made sure she was muted and tucked her thumbs into fists. She watched the inbox insanity issue forth as Mrs. Singh scrolled through. "What jumps out here?"

"Just to be clear, I resolved my questions about scheduling," Harry from Hawk Mills said.

"It would be helpful to have links to request forms as suggested," Mrs. Singh said. "I will look into that. And perhaps a more official way to assign empty desks when necessary."

Rebecca's screen went to black with the name Ben Heath. "Is anyone else a little concerned about Anon?" It figured that her nemesis took the meeting with his camera off. She was hiding the sneering employees of the nitro cold brew place and a dark wet stain ruining her white shirt. What was *he* hiding?

"While we do want the Office Life Inbox to be a safe space," Mrs.

Singh replied, "we must certainly be mindful of any posts that cross the line to create a hostile workplace environment."

"I also wonder about how best to enforce the Clean Desk Policy," Ben Heath was saying. Was he fucking kidding? Rebecca couldn't help herself. Finally, she was forced to engage directly with the enemy. She double-checked it was private, then sent him a message.

Rebecca sat back, blinking. Well, that had escalated quickly. Mrs. Singh was engaging in what sounded like a metaphysical dialogue with Richard about "Paul" versus "paul." Ben, who could apparently do two things at once without erroneously texting the group chat, made a comment about balancing privacy with safety and followed it up with another dig at Rebecca regarding desk cleanliness.

Me To Ben (Privately)

> KMarx? more like Inspector Javert

> you are really sowing the seeds of the cactus right now

> also kind of a suck-up tbh

Ben To Me (Privately)

> thought you were supposed to be a black hole of silence

Me To Ben (Privately)

> better than white man talking

Ben To Me (Privately)

> just trying to foster collaborative colleague communication unlike some people

Rebecca had started furiously typing a reply when her phone flashed a photo of Jane, who was calling her. Could everyone see the message "MOM CELL CALLING"? Of course not, right? Rebecca hit the red "deny" button, then somehow inadvertently logged herself out of Zoom. She looked at her phone in despair. Was her mom calling with an all-important update about her meeting with Rose? An employee

("Ask Me About Nitrogen Infusion") began aggressively wiping up the spill on her table. "Mop at table four!" they shouted.

"You hardly need a mop!" Rebecca protested. "It's mostly on my shirt. And I'm sorry, I tried to clean it up, but your napkins don't work." She hastily snatched her bag from the table as the employee got closer with a wet rag.

"You can order another one at the register," they suggested, with a hint of menace.

"It's okay, I'm leaving. Sorry about the spill!" Rebecca began gathering her things. A text from Chloe lit up her phone.

Really, Rebecca thought, *now Chloe is a detective?* She smiled apologetically at the unimpressed employee and left the chilly din of the coffee place.

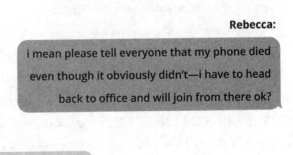

Then thank the lord for small mercies, Rebecca thought. Should she nip into the Gap and buy a shirt or should she show up at work wearing the stain as her excuse for botching the meeting? Which was worse, looking like a total mess or having to listen to Gabe rant about fast "fashion" (air quotes most decidedly his)? She bought a cute black T-shirt for $11 and changed in the store. After texting and calling back Jane with no response, she gave up in frustration. You would think her mother would do her the courtesy of telling her everything immediately! You would think her mother would want to share the suddenly very pertinent details of her life. Wait, had Rebecca BECOME her own mother, passive-aggressively disappointed in the level of communication between them? No, Rebecca decided, there was nothing passive about it. Her career hinged on what was going on between Jane and Rose. Was she being dramatic? Maybe! She glared at her phone. Nothing.

Rebecca headed back to the office and the desk she shared with an unhinged bully. She would get to the bottom of his photo of the Lion and its obvious provocation. She would get to the bottom of the mystery with her mom and Rose if she had to stay at the restaurant all night. She didn't care for mysteries! She had crammed her old shirt into the Gap bag to recycle later. No amount of soaking or bleach would save it, and she told herself to remember that she would never wear white again.

JANE

NEW YORK CITY
MAY 2022

Jane walked across Central Park from Mimi's to the East End town house. It should have taken about forty-five minutes according to Google Maps, but she slowed down as she got closer. The long blocks of wide sidewalks were familiar, and she remembered the flustered trek of her first day at the *East River Review*. The image of that black-haired girl in her carefully chosen "professional" outfit of velour top and pointy boots had come into her head as soon as she had heard about Teddy's death. She examined the photos and read the praise, the reassessments, the pages of biography, all with a practiced distance. It wasn't until Rebecca had called her with news of Rose's request that Jane's seemingly impenetrable self-protection ruptured. She had ended the call and left Sam behind in the kitchen. As she walked out the front door, Jane's thoughts were buzzing, each interrupting the next; as she walked around the block she wondered if she had always known that Teddy's death would, like a fairy tale's broken spell, bring back Rose. When she returned to the house, Sam was waiting in the foyer. He held her as she cried, murmuring words of comfort into her hair, but Jane's tears weren't sad tears, no, not at all. They were tears of relief.

The street emptied into a cul-de-sac with a cobblestone terrace overlooking the river. Jane sat on one of the wrought iron benches under an old-fashioned streetlamp. She had thought that maybe, after all these years, the town house would seem smaller than it had loomed in her memory, but that was not the case. Still imposing, still museum-like, its stone balconies and manicured evergreens in large pots signified generations of uninterrupted wealth. The unmistakable blue of the magazine's door drew her roving gaze. A young woman strode purposefully toward the town house, then past the iron gate and down the stairs, disappearing. Jane couldn't help but think of the building swallowing her; she imagined following and stepping down into the darker, cooler space of the office with its long, narrow aisle and desks lining the walls on either side. They would all have computers now, of course, and nobody had been allowed to smoke inside for years. A man in a fedora came out, letting the gate slam behind him and talking loudly on his phone. The office had never lent itself to discretion, Jane thought, and there was certainly no space for a pod or whatever it was Rebecca had described to her. All those times the phone cords were stretched across the way, all the personal calls they had made and been made to listen to, the cacophony of typewriters not enough to assure anyone's privacy.

The last time Jane had sat on this very bench she was with Rose; she didn't remember what they had been talking about, but it was soon afterward that everything had happened with Teddy. Jane thought about the phrase "everything had happened." A few hours, not even—really only a few minutes, if you wanted to be exact—and everything had *changed*, not happened. It was hard to imagine Teddy as an old man even though she had seen photos of him over the years, watched interviews, award shows. Through the screen or on the page, Teddy's charisma was obvious, but for Jane, the only real Teddy was the physical one, the one who had shaped her life like a natural disaster. He was forever in his prime, towering like a tsunami. (Here Jane revised her image; he was less water and more air, a centrifugal force that spun them all around his center.) Her son Ethan had done a junior high science project on tornadoes, and Jane remembered videos of cows and trucks being sucked up into the spirals. It wasn't inside the tornado that hurt you, Ethan explained; it was the ejection. Inside the tornado that was Teddy (*I'm really doubling down on this metaphor*, Jane thought, *but I'm going to follow it through*) there was chaos and excitement and access to everything she wanted. It was the ejection that changed everything. Was it banishment or self-exile? Even now, Jane couldn't say.

After the shock of Rebecca's phone call, it was unexpectedly easy to leave her contact information for Rose at the *East River Review*. And then to see the unknown New York number flash on her phone—not to answer, but to wait for the message, to hear Rose's voice for the first time in so long, telling her Teddy had written a book. They had arranged through short texts that Jane would come to the town house to read this book, that they would have dinner together with Rebecca. The terseness of planning seemed necessary in the face of the reality that they were going to see each other again.

The gate clanged, and Jane watched the man in the fedora reenter the office. She had the sudden memory of Parker arriving one day wearing a tennis visor, and the tension that had built among the interns: Would anyone say anything? Were they all just going to accept this sartorial statement? After the first incredulous eye contact, they were unable to look at each other. Parker was not as senior as Jonathan, not as intimidating as Ellen, not as confident as Paco, not as shameless as Deedle; nor was he one of them whom they could tease. It was impossible to concentrate, and Jane could still remember the dangerous giddiness threatening to spill over. Then Teddy had flung open the blue door, his arms full of books and papers, his broad shoulders blocking the light as he perused the room with avuncular fondness. "Why, Parker!" he exclaimed in astonishment. "Has Wimbledon come early?" First Rose, then Drew, then Jane had fled up the back stairs, trying and failing to stifle their helpless laughter. Smiling, Jane wondered what Parker was doing now. Many years ago, she had attended a reading for his well-reviewed, scarcely sold second collection of stories at the Penn State bookstore. She had waved at him from the back but hadn't stayed to have him sign her copy. His pink pants were adorned with lobsters.

Jane's phone buzzed in her bag, and she took the call from Sam.

"You picked up." He sounded surprised.

"I haven't gone inside yet," Jane admitted. "Rose doesn't know I'm here."

"How are you feeling?" Sam asked.

"I don't know," Jane answered honestly.

"You don't have to do anything you don't want to do," he told her. "You don't have to go inside if you don't want to. You can see Rose somewhere else. You don't even have to see Rose if you don't want to." Sam, who was often distracted and not particularly good on the phone—he preferred speaking in person and was disinterested in all technology—was focusing carefully, Jane could tell.

"I *want* to see Rose."

"Of course," he said mildly. *If Teddy was a tornado, Sam was a ballast,* Jane thought. All those years ago, when she needed refuge, Sam—slightly disheveled, brilliant, kind—had given her that and more; she trusted him absolutely. They had built a family together. Still, here she was on a bench outside the town house, the blue door in sight, on the phone with her husband in Philadelphia. "Well, you'll let me know how it goes?" Jane could hear running water and Fergus whining.

"I'll call you later," she said. "Love you." It was almost 12:45; she didn't want to be late. There was an earlier, unanswered text from Rebecca. She would give her daughter a quick call just to let her know she had arrived at the town house. It was difficult to keep putting her off, and Rebecca was rightfully frustrated. It was just that Jane had lived for so long with the past submerged in a deep part of herself. She was protective of that girl she once was; it was painful to hold her up to scrutiny. She was so young, and she had thought her choices, if they were even choices, were the right ones. It was foolish to imagine how it could have been different because it wasn't different. The call went straight to voicemail. Jane didn't owe anything to anyone. Except to the one person who was left.

She stood up at the same time as the town house's door opened. And there was Rose, framed in the doorway. "I thought that was you," she called out. Rose. Willowy, pale, striking. Jane took a few steps toward her and stopped. She brought her hand to her throat, where she could feel her pulse quicken. There was a moment when the old Rose would have rushed forward to hug her, but this Rose was still, composed in her elegant, tailored clothes. "Would you come in?" this Rose asked politely. "I hope it wasn't insensitive of me to invite you here. We could go somewhere else?"

"No," Jane answered. "It's all right." The moment of the reunion—the possibility of an embrace, the expected relief—passed, and somehow they were going to move forward in this formal, awkward dance as if they were strangers. *Were* they strangers? Jane had worked at a number of jobs; she had married; she had raised Ethan, Andrew, and Rebecca; she had thickened in the middle; her hair was silvery gray; she had reading glasses in her bag. Silently, Rose turned and Jane followed. The town house foyer hadn't changed: masses of flowers, light from the long windows falling across the graceful statues, the wide staircase curving upward. When they entered the enormous living room, Jane stopped at the pool table while Rose continued on. She hadn't played since she left New York. This one was a beauty. It must have been custom-built, judging from its size and polished walnut, its deep green felt unfaded. When she looked up, Rose was sitting on the window seat, and Jane had a moment of powerful, disorienting déjà vu.

"I found a manuscript in Teddy's desk after he died," Rose began directly. "I was in the process of gathering papers for the lawyers and collecting his unpublished stories and letters as part of the estate; I'm moving everything from PK Publishing to another house. His work could use younger, fresher eyes, as you can imagine." Jane could imagine. There had been a story of Teddy's published years ago that had kicked up enough controversy that even Jane had been aware of the social media backlash. "It's the only copy," Rose continued. "And before it's destroyed, I want you to read it. Not all of it." Here, her expression was wry. "I wouldn't put you through that. But there are a few relevant chapters."

"Is it a memoir?" Jane could see the stack of yellow papers held together with a rubber band. She remembered the lined notebooks she had filled. They were shelved next to the old *East River Reviews* in the guest room. Someone, most likely Ellen, had subscribed her to the magazine: she had received copies sent to her mother's house for years until, without her really noticing, they had ceased or hadn't been forwarded after her mother had moved into assisted living.

"Most decidedly fiction," Rose answered, with a flash of her old fire. "But as with all his work, it's based on his life. And ours." Jane wasn't sure if she meant hers and Teddy's or hers and Jane's. "I didn't want to copy it and I couldn't bear to read it over the phone. I don't even know the right questions to ask you. All I could think of was to figure out a way you could read it yourself."

"Through Rebecca," Jane said.

"Through Rebecca. Who is lovely, by the way." For the first time, Rose smiled, and Jane, just as she could always see the babies in the faces of her grown children, could glimpse the sparkling young woman behind Rose's sad eyes.

"How did you make the connection?"

"Ellen had your mother's name, and I occasionally googled it—after googling became a thing. When she died, I saw your married name and the names of your children in the obituary. I kept tabs on everyone. I knew Rebecca worked at Avenue. I promise I wasn't a stalker. I was hurt and angry for so long, but somehow it was soothing to me, just to know a little bit."

Jane felt a pang. "You were easier for me to track, of course."

"I did try to contact you, you know," Rose said. "Early on. But it was clear you didn't want that."

"I wanted to disappear," Jane admitted. "I wrote you letters, though. Instead of a diary, I suppose. That slowed down when I had the twins. But I still did. Write you, I mean. A few letters every year. There's a folder on my laptop."

"Jane." Rose unfurled from the window seat, her eyes shining. "I wrote you letters too!"

Jane gave a startled laugh. "You did? You didn't hate me for leaving like that?"

Rose tapped her chin in a gesture that Jane remembered fondly. "I didn't say that the first few years of letters were particularly forgiving, did I? I looked over some of the early ones last night. Textbook stages of grief at your abrupt rejection. At some point, maybe acceptance?"

Did Rose mean that she accepted the loss? Had Jane ever accepted it? But it must mean something that Rose had written her letters. Jane stepped closer. "I couldn't see a way forward. Either you knew what happened, and I couldn't bear it, or you *didn't* know, and I couldn't bear it!" She stopped and put one hand on the edge of the pool table for support. An image of Teddy—his booming laughter ringing in her ears, his blue shirt open at the neck, his dark eyes—flashed into her head. What would Rose think of her outburst? Teddy had—it was almost unbelievable—died. He had loomed so large for so long. And Rose had been his wife. Jane gave her head a little shake to clear it of him. All those years, it had been Rose and Teddy, and after so much time, who was Jane to need something from her? *This* Rose was a widow.

"When I read this"—Rose held the manuscript out toward Jane—"it confirmed some of what I had imagined. But of course *yours* is the story I need to hear. Not his."

Jane hesitated. It was as if her flare of emotion hadn't happened. They stood facing each other, and it seemed to Jane that Rose was holding the book between them to ward her off. What had Teddy written? What did Rose think? Jane flushed with a sudden twinge of guilt, of the long-suppressed shame. But she wasn't that girl any longer. She had her own story to tell. Jane took the yellow papers carefully. "How should we do this?" she asked.

"You sit." Rose gestured to the window seat. "I'll get us some lunch. As I said, you can skim it. You *should* skim it . . . or just read the pertinent sections. Prepare yourself."

There was a burst of animated talking from the kitchen. Two young people barged partway into the room, then stopped abruptly, mouths agape.

"Upstairs is closed today," Rose said firmly. "I thought I made that clear to Tom."

"We're so sorry! We just got here! He's at lunch!" one of them squeaked, while the other, face reddening, backed up hastily until he bumped into a chair.

"It's all right," Rose relented. "Please close the door at the top of the stairs. I should have locked it."

"Sorry! Sorry!" They darted away, chastened.

"Interns," Rose explained. She cocked her head and raised an eyebrow in an expression that reminded Jane, piercingly, of Drew.

"Interns," Jane repeated.

"Later, interns," Rose said.

"Gotta bolt," Jane replied. The air between them was charged with the memory of laughter and the laughter still inside them, swelling closer to the surface. But there was also the manuscript, heavy in Jane's hand.

"Read." Rose turned toward the kitchen. She looked over her shoulder at Jane as if she might disappear. "I'll be back," she promised.

Jane settled on the window seat, leaning against the window's cool glass, the spectacular view spread out behind her. She read quickly and kept reading even when she sensed Rose dipping into the room and back out again. A long time passed before she skipped to the end, then reread what Rose had called the "pertinent" section. She stood up and stretched. God, she was thirsty. Wandering over to the pool table, she couldn't help running her fingers over the smooth balls in the rack. Pushing and pulling the rack as the balls clacked against each other. Pushing and pulling until Rose came over and stilled her hands by taking them in her own.

"Tell me everything," she said gently, and Jane did.

CHAPTER TEN, PART ONE

MONDAY
HOME, REBECCA

While Rebecca sipped her 6 p.m. cocktail with Mimi and Jane, she could spy the neatly folded blankets and pillow next to the couch where she was supposed to sleep for a few nights. The couch was narrow, slippery, and perhaps stuffed with straw. It had been a slightly taxing early evening for Jane and Mimi as they reviewed photos of grandchildren and great-grandchildren and shared their high hopes for Rebecca's future. The point was, Rebecca thought, everyone needed a stiff drink in a tiny glass.

Turning to Mimi she said, "I'm sure Mom told you she hasn't seen Rose Adams in a million years. Did she tell you why? Did she tell you what happened today at the town house when they first laid eyes on each other after those million years? Because she certainly hasn't told me."

"Told you what, dear?" asked Mimi.

"Sweetheart," her mom responded. "Seeing Rose was overwhelming. I'm still processing everything. And we *are* having dinner together. You can ask us questions, I promise."

Rebecca didn't like the sound of this "us." In the past week or so, it had become apparent that while Rebecca's life was an open book to her mother, fair game for all kinds of queries and judgments, Jane did not feel obligated to return the favor. And now that Rebecca was asking the questions—plenty of them—Jane was the one resisting, hedging, withholding.

"Stella dropped off a Greek platter earlier, so don't worry about my dinner," Mimi announced, clearly not opposed to their worrying. "She marinates the chicken in an oregano-yogurt sauce before she cooks it, and the texture is sublime." Had she not heard Jane and Rebecca, or was she making sure they knew she would be eating alone? Or both?

"Mimi, I'm going to make you and Stella famous," Rebecca said loudly. "You're going to have your own TikTok account and then we'll take over YouTube."

"TikTok? Honestly, Rebecca," Jane said disapprovingly.

"I just watched an old lady with literally *half* of Mimi's personality stand there making chapatis and she has millions of followers!"

"Old lady?" Suddenly Mimi's hearing had improved.

"Millions of people have nothing better to do? This is why reading literacy is plummeting in this country," Jane scolded.

"And we're also going to start a YouTube channel for you and Stella," Rebecca continued, ignoring her mother. "You'll be an influencer in no time. Then brands and companies and music producers and all kinds of people will pay you to promote products and songs and places. The next thing you know, you'll be hiring a private car and driver to squire you about town."

"Well, that does sound as though it would keep me busy!" Mimi said agreeably. "Although I don't need a private car now that you showed me how Youbert works."

"Uber, Mimi. U-B-E-R." Rebecca was not at all confident that her Uber app lesson had been absorbed, but fortunately Mimi still enjoyed hailing a taxi by waving an umbrella, which she carried in her capacious purse, rain or shine.

"It was wonderful to glimpse Stella," Jane said. "She came by just before you got home. She was telling some incredible stories about the family she works for—and it sounds as though she and Miles are doing well."

"I know, it's crazy. Miles is great but he's never around. He's super-busy." Rebecca waited, one, two, three, and . . .

"Are you seeing anyone these days? How is that lawyer?"

It was unclear how much Jane knew about what had happened with Max, and Mimi refused to catch Rebecca's eye, instead busying herself with the last of the olives.

"Nope, nope, nope." Rebecca stood up to gather the glasses. "Free and single, yay."

"I approve," Jane volunteered, unasked. "The more time you devote to your career at this stage, the more it will pay off down the line."

"I never thought that lawyer was good enough for Rebecca," Mimi revealed.

"So I've heard." Rebecca turned and looked over her shoulder. "Mom, we need to get going. Fifteen minutes, okay?"

"Now, that doesn't mean there's not a wonderful young man out there who is just right for her," Mimi went on. "In my day, we weren't afraid to say 'soulmates.'"

"Fortunately, Rebecca lives in a day and age when her worth can be measured by more than her good fortune in finding a soulmate," Jane replied tartly.

Rebecca paused until she was certain this familiar throw down had led to a noncontentious discussion, then went to change for dinner and to text Stella.

Rebecca: thanks for the chicken—how was seeing jane?

Rebecca: your abiding love with miles and soon-to-be rocketing career used as bludgeon

Stella: easy to please jane if you're not her daughter

Rebecca: jane not telling me anything about rose

Stella: she did seem distracted

Rebecca: wtf should I expect at this dinner

Stella: patience is a virtue

Rebecca: NOT ONE OF MINE also almost got fired today after mtg debacle in nitro brew place by subway

Stella: everyone's so mean in there!!

Rebecca: desk share guy revealed as expected to be a complete ass

Stella:

gabe said he was hot

Rebecca:

that's according to mrs. singh! unreliable!!

Stella:

well?

Rebecca:

had his camera off like a sniveling coward

Stella:

idk but i feel sparks

Rebecca:

UGH NO

Stella:

you need to get back in there
👋🌷🥖📎🐿🍵

Rebecca:

I BEG YOU TO STOP

Stella:

👏🌰

Rebecca:

think you need to see miles soon

ok i have to go to world's most awkward dinner now

my true paternity revealed

kind of nervous tbh

Stella:

👉💧

Rose had already arrived. Bruno, the restaurant's proprietor, who had known Rebecca since she was a child visiting Mimi, ushered them to "the best *tavola* in the house: very *privato*!" Rebecca let her mom go first. She watched Rose's face light up as she stood and moved toward Jane. They hugged for a long time. Long enough to make Bruno uncomfortable. "May I bring some vino? Would the *signore* care to sit down?"

The *signore* did finally sit down, and Rebecca went to the bathroom to give them a chance to speak alone. They hardly seemed to notice her leaving but huddled together on the banquette. Rebecca peed, washed her hands, and texted Gabe.

Back at the table, Jane and Rose were deep in conversation. Mercifully someone had seen fit to order a bottle of wine that Bruno was pouring. Rebecca sat down across from them like a couple's therapist or a bank officer reviewing a loan. "Well, cheers!" she said, lifting her glass as soon as Bruno filled it. "Let's drink to . . ." She looked expectantly across the table. Had both of them been crying? Rebecca couldn't remember the last time she had seen her unsentimental mother cry.

"Friendship," Rose answered, raising her glass.

"Looking forward, not backward," Jane added. "To reconnecting."

"To always being connected, no matter what," Rose said meaningfully.

"To friendship!" Rebecca clinked her glass against Rose's, then Jane's. They all took a sip, and Rebecca seized her moment. "So I would love to know what's going on. Like, why you haven't seen each other in so long and why I have no idea about any of it?" She looked pointedly at Jane. Jane wiped her eyes with a napkin. Rebecca motioned for Bruno to bring garlic bread and caprese, the usual.

"Years ago," Jane began, and Rebecca nodded encouragingly, "we worked at the *East River Review* together. We were interns . . . Rose was a writer, a model, a wonderful editor—"

"And your mother," Rose interrupted, "is an amazing writer!"

Rebecca remembered what Rose had said at the town house. *Was Jane an amazing writer?* "Mom?"

"I did think I was going to be a writer," Jane admitted. "It was such an exhilarating world to be part of . . . We were around writers and writing all day, all night. It's hard to explain how it was the air we breathed. Everywhere we went in the city, we were talking about books, about art, we were reading everything . . . I remember all of it!" Jane concluded passionately. Who was this emotional woman impersonating her mother? Or could it be that her sensible, even-keeled mother had been the lie? When Rebecca thought of her mother's life before her, it was a self-described slog of raising twin boys and waiting for the day her beautiful daughter arrived. This was a narrative that served

Rebecca well, she realized, and, frankly, she was not proud that she had swallowed it whole and never looked beyond it. "Your story about the motorcycle, the job in Paris," Jane continued, turning to Rose. "I read it in *The New Yorker*."

"Your fingerprints were all over it," Rose claimed. "You were the one who suggested the cat! You shaped that last paragraph." She took a breath. "I thought maybe you would call after that. I understand now why you didn't."

There was a long pause while Bruno deposited the bread and caprese, read the room, and left without insisting on a dinner order. *The one who suggested the cat?* Rebecca poured everyone another glass of wine. When would *she* understand why Jane hadn't called?

"I wish I had," Jane said. She picked up her water glass and set it back down without drinking. "And now I'm old. It's been so long."

"You look exactly the same," Rose said lovingly.

"You're very generous." Jane laughed, almost shyly, her eyes damp.

"Oh, we were so young!" Rose exclaimed.

"Remember how old everyone else seemed? Susan Sontag was ancient!"

"She must have been in her forties then."

"And Tama Janowitz—the height of cool! But she was only a year or two older than we were—"

"And when we went to deliver manuscripts to Patti Smith at the Chelsea. And all those nights at the Odeon . . ." Rose was gathering steam. "That little room under the stairs! What we got up to in there, my god. Everyone smoking everywhere. Those amazing fries!"

"When Jay McInerney kept buying us drinks." Jane laughed. "In that trench coat he never took off. Years before *Bright Lights, Big City*!"

"I was telling your daughter a little about it," Rose said, and they both looked at Rebecca, not quite seeing her. Rebecca often met Gabe and Tor for drinks (and fries) at the Odeon, where it was still open on West Broadway.

"Teddy's tab at Elaine's . . ." Jane began again. "The fight with Mailer that time."

"When Teddy would storm into the *East River Review* office and yell, 'Daddy's home!'" Rose and Jane burst out laughing. Then Rose sobered. "How did we stand for it, let alone reward it?"

"We all thought it was charming, didn't we? We were all a little bit in love with him, weren't we?"

"We were," Rose said. "I was obliviously in love with him."

"When we were upstairs reading through the slush pile, and he would come down in his boxers and challenge people to play pool . . ." Jane paused.

Rebecca perked up. She had been entranced by the parade of famous 1980s names and places and entertained by the glimpse of their lives at the *East River Review*. But now the tone had shifted, become more fraught, and she sensed something was going to be revealed. Bruno slowed the momentum by appearing tableside and reciting the specials even though they never ordered anything but the *linguine alle vongole* and a side of sautéed spinach with garlic. There was a short discussion about the osso buco, but Rose quickly fell in line, and Bruno was sent away with three identical orders and a request for another bottle of wine. Rebecca knew they were making progress toward the heart of the rift, and as much as she was nervous about what might be uncovered, she was eager to know. "In his boxers?" she prompted her mother. "That doesn't sound HR approved."

"Yes," her mother said slowly. "This time . . . the pertinent time . . . Rose had gone to Paris for the Armani show. The week of a crazy April blizzard." She paused again.

"Will you tell me about what happened then?" Rebecca prodded. "Why it's been so long since you've seen each other?"

Jane looked at Rebecca. "I was good at pool." *More surprising information*, thought Rebecca. And possible non sequitur? "But I was overconfident. Teddy loved a wager. He was still married to Clara but already falling in love with Rose."

"Wait, hold up," Rebecca interrupted. "He was *married*?"

"Oh yes, to his second wife, Clara, Atticus's mother," Rose answered. "His first marriage, to the French actress Marielle Martine, ended when they were quite young. And Clara had Atticus *after* Teddy and I were together. As you could have read in the tabloids, their divorce was messy and took forever. Atticus was so young. I was so young! And then Clara got breast cancer. It was hard for years."

"What about you, Mom? What happened? Why did you leave?"

Jane put her hand on Rebecca's arm. "This is hard to talk about, even now."

Rebecca squeezed her mom's fingers, then let go. She looked across the table at Jane and Rose, and waited.

JANE

NEW YORK CITY
APRIL 1982

The local radio and TV stations had been blaring about the freak spring blizzard all morning. As far as Jane could tell, the snow was steady and, yes, surprising, but not what she would call a blizzard. Nevertheless, the city was in turmoil. Schools were closed, trains were late, and Rose's father called from the airport to say he was headed to the apartment, since his flight was canceled. Rose had left for Paris a few days earlier for a fashion shoot. The last place Jane wanted to be was alone with Anders Bergesen, so she decided to walk to work and then stay the night at her own apartment in the East Village. Drew had called to say he couldn't get to the subway station, and anyway, snow day! Jane stepped out onto the street clutching a small bag of overnight things and wearing her Russian hat. The wind almost knocked her over, and she was blinded by a swirl of snow. Traffic had come to a complete stop. Fine, Jane conceded, blizzard!

The ten-block walk was exhilarating. With the traffic stilled, Jane tromped in the muted city past a woman doing battle with an inside-out umbrella, a man unearthing his car with a broom, and a few gleeful children in puffy snowsuits hurling fistfuls of snow at each other. White heaps piled on each branch of the trees lining the streets, and Jane could make out the pink blossoms of spring, bright and surprised under a skin of snow. The air was cold, and she felt the clarifying sting of it in her nose and lungs. Just last week she and Rose had been sitting on the bench in front of the iron railing overlooking the river outside the town house. There were daffodils! They had been up late the night before having drinks with the *East River Review* staff, Teddy presiding over the table, ordering martinis and regaling them with stories. As it was anytime they were in his presence, the interns were rapt, Drew downing inadvisable amaretto sours, Rose catching Teddy's eye, and Jane trying to keep track of all the new names she was learning: which artist had a sold-out show, which writer had become a social pariah, which actor had a new mistress. After a spirited group discussion of John Irving's latest novel, Deedle got up to demonstrate an exercise from Jane Fonda's workout tape. This involved him flat on his back like a plump beetle, legs churning, a harried waiter sidestepping to avoid him. Jane had laughed so hard that she started coughing; everyone was howling; even Ellen, close at Teddy's elbow, had smiled indulgently. In the incandescence of candlelight, Jane thought everyone looked beautiful. She urged herself to remember the choice phrases she would scribble into her notebook later: "the plump beetle," "the incandescence of candlelight."

When she got to the town house, Parker was out front holding a shovel. "Oh, Jane!" he called, his words snatched by the wind. "Everyone left or didn't come in. I was going to do the steps, but it's useless." Jane didn't imagine that he'd tried very hard, but it was true that the snow was already drifting up against the blue door in the clearing he had made. He was wearing a thick woolen hat with braided strings that looked fairly ridiculous. "I know they have salt somewhere, but . . ." He trailed off, shrugging helplessly. "I'm going home before it gets worse."

"I have some things to do," Jane shouted over the roar. "If that's all right?"

"Just lock up when you leave! You know where Ellen keeps the key? And if you want to come to York Tavern, Deedle is seeking shelter there. I might stop by."

Jane lifted a mittened hand and skidded down the stairs. She had never been alone in the office before. There was a cigarette butt in Ellen's cactus, an open book on Jonathan's desk. Paco, who hadn't been there in weeks, had left a cashmere sweater draped over his chair. Jane shed her outerwear and sat down at Parker's desk. She depressed the typewriter keys and opened his top drawer. A roll of chalky Smarties, one brown leather glove, a stash of striped canvas watch bands in different colors, a copy of Strunk and White's *The Elements of Style*. It was so cold that Jane wondered if the heat had ever even come on. The radiator was ominously silent.

Teddy had gone to London to "sort things out" with Clara—though, as everyone had heard from his booming voice on Jonathan's phone, he was retaining a lawyer. The interns had seen Clara exactly once, when she and Paco arrived at a book party late and overdressed. Clara was an abstraction to them, and after she took up residence in the London flat, Teddy was visibly more relaxed and his visits to the office picked up. Every time he barreled through, the air was charged with his energy. Jane loved it when Teddy ran the editorial meetings that were usually handled by Jonathan: they all trooped up to the living room with their coffees, the discussions were free-flowing, and everyone vied for Teddy's attention. No matter who spoke—Jonathan, who had been at the magazine forever, or Jane, whose cheeks flamed when she opened her mouth—Teddy gave them his absolute attention, shaggy head cocked, his eyes aglow with interest.

Jane blew on her hands to warm them. She had pulled an amazing story from the slush pile about an English Pentecostal community and was determined to convince Ellen to take a chance on the writer, who was about the same age as Jane. She rolled a sheet of paper into the typewriter. Maybe she should call her mom, who was probably watching the news and worrying. Although a blizzard in April would certainly be a sign from her mother's merciless god, who often, it seemed, signaled his disapproval of sin with bad weather. Jane knew how the conversation would go: Was Jane safe? Were there crackheads on the streets? Had Jane been to Mass? Would Jane please consider coming home and helping out at the store? Did Jane know that there was a crime epidemic raging in New York City? When would Jane get "all this" out of her system? Jane decided not to call her mother. Her hands were still too cold to type. If the door was unlocked at the top of the back stairs, it would be a sign that she should read on the window seat.

The window's thick glass swallowed a crack of thunder, and Jane tucked her stocking feet under a cushion. Snow dropped furiously onto the river, disappearing into the dark water. It was much warmer upstairs, cozy even. She opened a cover letter. "Dear Edward David Adams, I guess you could say I am a Renaissance Man much like yourself . . ." Jane laughed out loud. This was one to save for Rose and Drew. She skimmed the predictably awful poetry and tucked it back into the envelope with a form rejection letter. "We regret that we are unable to publish it" always struck Jane as untrue: certainly they were *able* to; they just chose *not* to. The interns spent quite a bit of time regretting to inform each other that they were unable to find a subway token, that they were unable to sanction Rose's desire to watch *The Love Boat*, or that they were unable to meet Deedle for a nightcap.

There was a sudden thump. Jane leaped up from the window seat, her heart galloping. "Hello? Is someone there?" It was Teddy's deep voice calling down the spiral stairs.

"Yes! I'm so sorry! It's Jane!" she called back.

Teddy strolled into the living room barefoot, his thick hair tousled. "What a delightful surprise," he said amiably. "Good heavens! Has the world ended?" He gazed out the windows. "How very Joycean."

"I'm so sorry," Jane repeated herself. "I thought you were in London, and I had some work to do. Parker told me it was fine to go upstairs." Parker had *not* told her it was fine to go upstairs, but Parker was most likely on his third hot toddy with Deedle.

"They canceled my flight last night," Teddy told her, stretching. He was wearing an untucked blue button-down shirt and chinos.

"I can leave." Jane started gathering her things. "I don't want to disturb you."

"Nonsense! Where would you go in this tempest? I'll do some work, you carry on, then we'll reconvene for sustenance." He wandered off toward his office, where Jane had once been sent to consult the enormous *Oxford English Dictionary*, perched on its own pulpit.

It was hard to concentrate at first, but Jane found she had read through a large pile of submissions by the time Teddy came back, singing in a rich baritone, "*Oh, the weather outside is frightful . . .*" He motioned to Jane. "You stay right there and I'll see what sort of provisions Lorraine has left us." He disappeared and Jane could hear him singing. Should she leave? Should she stay and eat with him? Rose and Drew would be jealous. But it was sure to make a good story, right? She had never been alone with Teddy. Since their intern lunch, he had given Rose some of his work with the instruction to "do what she could with it." He had taken Rose out, just the two of them, and listened with great openness, Rose explained excitedly, to her praise and suggestions. He had arranged for the interns to visit Keith Haring's studio, and Ellen had asked Jane what she thought about staying on at the magazine. Jane had been too enthusiastic, perhaps, and scared Ellen off; she hadn't mentioned it again, although Rose and Drew assured her it would happen. But there had been no sign from Teddy that he had read the story she had given him after their intern lunch.

Teddy came back from the kitchen with a baguette, a knife balanced on a plate of cheese, and a bottle tucked under his arm. "Spread that out and we'll have a feast!" He nodded toward a blanket on one of the armchairs, and Jane hastily set up a picnic on the floor. She was nervous but he put her at ease, telling a funny anecdote about expats in Tangiers, detailing the provenance of the wine, noting again her keen eye regarding the Cisneros story. The snow continued to fall, so thick and fast that it obscured the view and gave the illusion, Jane thought, of their being alone in the world, everything else muffled, the movement outside merely white noise. Teddy's tan feet made her think of a beach; she found them endearing, intimate. Jane was careful to take her time with one glass of wine; she wanted to stay alert in this fairy tale.

She told him about the Renaissance Man cover letter, how she hadn't gone swimming since seeing *Jaws*, how she stayed up all night to finish *Middlemarch*, how she and Rose won tickets to see Grandmaster Flash by calling a radio station. Teddy recited a poem by Kenneth Patchen (Jane admitted she had never heard of him), his voice shifting to a deeper register:

The snow is deep on the ground.
Always the light falls
Softly down on the hair of my belovèd.

This is a good world.
The war has failed.
God shall not forget us.
Who made the snow waits where love is.

Only a few go mad.
The sky moves in its whiteness
Like the withered hand of an old king.
God shall not forget us.
Who made the sky knows of our love.

The snow is beautiful on the ground.
And always the lights of heaven glow
Softly down on the hair of my belovèd.

Jane, who might have been embarrassed, was instead moved by the theatrics of his performance, shivering a little when Teddy fell silent and the poem still resonated. This was the life she had scarcely dared to imagine when she first moved to New York: poetry and bread and cheese and real friends who spent hours browsing books with her at the Strand or drinking cheap wine at art gallery openings. Who would believe that she was sitting on the floor with Edward David Adams, whose books she had studied, whose striking face she had admired in magazines?

"'The sky moves in its whiteness' indeed." Teddy clapped his hands. Jane started gathering the empty plates. "No, no, leave it," he commanded. "Enough poetry! Shall we exercise our bodies as well as our minds?"

Jane laid the knife down carefully and said nothing. "I speak of course of billiards," Teddy continued, in a gently teasing way. "Have you played?"

"I have." Jane's pulse quickened. In all the time she had been at the *East River Review*, she still hadn't dared to disturb the table.

"Perhaps a small wager, then?" Teddy rose to his commanding height and offered Jane his hand. It was warm and dry, and he pulled her easily to her feet. "Two out of three. Winner of each game gets one thing he or she wants. Grand winner gets bragging rights."

Jane's confidence surged. She knew what she wanted. "I accept your terms," she said formally, turning their hands, still clasped, into an official shake.

"Shall I break?" Teddy was already racking the balls, the noise familiar and exciting. It reminded her of her uncle's bar and the times she had felt most powerful, most in control. Jane knew that they should have flipped a coin to determine who broke first. Breaking gave you an advantage, but Jane didn't say anything. She watched as Teddy made a hard, clean break, then sunk three stripes. "I'll take high balls," he instructed her as he handed over the cue. Jane resisted lifting all the cues in the holder to find her fit. Instead, buoyed by skill and luck, she ran the table, winning on a decisive smack of the eight ball into the corner left pocket. Teddy laughed in delight. "Why, Jane Kinloch!" he roared. "You surprising little thing!"

In the glow of victory, Jane realized that up until that moment she had been unsure if Teddy even knew her full name.

"And now I must pay up!" He looked down at her, eyes twinkling. "Tell me your heart's desire, Jane Kinloch."

Jane began racking the balls so she wouldn't have to look directly at him, his dark, shining eyes. "I want you to read my story. The one I gave you. 'Tomboy.' And tell me what you think. And be honest."

"Agreed! I would be delighted!" Teddy stepped back to give Jane space. She broke with easy force, sinking three solids, but leaving her path forward blocked. Handing the stick to Teddy, she said breezily, "I'll take low."

Teddy laughed again, then switched to deadly serious, stalking around the table, his big body agile and his span allowing him to make seemingly impossible shots. The game was over quickly. "Shirt off, my dear," he announced casually as he chalked the cue tip.

For a minute, Jane's brain lagged. Shirt off? She worked hard to make sense of it. Was it a kind of dare? Okay, *this* would be the story for Rose. Playing pool in her white cotton bra! With Teddy! Everyone knew Teddy sometimes ambled downstairs in his boxers and challenged whoever was around to a game. Jane had been secretly waiting for her chance. They even had a drinks fund made up of his winnings: a coffee can that Ellen kept in the galley kitchen. Jane knew that Teddy was interested in Rose. Obviously in a different way than he was interested in her. There was no comparison. Everyone was interested in Rose. Rose was Rose! Anyway, Rose and Teddy were just circling, flirting. There was the matter of nineteen years. Also, Jane was sure she could win. She was too flushed with competitive spirit and the indignity of being hustled to fully think through the implications of continued stripping. Anyway, they only had one more game. She tossed her shirt on a chair and tried to be as nonchalant as possible. The next game lasted much longer, both of them playing defensively, thinking ahead, planning angles and blocks. Eventually, Teddy executed a trick shot that sank the eight ball over her one remaining ball. "Pants," he ordered.

Jane unzipped her jeans, folded them carefully, and stood, arms crossed, in her white cotton boy shorts. "Splendid!" Teddy made a show of taking off his watch and belt, placing them on the pool table, and unbuttoning his shirt to reveal a wide expanse of tan chest with a dark strip of hair below his navel. "Now we're both more relaxed. Shall we?"

Jane didn't move. There was still time to stop this. Whatever "this" was. It wasn't really anything, was it? Jane didn't have to move forward. She didn't have to move at all. It would be beyond humiliating, but she could gather her things and walk downstairs. *It's not too late*, she told herself. *It's not too late!* Her heart was pulsing in her throat. "Come, now," Teddy rumbled. "I must make good on my bet, mustn't I? I'd never leave you, fetching as you are, only fulfilling *your* word. I'm no welsher, Jane. I believe your story is in my den." He walked out without looking back to make sure she was behind him.

Jane wavered. Should she put her shirt back on? But if she didn't stick to the bet, would *he* not stick to the bet? Should she grab everything and slip quickly downstairs, out into the snowy street, down to her tiny apartment? How could she ever come back if she did? Agonized, Jane thought of Rose. What would Rose do? Jane conveniently blocked the fact that she was half-naked. She didn't think of Rose's crush on

Teddy that kept them up many nights spinning elaborate fantasies. She didn't think of Teddy's solicitousness with Rose, his hand on her lower back when they all left the restaurant the other night, or his reportedly gushing appreciation of her edits. She didn't want to think of anything except her story and the chance she had now. "Don't chicken out," she remembered Rose saying the night after the intern lunch. She followed him into the office.

Teddy was rummaging in a pile of papers. The air smelled of pipe smoke and leather. "Aha!" He pulled a few typewritten pages that Jane recognized and waved them triumphantly. He brushed past her and lowered himself onto the couch. "You stay over there; you're far too distracting," he directed. Jane leaned against the heavy desk, watching him read. It was unbearable. It was intoxicating. She followed his eyes scanning her words and it was as if they were moving over her exposed skin. Although she knew in the back of her mind that she should be nervous, she wasn't. All she could think about was his validation. She wanted him to keep reading her work forever and she couldn't wait another minute to hear what he thought.

It wasn't a long story, and when he finished reading it, he started back at the top and read it again. Jane stayed absolutely still, as if any movement might diminish his focus. Finally, Teddy placed the papers down beside him. He gave her a long, unreadable look. Jane held her breath. It seemed that he hadn't seen her before this moment. His eyes narrowed a little, and when he spoke, his voice had lost all its flirtatiousness, its seductive teasing. "You're a real writer, Jane Kinloch," he said.

Relief and pride coursed through her. Because he was still sitting and she was standing, she could meet his eyes frankly. "I am," she said.

"Raw," he continued. "Untutored. But you have it." There was something almost grudging in his tone. He tapped his head. "A bit here"—he tapped the left side of his chest—"a bit here," and then he spread his hand across his stomach. "Here is where you have it, Jane. You have the *guts* for it. Can't be taught."

Jane's first thought was that she couldn't wait to tell Rose. In fact, maybe she could call her in Paris from the downstairs office phone? She was chilly but elated. Why was she undressed? All of a sudden, Jane became keenly aware of the fact she was half-naked and alone with Teddy. For the first time since she had met him, Jane had the realization that he was a man. Not a monument, not untouchable. A minute ago he had looked at her with respect, writer to writer. She knew it. Now he was looking at her with darkening eyes, and she felt a prickle of fear. It wasn't far to the door. Teddy rose to standing and in one step was in front of her. "Jane," he said huskily. "You know I can't control myself. Not when you're wearing those white cotton underwear. My Achilles' heel. You little gamine. Hoyden." He was working himself up, Jane thought. If she could just get him calmed down, if she could just get to the door, get her clothes on.

Teddy slid his big hands over Jane's bra and tugged the hair off her neck. Despite herself, Jane's body responded and she softened. *Maybe a few kisses*, she thought desperately. It wasn't too late. Just a few kisses, then she would leave. He was so handsome. Teddy was grappling with his pants and moving her against the desk, its edge pressing into her back. He pushed her underwear aside and ordered her to lift up, to move her leg, to get ready for him. "Wait," Jane whispered, then louder, "Wait a minute," but he must not have heard her because she felt him probing, fumbling. But still it wasn't too late! She twisted a little, but he gripped her firmly.

Then it was too late. She held on to the bulk of his back, her eyes focused on the painting of a ship tossing at sea. "Oh, you little tomboy," he groaned into her hair. It was over quickly. He stayed inside of her. "You naughty girl," he murmured. "Now look what you've done. You are positively irresistible, my dear."

Her back was going to be bruised from the desk. Teddy was still close against her. It was too late. It was too late. She could never take it back. Jane tried to breathe, but panic swelled in her chest. What had she done? She scrambled backward in her mind to all the places she could have—should have—stopped it. She had to show off playing pool. She had to take off her clothes. She had to follow him into his den, so desperate she had been to have him read her story. Suffocating, she still couldn't bring herself to move him off her, to give him the slightest hint that he was crushing her. Why? She didn't want to upset him or let him know that she was upset. She waited numbly until he sighed deeply and pulled out. It was wet and painful between her legs.

Teddy zipped up his pants and smiled at her. *He is so handsome,* Jane thought again. She looked around the room, anywhere but at him. There was a pile of hardcover books stacked on the floor, and Teddy noticed her seeing them. As he reached toward her, she flinched, but he was only getting a heavy gold pen from his desk. "Allow me," he said, and picked up a copy of *The Coldest War*. "Hot off the press!" He opened the book and wrote something quickly inside, then handed it to Jane.

"Thank you," she said, clutching it in front of her chest.

"If you don't mind, I will hold on to your story," he said, collecting it from the couch and slipping it back among the pile of papers. "Perhaps one day you'll do me the honor of signing your book for me!"

Jane stood stupidly, she knew, unable to move. Her thoughts stuttered like an old black-and-white movie, the frames jerking along: her back against the desk, the ship over his shoulder. It had happened so quickly. She was freezing.

"Well, my dear," Teddy said. "I do have more work to do. You are of course welcome to stay as long as you like. Perhaps it's clearing up?"

"Oh, no, I have . . . I have plans," Jane blurted. Still holding the book, she almost ran out of the room, dressed hastily, and picked up the manuscripts. There was a little puddle of water where her boots had been. Teddy followed her leisurely.

"Yes, it's really slowed down." He gestured out the windows. "I'm sure they've been salting and plowing all day. And nothing stops the subway."

"I'll lock up downstairs," Jane promised. She couldn't wait to get out of the town house.

"Then you'll return the key to Ellen?" Teddy asked. He was buttoning his shirt and buckling his heavy watch.

"Of course." Jane's lips trembled.

"Now, now." Teddy came over and pulled her into a warm embrace. "None of that. You keep your chin up. 'Best words in the best order' and all that."

"I know," Jane whispered into his chest. Then she was flying down the stairs, pulling on her coat and hat, finding the key, and heading out the blue door. She had to tug the mitten off her shaking hand to lock it behind her. There were only a few flakes in the cold air.

One of the doormen from a neighboring building was scraping a shovel against the sidewalk, his coat open. "Can you believe it?" he asked her in a friendly way. "Not two days ago it was seventy degrees! What does it mean? What *could* it mean?"

Jane didn't trust herself to speak but instead shrugged and moved her mouth in an approximation of a smile. Above him, the lights in the town house came on, illuminating the big windows. She looked up, but there was nothing to see.

CHAPTER TEN, PART TWO

MONDAY
HOME, REBECCA

When Jane stopped speaking, restaurant clatter and hum filled the silence.

She suddenly leaned her forehead against Rose's in a surprisingly intimate move. "I'm so sorry."

"No, *I'm* sorry," Rose insisted. They remained like that for a moment. Rebecca's words stuck in her throat. She wanted to reach across the table to touch her mother, but she recognized a private moment, and for once, she thought, she would restrain herself.

"What I thought back then"—Jane turned away from Rose and fixed her gaze on Rebecca—"was that I had had sex with my best friend's crush. That I had betrayed Rose. What Teddy would say—what he *has* said—was that I seduced him, that I would try somehow, like Clara, to entrap him. The words I might use today are different, now that I have more sympathy for the girl that I was then."

"Words like 'power imbalance'!" Rose broke in. "Words like 'assault.'" She too looked at Rebecca, who leaned back under the double intensity. "You have to understand, we didn't have these words for what happened between Teddy—who, may I remind you, was like a god to us—and your mother, who was a young intern."

Rebecca found her voice, put her hand over Jane's. "Oh my god, Mom. I'm so sorry. I'm sorry that happened to you and I'm sorry I've been harassing you for details." She had revictimized her own mother!

Jane pressed Rebecca's hand back. "As hard as it is to talk about, I wish I had done it much sooner. With Rose, obviously. With you."

"Mom, it's *your* story." Rebecca wanted to encourage her mother's openness and reward her courage. She could sense Jane's relief in the telling, the calm after a good cry. Perhaps another piece of garlic bread all around? She offered the basket across the table. "You can tell it how and when you want. Or if you don't want."

Rose smiled sadly. "Except that Teddy wrote an entire book about it."

"What?" Rebecca choked on her garlic bread. "Mom, did you know?"

"I read it today at the town house."

"Wait—so this unpublished manuscript is all about what happened with the three of you?"

"Let me clarify," Rose said. "*Teddy's* version of what happened. And such as it was, it was the first I'd heard of the most important details. Once I read it, I knew I had to find Jane again."

"Is it a memoir, then?"

Rose paused. "He writes in our voices."

"Fiction," Jane said. "Self-serving. But close enough that it wouldn't be hard to piece together who's who."

"Wait—what?" Rebecca said, incredulous. "He writes in the first-person voices of you and Rose?"

"It's an invasion of privacy, to be sure," Rose continued. "And at best, yes, it's self-serving. But the worst of it, the truly unforgivable part, is that it's just bad. Bad writing, defensive, trying too hard to argue against what he became obsessed with in the years before he died: the sense that this new world was passing judgment on him, as I suppose it does."

"Mansplaining our friendship, the affairs, your marriage." Jane shook her head. "Putting words in my mouth. The wrong words!"

Rebecca took a moment to appreciate that her mom had retained her explanation of "mansplaining" as the name for a concept she was apparently well aware of, probably more so than Rebecca.

"You'll see. Everything he did well in *The Coldest War* he did poorly in this. If this ever got published, *it* becomes his legacy. Though I would never allow Jane to be exposed like that. Fortunately, there is only the one handwritten copy. Teddy never took to computers." Rose sat back as Bruno delivered the pasta, refilled the wine, and intuited that no one wanted to banter.

Rebecca concluded that this unpublished novel was definitely going to stay unpublished. As it should! She could still feel the chill of unseasonal snow, hear the crack of pool balls, imagine her mother pulling on wet boots with shaking hands and fleeing the town house. Her heart hurt for Jane. Was it wrong that she was curious about the Lion's book? Had Rose intimated that she would be able to read it too? Before they shredded it? Before she could raise the topic, Rose changed the subject.

"What about you, Jane?" Rose asked. "Did you still write at all? All these years, were you able to do your own work? Did you keep at it? You were so good!"

"Not at first. But, yes, eventually I did. I kept writing when I could. Children exhaust you in ways I can't explain." Jane looked fondly at Rebecca. "They're worth it, of course. But they do make it hard—in my case at least, almost impossible—to find the self-centeredness you need for it."

Rebecca flinched. They were certainly going to have to circle back to her and her brothers sucking the life out of her mom and derailing her career as a writer! And exactly when and for how long had her mother been writing? Jane had been so secretive!

"Teddy was demanding and needy as any child," Rose said. "And his inability to stay away from other women suffocated my desire to have any children of my own. I don't regret it, though I wish we had been better parents to Atticus."

"But you loved him?" Jane asked suddenly, looking intently at Rose.

"I loved him," Rose answered slowly. "I did. Less than he needed. More than he deserved."

"The Lion." Jane shook her head. "The fucking Lion."

Rebecca blinked. First the crying, then the revelations, now the swearing? Her mother herself was the mystery!

"And you?" Rose asked. "You're happy in your marriage?"

Jane paused for a few excruciating seconds. "I love Sam," she finally said, and Rebecca let out a breath she didn't know she had been holding. It wasn't exactly an answer to the question, but maybe that was the point.

"And after all that, you have three wonderful children. And now grandchildren!"

"Oh, that makes me sound so old." Jane, who had never seemed to care about her age, gave a rueful laugh.

Rose took a long sip of wine. "Your writing, though, Jane. I'd love to see it."

"I'd love to show it to you."

Yes, Rebecca appreciated the tenderness and support between her mom and Rose, but what the fuckety fuck were they going to do about this unpublished book? Bury it, right? Burn it? And would *she* get a look at it first? "May I interrupt to ask what happens now? What's the plan?"

Rose sighed. "The real complication is Teddy's son, Atticus. Due to my carelessness, he knows about the manuscript. There are stipulations in the will about what Atticus inherits and how. For Atticus to gain access to his portion of what is, frankly, an obscene amount of money, he has to successfully complete an inpatient rehab program. He sees the manuscript as a way to seize some control, perhaps to make some money for the estate. I'm not sure *what* he wants, and I'm not sure he does either. If the book were ever to get out, it could be, as I said, damaging for Teddy's reputation as a writer and, more importantly, difficult for Jane—for both of us."

"But you're the executor of the estate. You own all the rights including anything unpublished, right?" Rebecca retrieved the lessons Ami and Frank French had imparted as they prepared her to plead Avenue's case to Rose.

"I do. But I truly want what's best for Atticus, and I want him to enter rehab in the right state of mind. His whole world is being turned upside down: his father's death, my selling the town house, the stipulations in the will. I owe it to him to proceed carefully. Jane and I weren't the only ones who suffered in Teddy's wake."

"But you can't possibly let him publish it!" Rebecca wanted to protect her mom. Anyone could do a little math, a little poking around . . . and the next thing you know, her mother would have to relive it all in public. This whole thing was unsettling. Rebecca couldn't even finish her *linguine alle vongole*!

"Rebecca"—Jane touched Rebecca's arm—"Rose and I discussed this. We have a plan." *Also, calm down and mind your tone* was the subtext that Rebecca heard.

"You've been a wonderful advocate for Avenue Publishing," Rose said kindly. "But I want Atticus to feel involved in these decisions. He hasn't read the book, so he doesn't understand the damage that publishing it would cause. But he's not listening to me right now. He has a friend, an editor, a young man who was connected to Teddy in his last few years. I'd like us to meet with them at the town house to hash this out after you read it. I hope his friend can help us to convince Atticus to let it go on his own. Rebecca, I realize this is very unorthodox."

Rebecca bristled. Young man? The Lion had written in her mother's voice. Badly! And defamed her mother! Wasn't that enough to kill the book right now? On the other hand, hadn't Rose pretty much just confirmed that she would hand the estate over to Avenue? And if so, why introduce another editor? Probably a more senior editor. Annoyingly, a man. This editor would be there in his capacity as Atticus's friend, not as an impediment to Rebecca, right?

"Would you like to come by the town house tomorrow after work?" Rose asked. "You could read the book to see what we're dealing with here. And then we could all meet on Wednesday. I'll let Atticus know."

Rebecca looked at her mom. "Is that okay with you? Do you *want* me to read it?" She held her breath, hoping Jane would agree.

Her mother nodded. "As long as you understand that it's a skewed version of what happened."

"Of course," Rebecca assured her. Bruno whisked away their plates and, because he was an angel, replaced them with tiramisu. She gave him a grateful smile.

"Jane and I were talking this afternoon," Rose began. "We have unsent letters that we wrote each other. We have stories. We have memories. We were thinking we might want to put it all together somehow. In our own words."

"I'm going to do a round trip to Philadelphia tomorrow," Jane announced. "I've got some things to collect from the house—letters and journals for this project we're considering—and then, after Wednesday's meeting, Rose and I are going to go out to the Southampton house."

"Where the party is next week?" Rebecca could hardly keep track of what was going on. What had happened to Jane. The Lion's stupid book. Rose and Jane together in the Hamptons? Atticus. The estate. The party!

"Which you are invited to, of course," Rose said graciously. Rebecca looked yearningly at her phone. There was so much to tell Gabe and Stella.

The rest of the dinner was a blur of wine, tiramisu, and more stories about Jane and Rose's adventures at the *East River Review*. They parted with plans for Rebecca to read the book the next day and for a meeting with Atticus at the town house on Wednesday.

Jane went to bed immediately after they arrived back at Mimi's, but Rebecca tossed sleepless on the torture couch, thinking about the Lion and Jane, texting Gabe, FaceTiming Stella, doing a deep dive into CookTok, and eventually pulling up BLURB.

BLURB ERR party moving to Hamptons deets please

Anon, please blowout with HUGE budget

NoPoAveBooks can confirm they have called in Tor Productions 🦁

RSD0513 ERR has mad EDA $$$

MBeeWrites eat the rich

BLURB EDA estate update: avenue lock?

MargaretTate hawk mills still in the game

Anon, please can confirm atticus will be in the mix

leslieGbergerbrooklyn is that even legal

bookguy2130 [meme of Michael Jordan crying] Did Not Get My Invite to ERR 60th

FlaxFineReads estate update: amateur hour! 🦁

Rebecca turned off her phone. "Amateur hour"? Seriously? Fine, she *was* an amateur! An amateur who was about to reel in the entire EDA estate, thank you very much. Only one thing stood in her way: Atticus and Atticus's editor friend, the "young man." Maybe that was two things. For some reason Rose wanted to hear from him. Why did anyone want to hear what yet another man thought? Rebecca kicked off her sheet in annoyance. She tried to turn over, but the couch was inhospitable to any movement. Her heart was still racing from the many coffees she had consumed. Also, tiramisu had caffeine in it! She would never sleep again.

What would she discover tomorrow after reading the book? Did she even *want* to work on the Lion's estate after what he had done to her mother? Rebecca entertained buzzing thoughts. Were her eyes really the fresh, new eyes to cast on his work? Her eyes were angry! Not to mention literally and metaphorically wide-open. Snapping them shut, she thought of her mother's face soft with tears. Maybe there was a way to avenge Jane and Rose by working from the inside, a way to hold the Lion accountable. Once she knew what was in his book, she would make it her mission to destroy it. What was the cliché? Keep your enemies closer than your friends? Maybe she was in fact the *exact* person who should handle his estate. Whatever it took, Rebecca would be ready on Wednesday.

CHAPTER ELEVEN

WEDNESDAY
WORK, BEN

It had been a week since what Ben thought of as his epic night with Atticus, and by "epic" he meant only that he had held the Lion's manuscript in his hands. Atticus, as usual, had been sending a stream of nonsense texts, but no word on any fallout from that night, nor had he made good on his claim that he would get Ben a meeting with Mrs. Adams. And then, to his surprise, yesterday Ben had received an email invitation from Mrs. Adams herself to meet at the town house this afternoon. He hadn't even made it to his desk when Caro waylaid him.

"Ben. I'd like to prepare a game plan. From what I've heard, Avenue is doing a victory dance. Ty and I have been shut out so far, so your pitch meeting is our best hope of landing the estate. The Lion's widow seems as unconventional as he was, and it's still unclear what exactly is going on." She looked at him sternly, and he refrained from admitting he too was at a loss to explain what exactly was going on. "I don't love being held at arm's length, but I trust your friendship with Atticus Adams will give us some insight into how Hawk can win a share of the estate."

Ben's "friendship" with Atticus was not exactly the pillar to support

Caro's expectations. Ben thought it best not to mention that but instead to see how the meeting played out first. After promising Caro he would stop by before he left, Ben began the now familiar process of unpacking his belongings onto his desk: laptop, water bottle, and Bill Russell. Was he really going to keep lugging the bobblehead doll back and forth every week just so Howie could play with it? Probably. He had left the photo of the Lion leaning against the monitor by mistake. Or maybe not exactly by mistake? He had been so annoyed by Rebecca Blume during the desk sharing meeting that maybe he had subconsciously left it there. Her attitude was terrible. Her Zoom etiquette was subpar at best. He was swabbing the desk with Clorox every night and she was slowly killing a cactus and leaving more traces of her presence, which, as a member of the Cooperative whatever-Orwellian-name-it-was Committee, she of all people should know was not cool. *Aaannnd* there it was. Another Post-it, cut carefully into a speech bubble and stuck to his photo. The Lion was saying, **"OF COURSE MEN KNOW BEST ABOUT EVERYTHING EXCEPT WHAT WOMEN KNOW BETTER." -MARY ANN EVANS, A.K.A. GEORGE ELIOT.** In the middle of the monitor was a flagrant pink Post-it: **"EVOLVE, BEN."**

Evolve? Was Rebecca Blume kidding? Ben was willing to bet he was the only person she knew who had actually read George Eliot. His English teacher mother had requested that he do so for her fiftieth birthday, and it had taken him all summer. His mom had been thrilled, and *Middlemarch* was actually pretty good, so screw Rebecca Blume. He ripped the Post-it off the photo of the Lion. Sure, a man who came of age in the 1950s and '60s was bound to have the occasional antiquated and possibly—okay, probably—problematic view, but it was reductive and merciless to hold everything the Lion had ever done to today's standards. Evolve? The person Ben loved most in the world was a queer Marxist feminist! And if Ava had taught him anything, it was that being a good person meant being able to learn from discomfort, from being challenged, and, yes, to accept that you were never finished evolving. He tore the speech bubble Post-it into tiny pieces.

"Dude. Are you okay?" Howie had sneaked up behind him. "Just here to remind you about the eleven a.m. meeting. And Caro wants you at the task force meeting tomorrow about Jennifer Aniston's memoir." Howie picked up Bill Russell and spoke in a squeaky voice: "The One When Jennifer Aniston Tells All!"

Ben had naively hoped that being a book editor would involve reading manuscripts all day, perhaps broken up by inspiring author and agent lunches. So far, his days were filled with meetings and emails. Almost all the reading he did—and there was a lot of it—was at night after he got home, working around his shifts at the bar. The background to his conversation with Howie was the steady ding of emails arriving to his inbox. Ben reminded himself that this was his dream job. His phone alerted him to a text. He bid farewell to Howie and watched as the texts multiplied.

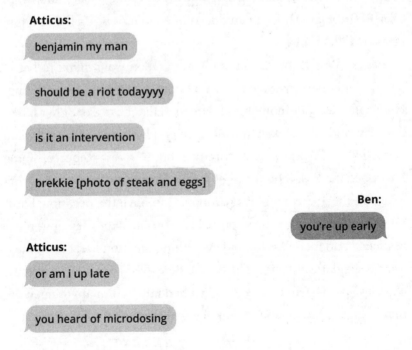

how about macrodosing 😜

Ben:
do you mean overdosing?

Atticus:
chill chill

ttrlkosdo0wu8jdw3e

Ben:
are you ok

Atticus:
mgoejdpor93ujkjg

Ben:
??

Atticus:
mallor on my lappppp

mally

mallory

[photo of long blonde hair and shoulder]

jacks wife freda

Ben:
who?

Atticus:
where we r in west village come join

Ben:
at work but will see you later

Ben checked the drawer to make sure Rebecca Blume hadn't left chocolate or kombucha. Or maybe another Post-it? There were three Biscoff cookies but at least they were still wrapped. Was there any chance Atticus would be sobered up by 2 p.m.? Maybe they *should* have an intervention. In a battle between Atticus and Rose Adams, Ben would not bet against Rose. She was calm in the face of an intruder and had the entire New York publishing world holding its breath to see what she would do next. Unfortunately, he was now aligned, for better or worse—and he understood it was for worse—with Atticus. He checked his emails, which were still coming in at an alarming rate. There was an encouraging one from the agent about the offer Ben had made on Marc Cooker's book of short stories (linked!).

As he was scrolling, a new email arrived from Rose Adams suggesting that Ben come to the town house early so that he could look through the Lion's book. Soon he would be among the first people to lay eyes on an unpublished work by the Lion. He stood up quickly and headed to Caro's office to tell her about this new development. He was going to read the manuscript this time. He was going to meet with Rose Adams. Officially.

Ben got out of the Uber that Caro had insisted he take to the town house. His phone dinged and he checked a text from Atticus: a selfie composed mostly of white teeth and cigarette smoke and the mysterious Mallory's hair. What were the odds that Atticus would show up by 2 p.m.? Maybe it would be more advantageous if he wasn't there, Ben thought. Once he skimmed the novel—Ben shivered a little in anticipation, even in the unseasonal warmth of the May afternoon—he would appreciate a chance to speak about it to the person closest to the Lion. He had felt a connection with Rose Adams that night; she hadn't freaked out when she'd found him in her living room at 3 a.m., secret manuscript in hand, glitter on his face. She didn't have to tell him that the Lion had appreciated his emails, but she did. She was entirely more reasonable and responsible than Atticus, though Ben knew that was not a high bar.

In the light of day, the town house was even more impressive, and Ben was tempted to take a look into the *East River Review* office. As he gazed down the stone stairs at the blue door, a man in a hat spun by him on a bike, aggressively ringing a little bell. Ben moved hastily out of the way as the man came to an abrupt stop, dismounted, and chained his bike to the iron fence in front of the entrance to the magazine. Ben recognized him as Thomas O'Flanagan, successful novelist, disciple of the Lion's, and present editor of the *East River Review*.

Under O'Flanagan's vaguely unfriendly gaze, Ben approached the door and rang the bell. Since Howie had introduced him to BLURB, Ben had reactivated his Instagram account to stay on top of the industry news. What he had learned was what he already knew (he was underpaid, overworked, lucky to have a job), and what he didn't know (the process of buying and selling books was murderously competitive, and the industry was littered with beaten-down English majors whose love of books was being slowly crushed by the corporate machine). But here he was, at the Lion's house.

The town house door opened and a woman who introduced herself as Lorraine ushered him inside. The foyer was cool and quiet, but Ben could hear laughter from upstairs.

Rose Adams was sitting shoulder to shoulder on the window seat with a woman about her age. When they looked up at him, Ben had the feeling he had interrupted an intimate conversation. "Oh, Ben, welcome," Rose Adams said, almost as if she had forgotten he was coming. "This is Jane Kinloch, an old friend." Both of the women smiled as if in possession of a joyful secret. "Jane, this is Ben Heath. He's a big fan of Teddy's and he's seen me in my bathrobe."

Ben felt his face redden. He was used to older women finding him charming, but he wasn't sure how to read these two. "I apologize again, Mrs. Adams."

"Please call me Rose," Rose said breezily.

"Especially since you've already seen her in her nightclothes," Jane added. From across the room, where they were still sitting, the women looked suddenly young and conspiratorial. Jane was wearing a stylish printed dress and her silver-gray hair fell neatly to her shoulders. Mrs. Adams—Rose—was wearing cropped pin-striped pants and an oversize white shirt. A pile of thin gold bangles slid up and down her arm when she gestured.

"We have about an hour until the others join us," Mrs. Adams—Rose—said. "That should give you enough time to take a quick look at Teddy's . . . novel. Lorraine will bring you some water or a coffee if you prefer. We can set you up in the study." She pulled herself away from Jane and stood up. In her heels, she was even taller than Ava. She motioned to the pool table, bracelets clinking. "There you go."

The manuscript Ben had held with awe the other night was still neatly bound with a rubber band. *Making the Sun Run* by Edward David Adams. Ben scooped the pages from the green felt surface of the table, turned off his phone, and left it in the manuscript's place. Maybe Rose hadn't asked, but he didn't want her to think he would abuse her trust and photograph anything. He said a polite goodbye to Jane and followed Rose.

The Lion's study was furnished with the same heavy desk from his author photo, bookcases crammed with a jumble of volumes, a stone fireplace set with wood, above it a large painting in a burnished gold frame of a ship on the ocean, and a faded red vintage rug. It smelled faintly of tobacco and vanilla. The vanilla, Ben knew, was the "old book" smell, the scent of family vacations in Maine with ancient games of Monopoly and swollen bird-watching guides, the scent of paperbacks in cardboard boxes that his mom loved to sort through at garage sales, the scent of the compounds in the paper breaking down: *bibliosmia*. The smell of books dying. It was a metaphor for something, Ben thought, but not the end of books.

Ben sat on a leather couch the color of a cigar, cool to the touch. Lorraine brought him a pitcher of water and a glass. When he was finally alone in the Lion's study, breathing the same air the Lion had breathed while he composed some of the best literature Ben had ever read—right there, between the gold pen and the pipe stand, the Lion had probably written *The Coldest War*—Ben held very still. *Be in the moment*, he counseled himself. *Don't forget anything about this.* He thought again of his younger self, the glittering stars in the

Vermont sky, the Lion's voice resonating. Then he carefully slid the rubber band off the stack of yellow papers and turned the first page. The epigraph, written as all of it was, in the Lion's strong, blocky handwriting—"Thus, though we cannot make our sun / Stand still, yet we will make him run"—was by Andrew Marvell, from a poem Ben dimly remembered about making the most of life, something about devouring time. Yes, the Lion had died and his study bore the smell of decaying books, but there was immortality here, under Ben's palm. He began to read.

An hour later, Rose appeared in the doorway. Ben looked up at her. He knew his face had drained of color. "Have a sip of water," Rose suggested gently. Ben obeyed. He tried to pinpoint his emotions. Disappointment loomed the largest, obviously, followed by a streak of anger, then a sliver of . . . what was it? Oh, right: embarrassment. Embarrassment for the Lion and, if he was being honest, embarrassment for himself, Ben Heath, who had clung to his idea of the Lion. He had clung to his reverence for this writer who had had such an outsize influence on him. From that evening at Bread Loaf to his graduate thesis to his job at Hawk Mills to this very point in time. Here where his hero worship, his stubborn *lionizing*, had landed him: with a bad book in his hands. Granted, in the one hundred pages or so that Ben had read, there were some surprising metaphors and the Lion's trademark precise, rich sentences. But not even the occasional masterful turn of phrase could obscure the fact that this book was not written by a great man. In fact, the man who wrote this book, Ben thought despairingly, was an asshole.

"Not quite as you had hoped," Rose said rather than asked, in what Ben could only call a complete understatement.

"Not quite, no." Ben couldn't bring himself to meet her gaze and busied himself pouring another glass of water. He didn't even know how to start, so he asked the obvious questions: "So Janet is a real person? And Roberta is supposed to be you?"

"Yes." Rose paused. "Quite unforgivable, really."

"Unforgivable that he wrote them in the first person?" Ben was a firm believer that women could write in the voice of men, that men could write in the voice of women, that authors could and should use their imaginations to get in the heads of people different from themselves. He understood appropriation—he wasn't clueless—and certainly he believed representation, opportunity, and access were essential. So if you were going to write in a voice not your own, it had to be believable. It had to be good. It had to *mean* something.

"Well, that and his renaming us Janet and Roberta."

Ben wasn't ready to smile yet. "Do you mind my asking . . . is it true?"

"Do you mean did my relationship with Teddy begin in layers of deceit and infidelity? Yes. Did we have an affair that finally broke up his marriage? Yes. Did he seduce and assault my best friend and did we not speak for almost forty years because I had no idea until I read this book? Yes. Does being a genius mean that everything you do should be excused and that everything you write is genius? Quite obviously, no."

Somehow, Ben felt chastised. "I'm sorry," he found himself saying. He meant it. He really was sorry. He *had* believed that everything the Lion wrote was genius.

Rose gathered the manuscript and snapped the rubber band around it. "I hope you're not put off by my candor. But you've read enough to know what we're dealing with here. It's emotional for me, obviously."

"Of course," Ben assured her. It was emotional for him too, but even in his dismay, he recognized that his reading this book was nothing compared to Rose's reading it. How had the Lion thought for a minute that it was a good idea to write in the voice of a young woman he had, in her words—meaning his words—"ravished"? How had he thought it was a good idea to use the word "ravished"? Was it *ever* a good idea for *anyone* to use the word "ravished"? The book displayed the Lion's paranoia, his defensiveness. It was hard to reconcile with that unforgettable short story he had heard so long ago. What was he going to tell Caro? Had he really imagined striding back into the office with breaking news of a new novel?

"Other than a few facts," Rose said, "there is very little that is *true* in here. And trust me, I've since learned that his version was beyond self-serving. I lived in a kind of cage, Ben, and that was never more obvious to me than when I read this book. You see my dilemma. I can't think of one good reason why it should be published. Can you?"

Ben shook his head. To be good for his own career didn't seem worth a mention. "It would tarnish his legacy," he said slowly. He thought about Rebecca Blume's rude Post-its. Maybe his legacy deserved to be tarnished? The Lion had literally stolen the women's voices.

"I agree. There is enough in his existing work that is ripe for reevaluation, for—what do you say these days?—calling out. And that's in his best work. That writing, with its flaws and its brilliance—*that* should be engaged with . . . not this." Rose brandished the manuscript. "*This* would be excoriated. Rightly so."

"Yes." Ben felt deflated. But Rose was right that the Lion's best work had value, that it could spar with and, Ben still believed, withstand what people could throw at it. But not this mess of a book.

Rose turned in the doorway and asked over her shoulder, "So, Ben Heath, would you like to come talk to 'Janet'?"

Ben followed Rose back toward the living room. The disillusionment of reading *Making the Sun Run* was slowly making space for an idea. He was thinking about what Rose had said about the difference between what was a fact and what was true. Good literature was about what was true. The Lion's unpublished manuscript was a version of a story in which he inhabited (badly) "Janet" and "Roberta," to make himself look better. Ben knew fiction often traveled alongside "facts" and sometimes came together with what was "real" in the service of what was "true." Writers stole and manipulated and spied and betrayed to benefit their stories. It wasn't wrong that the Lion had wanted to chronicle his version of what had happened, but it was too bad that he had asserted a particularly tone-deaf authority and used "Roberta" and "Janet" as first-person mouthpieces for his grievances. Ben knew Rose Adams had been a writer herself. According to *Making the Sun Run*, Janet had been a writer too. A good one. What if Rose and Janet/Jane wrote *their* version?

When he came through the doors, Jane was standing by the pool table, idly cracking the pool balls together with her hands. She gave Ben a wry smile. Ben resisted the urge to keep apologizing. It was awkward to be face-to-face with the two women he had just read about in what could only be described as cringey sex scenes. He knew from the book that Jane and the Lion had played a high-stakes game of strip pool. "I trust you see why we would prefer this book never see the light of day." Jane gave one of the balls a hard whack, knocking it into the corner pocket.

"Yes, of course."

"And we were hoping you might be able to talk some sense into Atticus," Rose said, adding, "He should be here shortly."

Ben wondered at the assumption that he could control Atticus, let alone that Atticus would show up. He supposed he had only brought it on himself by playing up their relationship in hopes that he could get his hands on the Lion's new book. Did Rose think he was Atticus's only friend? *Was* he? Ben thought again about the possibility of Rose and Jane writing a response. Something along the lines of how Liz Phair had written an entire album taking on the Rolling Stones' *Exile on Main St.* song by song, which Ben was intimately aware of, since Ava and his mom had played Phair's *Exile in Guyville* approximately a thousand times on a family road trip.

"You said there were also letters and unpublished short stories, right?" Maybe he could salvage something to bring back to Caro. Even if the book was never published, Rose was still interested in moving the estate away from PK, right? Why not to Hawk Mills, then?

Rose started to answer when there was a sudden commotion behind him. Someone was rushing up the staircase, calling out, "I'm so sorry I'm late! It was unlocked!"

Ben turned around just as a young woman arrived breathless at the top of the stairs. Ben instantly recognized her as the woman he had seen on the big screen at his office. How could it be? She was even more beautiful in person, Ben thought, radiating vitality, her dark hair escaping a bun and spilling to her shoulders, her eyes sparkling and face flushed. He couldn't control the huge smile that burst out of him. He'd found her by sheer stupid good luck! She had stopped suddenly, her oversize bag sliding down her shoulder. Then her entire face lit up as she smiled back. Ben could swear that there was an actual jolt of energy that flowed between them and rocked him back on his heels. All the clichés that he would delete from a manuscript took over his body: pounding heart, quick breath, a heightened awareness of her every expression, an inability to stop smiling. Her dark brows, her intensity, her perfect mouth. She was ravishing. The word had just leaped into his head! "Ravishing" was worlds away from "ravished," right? Was *he* the objectifying asshole now? What was happening? Something, Ben was certain, even though he had read about it a thousand times, that had never happened to anyone ever before. An instantaneous, powerful physical connection that left him helpless to do anything but let the moment stretch out forever while they kept smiling at each other, the lightning sparking back and forth between them.

"Ah, Rebecca!" Rose called from behind him. "Ben, this is Rebecca Blume. Rebecca, meet Ben Heath, a good friend of Atticus's and an editor at Hawk Mills. Ben, Rebecca works with Avenue, the imprint that's going to release Teddy's backlist. I'm so glad to have the two of you here to help us hash out the situation with *Making the Sun Run*."

It was as if a record needle had screeched across an album, a terrible sound Ben was acquainted with since Ava had gotten her hands on his stereo when they were children. What the actual fuck? Even as everything in his body was still leaning toward her, his brain was racing to catch up to the words "Rebecca Blume." Even now, her face was a mirror of his, her radiant smile dimming, her eyes darkening in dismay. "Wait. What? Ben *Heath*?" They glared at each other.

"Come, come," Rose said, oblivious to what Ben was sure had to be obvious: the currents snapping dangerously around him and Rebecca Blume as they stood rooted, eyes flashing. "Lorraine is bringing out some cheese and her homemade fig jam." As Ben watched intently, Rebecca's face flushed even more and she dragged her gaze away from his, breaking the spell. She walked quickly past him, and since, unable to move, he was blocking her way, she brushed against his arm. They leaped apart, electrocuted. Ben's pulse was thudding as if he had played full court all day.

"Hello, sweetheart," Jane said, giving Rebecca a quick kiss.

"Hey, Mom." Rebecca dropped her bag and sat on one of the high-backed chairs across from the couch. She crossed her legs and studiously looked away from Ben.

Mom? What, Ben asked himself again, was happening? He willed himself to go into the room where Lorraine had placed a large plate of charcuterie on a table next to the low couch. Rose dropped the manuscript back onto the pool table, Jane slid a last ball into the side pocket, and Rebecca Blume stared out the window at the river as if it were her job. Ben made his way to one of the chairs, but Rebecca picked up her giant bag and plunked it on the seat. "Are you saving that for someone?" Ben asked incredulously.

"Yes," Rebecca replied frostily. "For my mom."

"Is this the middle school cafeteria?" Ben muttered.

"The couch is comfortable." Rebecca still wouldn't look at Ben directly.

Ben peered at the couch dubiously. It was a long way down. Rose settled on the window seat, and Jane, after filling a small plate with prosciutto and melon, waited until Rebecca swept her bag off the chair. Ben knew he was looming. "Have a seat." Rebecca waved her hand at the couch and gave him a quick glance under thick lashes. She was wearing a short flowered blue dress and high brown suede boots. Her hair was curling around her face, and he could see a little sheen of sweat above her perfect lip. No! She was the enemy and not at all attractive to him anymore! Ben was not the kind of guy who didn't take personality into account. Rebecca Blume was an alluring vessel for a flawed character: at best supremely annoying and at worst possibly deranged. Ben could and would master his disobedient body, which was even now bending toward her where she sat. He dropped onto the couch, a terrible mistake that he realized as soon as he hit bottom and his knees were almost taller than his head.

"So now that we've read it, let's begin where I think we all agree," started Rose. "That *Making the Sun Run*, for numerous reasons, should not be published."

"To start with," Rebecca said, her gaze somewhere above Ben's shoulder, "that title? Fitting that he's quoting a poem about sexual harassment."

If there was ever a time for Ben *not* to mention that he remembered the Marvell poem differently, this was that time. Still, he chafed a little under Rebecca's selective memory and obvious exaggeration. He would not be drawn into defending this particular (indefensible) work of the Lion's, but he was not ready to dismiss everything the man had written. "It's really disappointing," Ben began. "But it's not published, and it doesn't have to be—"

"Obviously!" Rebecca interrupted. "I mean, we've all read it. If it were published, it would expose the Lion to ridicule and cancellation! Which, I might add, would be richly deserved."

"But not," Rose said gently, "the best idea in terms of Avenue's plans for reissuing and repackaging his work . . ."

Ben processed what Rose had said before and was confirming now. Avenue was winning the estate. For no other reason than Rebecca Blume was Jane's daughter? Rebecca Blume, who clearly despised the Lion and was not remotely the right person to guide the process of protecting his legacy? Rebecca had flushed at Rose's correction, and Ben had never seen such luminous skin. No! She was an undeserving nepo baby! "I know it might not be appropriate to ask," he said, "but is it a done deal that Avenue is handling the estate?"

Rebecca shot him a furious look. "Seriously?"

Ben ignored her and looked up at Rose. "I mean, I guess I'm not 100 percent sure why I'm here."

Rose offered Ben the charcuterie, which he politely declined but only because there was no way to eat it from his position. "Yes, I'd like to have Avenue handle the estate: Rebecca has offered some very thoughtful ideas about how best to reintroduce Teddy's work to today's audience. In particular, I was impressed with the plan to reach out to young women."

"By canceling him?" Ben said under his breath. Something about Rebecca Blume brought out the worst in him. Although, in his defense, this was the least professional meeting he had ever attended, and he had once negotiated a deal for a book about maple syrup during a Grateful Dead tribute concert at Nectar's Bar in Burlington.

"I know that you have a close relationship with Atticus and that you had a connection to Teddy. Your opinion is important to me, especially since it's less biased than the other readers so far." Here, Rose smiled at Rebecca, who was fuming above Ben, her booted foot swinging in agitation.

"And again," Jane said, "we really hope you can help us convince Atticus to let this book go without a fight. He doesn't, as far as I understand it, have an actual claim on it, but he's being difficult."

"I want him to feel as though he has some agency," Rose said. "The stipulations of Teddy's will are a shock to him, and I know he's in pain."

Ben thought about how Atticus had said that Rose was disappointed in him. "I can talk to him, of course, but . . ." So he was here in his capacity as Atticus's "close" friend? And not representing Hawk Mills as competition for Avenue? How had this all gotten so far away from him? Between Rose and Caro, he was going to have to seriously tamp down everyone's expectations. He was still reeling from the experience of reading the Lion's terrible book and, if he was honest, the shock of the collision between the imagined Rebecca Blume of desk sharing and the actual Rebecca Blume scowling at him. Somewhere in the mix was the cherished image of the green-eyed woman he had been holding close.

There was another sudden cacophony on the stairs, and Atticus himself appeared in the doorway, his white shirt untucked, his eyes pinwheeling. It was clear that he had been up all night. "Making some decisions? Figuring ways to cut me out?" Atticus addressed the room in general, and Rose stood up.

"I invited you to this meeting," she said calmly. "I'm very interested in your input about the estate, Atticus. I wanted you to meet Rebecca Blume from Avenue. I think you'll be impressed by Avenue's ideas about how to reissue Teddy's work and to introduce his unpublished stories. And this is Jane Kinloch, an old friend of mine. We'd like to explain why we're not going to publish the novel. I know your friend Ben can back us up . . ."

"Benjamin! My man!" Atticus spotted Ben, who began the Herculean task of trying to heave himself up off the couch. "What's your verdict? What did you think of the great man's last tome?" Atticus propped himself against the doorframe, his glassy eyes darting around the room.

"Have you read it?" Ben couldn't converse and stand at the same time; it would take all his effort to get up.

"What does it matter? It's the Lion, man. It's worth its weight in gold, am I right? Or was it Bolivian powder?"

"We should talk about it." How was it that he was in basketball shape but not haul-himself-off-a-low-couch shape?

"*Et tu*, Benjamin?" Atticus stumbled into the room and leaned against the end of the pool table. "You've all taken a vote? Thumbs down on the Lion's last book? Is that what this little committee decided?"

"Use your core," Rebecca said to Ben unhelpfully as he struggled.

"Screw it." Atticus snatched the manuscript off the pool table and clutched it to his chest. "This is my dad's book." His voice broke a little.

"Hold up," Ben said, finally lurching to his feet with a powerful combination of adrenaline and quad, not core, strength. The vulnerability in Atticus's stance moved him. They just had to convince Atticus that this book would hurt the Lion, no matter how much money it might make. He caught Atticus's eye, trying to convey sympathy. Atticus winked at him. What the fuck?

"Atticus," Rose said firmly. Ben and Rebecca moved forward at the same time and bumped each other. Rebecca recoiled dramatically. Ben was trying to focus while the entire side of his body near Rebecca was vibrating. He took a few strides toward Atticus, who stumbled backward. Rebecca was advancing around the other side of the pool table, trying to be sneaky. In monitoring her progress, Ben took his eye off Atticus, who was able to stagger out of reach.

"If you'd just listen for a minute." Ben snapped back to attention and raised his hands to indicate his innocent intentions. How was he always a threat in this place?

"I'm done listening," Atticus responded, tightening his grip on the manuscript. "I came here in good fraith. Fainth."

"*Faith*?" Ben took a small step closer in this demented game of Red Light, Green Light. Atticus danced back, suddenly surprisingly nimble for someone under all the influences. Ben glimpsed Rebecca out of the corner of his eye, also tiptoeing closer but with far less stealth than she obviously intended.

"Not to publish this?" Atticus turned to catch Rebecca, who stopped abruptly in her tracks. "Unconshusshunable."

"Unconscionable *to* publish it!" Rebecca, as Ben suspected, was constitutionally incapable of not arguing, even when placating was clearly the wiser path. Also incapable of not showing off her ability to smoothly pronounce "unconscionable," which was, in fairness, a mouthful.

"The last thing my father ever wrote." Atticus kept his eye on Rebecca beseechingly.

Recalling the wink, Ben knew Atticus was full of it, and he hoped Rebecca was savvy enough to see through his manipulations. No such luck. She was obviously softening. Ben crept close enough to smell the potpourri that was Atticus: sweat, bourbon, weed, something bitter (cocaine?), and something really good (expensive cologne?). What was the actual plan? Tackling him? Rebecca was clearly distracting Atticus with her distracting beauty. Ben took another quick glance at her. Her expression was compassionate, earnest, kind. She was completely taken in by Atticus's bullshit!

"If you just hand it to me," she said sweetly, "we can talk about it."

"Seriously?" Ben couldn't help but mutter.

"Seriously?" Rebecca snapped. As they glared at each other, Atticus leaped for the doorway.

Ben and Rebecca lunged at him but managed to collide and spring apart as Atticus ran swiftly if unsteadily down the stairs. "He had no intention of giving it to you!" Ben said, rubbing his arm where he could still feel the heat of her body.

"I was placating him!" Rebecca retorted. "It was working!"

Ben revised his theory that placating was the wiser path. "He saw right through you!" he argued.

"And what, pray tell, was *your* plan?" Rebecca continued furiously. "*Ninja* him?"

Before Ben could reply—*Ninja him?!*—he caught sight of Rose and Jane, their expressions revealing both bewilderment and mild alarm.

The door downstairs in the foyer slammed. Atticus and the manuscript were gone.

CHAPTER TWELVE

WEDNESDAY
HOME, BEN

Ben finished describing the most confusing day of his life to Ava. They were on a park bench by the court, and he was lacing up his basketball shoes. "Jeezum Crow, B," Ava drawled in her best Vermont accent.

"Jeezum Crow, A," he replied in a better one. Butch sighed loudly and kept an eye on the basketballs.

"So your boy is just out there with the one and only copy?"

"Yeah. I mean, maybe he'll leave it in an Uber. Better yet, drop it in the river. But I'll bet he's trying to get publishing houses to pressure Rose. Or worse: he's actually showing it to people. What if he goes to the media?"

"You really have evolved," Ava said admiringly. "Look at you, advocating for the destruction of the Lion's posthumous masterpiece."

"First of all, how is 'evolve' the word of the day? Also, 'masterpiece' hurts."

"It's good for you to examine and discard your slavish adherence to the hegemony." Ava yawned. "The Humble Brag girls and I were out until four." Ava was already doing summer research for her art history professor and living in the same dorm as a surprisingly successful indie band of seventeen-year-olds. No one was exactly clear on why they were also in the dorm after the term had ended, but Ava had surmised it had something to do with the most pierced member rumored to be a daughter of the provost. "We were celebrating their song debuting on the XMU Download 15."

"I thought they only had one song?"

"Well, it's number six on this week's countdown. Anyway, back to your love life." Ava was wearing what appeared to be a wedding dress with a crocheted cardigan and what he thought of as restaurant clogs.

"It's not love I'm feeling." Ben yanked the laces and adjusted his ankle brace.

"I don't know. You seem pretty shook."

"Obviously! I mean, she comes out of nowhere and not only is she the worst desk sharing partner on the planet but also she's getting the estate because her actual mom is best friends with Rose Adams, and after Atticus stole the manuscript she actually said she felt sorry for him, which I know she said only to piss me off and now I have to go empty-handed to Caro. She knew about that fucking couch! I think I pulled my hamstring getting off it. Seriously, if you want to know *who is the kind of person who would kill a cactus*, Rebecca Blume is that person. What?"

Ava was giving him a look. "That may be the most impassioned speech you've made since you petitioned Doug and Jeanie for a dog in fifth grade."

"Which, by the way, you're welcome. RIP, Luna."

Ava clamped her hands over Butch's ears. "She was the best dog. RIP, Luna."

Ben stood and stretched his leg gingerly. No, not injured playing no-holds-barred streetball. Injured getting off a couch. Jesus. He raised his hand to acknowledge a cluster of regulars milling by the court. "We got next! You're with us, Luka!" the guy in a green bandanna yelled, pointing at Ben.

"Why is he calling you Luka?"

"It's a compliment, trust me. The first few weeks I was just 'the White Guy.' Luka Dončić is a Slovenian killing it in the NBA."

"Oh, I get it." Ava squinted at the court where a small crowd had gathered to watch. "Are they nice to you now?"

"If by 'nice' to me you mean jeering and mocking the dudes who try to guard me, then yeah."

"Flex much? Okay, Butch and I will stay for a little, but I'm going to bring him by the dry cleaning place. They have treats and a water bowl."

Butch's ear twitched at the word "treats." "Good boy, Butch," Ben said, then took a swig from his water bottle and tried to get in the right headspace to play. He would not think about Rebecca Blume. He would not think about Rebecca Blume. He would not think about Rebecca Blume.

"One thing," Ava said, reaching into her overstuffed bag to pull out a paperback. "Do you think you could put a word in with Rebecca Blume about reservations for *salute!*? She and Stella Marino-Miller are tight. Remember I told you about her? What? Too soon?"

Ben gritted his teeth. The image of Rebecca Blume's green eyes and heart-shaped face flashed into his mind. It was the Rebecca he had seen on the screen in the office in the innocent days before he knew who she was; that image swelled his heart. The Rebecca Blume of a few hours ago with her arrogant suede boots and flash of white thighs and obnoxious seat saving and argumentative nature—*that* Rebecca Blume filled him with rage. The Rebecca Blume of annoying Post-its and scattered desk trash and complete disregard of the agreed-upon bonds that held together work society and the misplaced sympathy for Atticus—*that* Rebecca Blume disturbed the fuck out of his peace. He plucked a basketball out of his gym bag, slammed it on the concrete, palmed it, and smacked it down again. Butch gave him a reproachful glance.

"Just keep it back of mind, okay?" Ava opened her book and ignored Ben as he heard what could only be described as a low growl emerge from his own throat. Butch registered mild concern. Ben jogged to his team, which was now taking over the court and starting a quick warm-up. He fist-bumped and head nodded his way under the basket, snatching the errant balls and sizing up the competition. The loudest guys were never the problem. They would put a tall guy on him, then a faster guy, then their best player, but it wouldn't matter. Ben circled out to midcourt, sank a three through the hoop, and ignored the hoots from spectators crowding up on the chain-link fence. Give him an elbows-out, loudmouthed motherfucker to mix it up with today. Maybe Ben was consumed with Rebecca Blume, but Luka wasn't. Luka was going to sweat Rebecca Blume out of his system; he was going to punish anyone in his way; he was going to play hard enough that his head had nothing in it but basketball.

Later that night, Ben's aggravated hamstring was starting to bother him. He had kept his head down, ignored the fouls, and channeled his aggression into the game. He got in that zone he loved where everything slowed down and he could see three, even four moves ahead: Pass it, go, catch it, shoot it. The satisfaction of running the court until the shadows deepened and he was going to have to hustle not to be late for work; the thrill of sinking shot after shot while opponents fell away; the respect from the quietest, toughest players on his team—all of it was enough to carry him through a long shower, a quick dinner, and a busy few hours at Betty Jack's. But now that his adrenaline was fading, his body was letting him know that, even at twenty-six, he was not as young as he used to be.

After work at the bar, Ben got a slice of pizza to tide him over until morning, but instead of going back to his apartment he decided to walk for a while. Ava was not sympathetic to the crushing blow he had suffered while reading the manuscript. He knew that the Lion wasn't perfect—far from it. Ben had known about his affairs, his younger wives, his less-than-enlightened portrayal of women in his work. Ava was right: Ben *had* been an apologist. Meeting Rose and Janet—Jane—had made it pretty difficult to intellectualize or rationalize the pain the Lion had caused. Ben needed another slice and probably a beer. He was too agitated to sleep anytime soon.

And that was how he found himself sitting at the bar of a dark, emptied-out little Italian restaurant, the kind of place he probably wouldn't be able to afford to eat at even if he could get a reservation. It was also the perfect place for a date: open late, red-checked tablecloths, candles massing wax over the sides of wine bottles, the lingering smell of garlic butter, a quiet playlist bouncing between Ella Fitzgerald and Mitski. Ben wasn't sure how a slice and a beer had turned into a plate of *penne alla vodka* and a Manhattan, but it had to do with the bartender, who, instead of turning him away since the kitchen was closing, had brought him the pasta and leaned on her elbows while they talked and given him her attention as if she had all the time in the world. Ben had to admire a pro. She poured herself a small glass of Fernet-Branca and they clinked.

His phone buzzed in his pocket. The bartender smiled, set the drink down, and began drying glasses at the other end of the bar.

Atticus:

miss me? 😂

There was an unknown number on the group text that Ben assumed was Rose Adams. He took a sip of his Manhattan. Perfectly balanced. He had not been called on to mix many Manhattans at Betty Jack's. He hoped that Atticus had gotten some sleep since he had seen him at the East End town house and that he still had the manuscript on him and that it wasn't being passed around to all the publishing houses in New York City. According to Rose, the Lion's will had stipulated that Atticus go to rehab or he would inherit nothing. Was Atticus making the most of his time left before then? Ben needed to convince him that publishing *Making the Sun Run* was a bad idea. Atticus hadn't even read it yet. Did he care about his father's legacy or was it just control, or more likely chaos, that he was seeking?

Atticus:

verrryyy interesting day

just opening the negotiations here

Ben finished his Manhattan, noticing that the bartender had given him a few extra cherries. Merely solidarity with a fellow bartender? Or did he still just look hungry?

Ben:

where are you?

Atticus:

lots of interest in running sun

making sunning run

Ben:

do you have it?

Unknown Number:

?

Ben imagined Rose Adams worried about Atticus, worried about the missing manuscript.

Ben:
> you should get some sleep

Atticus:
> ahahahahahahahahahahaha

Unknown Number That Was Unlikely Rose Adams:
> ?????????

Ben:
> it's late let's talk tomorrow

Unknown Number That Was Definitely Not Rose Adams:
> who even is this??? WTF?

Okay. Ben paused. His thumb hovered over his phone. He had what his mom called "a sneaking suspicion."

Atticus:
> not sure why rose called in the JV squad
> but here we are

Unknown Number That Was Most Likely Rebecca Blume:
> seriously who is this

Ben:
> JV squad?

Atticus:
> my man! dont get pissed just truth telling here

Atticus:
> negotiations right? how about hawk eye?

Ben:
> that's rose's decision

Rebecca:
> atticus? BEN HEATH??

Atticus:
> does rose have the bush in bird?
> bird in hands? hand in the bush LOL

Ben:
> it's not good for anyone if that book gets published

Atticus:
> you were his biggest fan 😉

That stung. Ben told himself again that Atticus hadn't read the book. He thought about that wink at the town house, just when he was feeling sorry for Atticus. Even if he had read it, there was a good chance he would still be championing it, still trying to get it published. Whether for the money or to hurt Rose or even if it was to see his father's last work in print, it didn't matter.

Rebecca:
> lose my number both of you

Atticus:
> becca! maybe avenue buys it to squash it
> know what i mean

Rebecca:
> gn don't text me again

Atticus:
> don't be mad becca

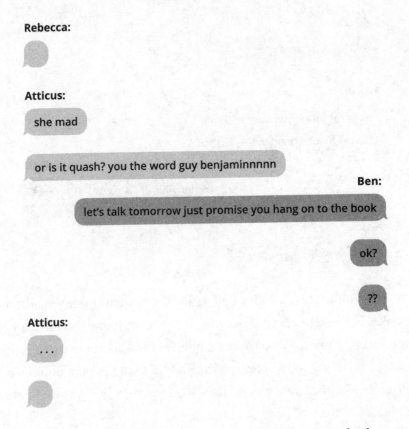

Ben waited another minute. Rebecca and Atticus were both gone. He shook his head in annoyance.

"All good?" The bartender pointed to Ben's empty glass. "Another?"

"No, thanks. I know you're closing up. I'll let you get to it." His phone buzzed and he sneaked a quick look. It was Rebecca Blume's number.

Rebecca:

get your friend under control and make sure he doesn't fuck everything up

He was going to ignore Rebecca Blume's rude text. He was going to walk home, clear his head, and think about his next step. Probably talk to Caro tomorrow and raise the idea of Rose and Jane writing a memoir together.

Ben pulled out his wallet. "What do I owe you?"

"No, no. We're both in the business, right? You'll get me next time."

Ben found a twenty and tucked it under his glass. He would love to reciprocate but she was clearly too elegant for Betty Jack's. "Thank you."

On his way home, Ben kept pulling his phone out, rereading Rebecca's text, thinking of a response, then shoving his phone back in his pocket. Finally, the Manhattan got the best of him.

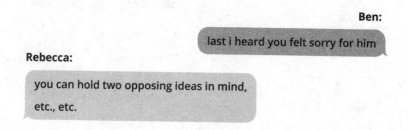

Ben tried to think where he had just heard that F. Scott Fitzgerald quote. Ava? Yes. He sat down on a stoop so he could concentrate, first scoping the vicinity for rats. All clear.

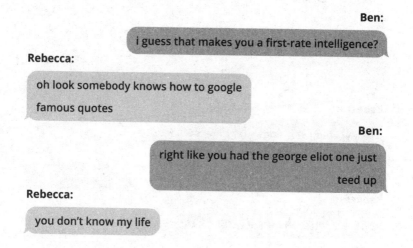

Ben: i know george eliot

Rebecca: personally?

Ben: are you always like this

Rebecca: a first-rate intelligence?

Ben: guess that's why rose adams asked you to represent the estate

Rebecca: don't be a sore loser

Ben: it was hardly a competition

Rebecca: lucky for you

Ben: srsly i would love a competition

Rebecca: ok here's an idea

Rebecca: get the book back from your friend

Ben: not my friend

Rebecca: really?? then why does rose think so

Ben: i can get the book

Rebecca: i have a better chance of getting it than you

Ben:

haha seriously??

oh you're serious

i'll take that bet

Rebecca:

if he hasn't already left it at a publishing house

Ben:

cold feet?

Rebecca:

these are the terms

book needs to be delivered by monday all in one piece

and if it's been copied it doesn't count

four days do you accept the terms

Ben:

what is this mission impossible

Rebecca:

maybe for you

Ben:

winner gets what

Rebecca:

to give rose the book back

Ben:

and

Rebecca:

clear validation of superiority

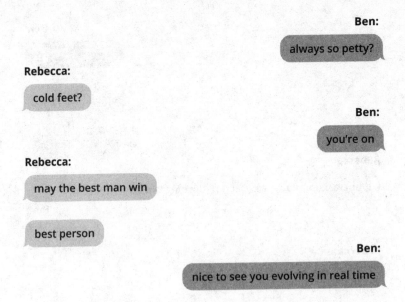

Ben: always so petty?

Rebecca: cold feet?

Ben: you're on

Rebecca: may the best man win

best person

Ben: nice to see you evolving in real time

He turned his phone off before she could respond and enjoyed a momentary glow of satisfaction. It lasted until he began the long slog up to his apartment. Was he just playing into her hands? She had a lot more to lose if the book got published than he did. Had she set this whole thing up to motivate him to get the book so she and Avenue could go ahead and rake it in with the Lion's backlist and new work?

The door on the third floor creaked open a crack. "Well, aren't *you* a tall drink of water!"

Ben saluted and continued up the stairs, his mind racing. He would get the book for Rose. He would get the book to prove his—what had Rebecca said—clear superiority. Of course, if he got the book, he would see her again. He stopped on the final flight of stairs and stretched his hamstring. Maybe he would just take a quick look to see if she had responded. Ben pulled out his phone. Nothing. Fine. He pressed info on her phone number. Create New Contact. He hesitated. Better to be prepared next time. He couldn't deny the frisson of something, be it irritation or excitement, as he typed into his phone: "Rebecca Blume."

CHAPTER THIRTEEN

MONDAY
WORK, REBECCA

Rebecca regarded the cactus with suspicion. Someone had watered it and placed it in what she had to admit was a tasteful white ceramic pot. Could that someone be Ben Heath? It would make sense that he felt the need to make a conciliatory gesture after last week, even if it was only to rescue his own plant. How he had ended up at the town house or been asked to weigh in on anything to do with anything was a mystery. That she had failed to track down Atticus or the manuscript was maddening, but at least Ben hadn't succeeded either as far as she knew. And based on their interactions, he would surely be needling her by now if he had. Yes, it was a shock that he was so . . . tall. Rebecca knew the word "tall" was doing a lot of work here. What did it mean that she couldn't get the image of him out of her head? She hadn't conveyed to Stella or Gabe the rest of it: the broad shoulders, the dark blue eyes, the NOT ginger thick brown hair with *maybe* a hint of auburn, the unguarded smile he had given her at the top of the stairs, and the way it had literally made her knees weak (and she was using "literally" correctly, thank you very much), the sheer presence of him . . . fuckety fuck!

"And a fuckety fucking good morning to you too!" How long had

Gabe been standing at her desk? And was Rebecca now someone who muttered her thoughts out loud like the wizened old lady who haunted the Ninety-Sixth Street station? "Late night?"

"What? Why?" Rebecca hadn't slept and it was not because she was out having fun. Just as she would drift off, her eyes would snap open and she would squirm in shame remembering that she had texted Atticus Adams in at first beguiling and then increasingly desperate attempts to provoke a response. Nothing. She was sure that he and Ben Heath were smoking cigars at a private club or whatever it was that rich assholes did all weekend. Ugh!

"Why are you blushing?" Gabe leaned in to peer at her.

"Why are you so close? I can smell your aftershave! Back it up!"

"And it smells delicious. Tom Ford."

"It *is* woody and spicy," Rebecca conceded.

"Notes of leather and sage. What's going on?"

"I'm just tired from launching Stella's YouTube channel all weekend! That was more research than I had anticipated. I had to watch YouTube videos on launching YouTube videos."

"I saw . . . It's going to be huge. You're good at this." Gabe had, thankfully, lost track of his inquisition. "Luckily for Stella." They both knew that Stella, for all her talent, was hopeless with technology. Like Rebecca's father, she needed to be given precise instructions—more than once—on the basics. While the Professor, pecking out texts laboriously with his index finger, could be excused based on his age and preference for pondering the weighty questions of ancient history, Stella had no excuse but no patience for social media, so Rebecca had been forced into taking over for Stella's own good, subsequently discovering a talent for promotion and a surprising facility with digital platforms.

"Right? I mean it has everything: the Black, Italian, and Jewish grandma influences; their anecdotes; the recipes; and, of course, Stella the star." Over the weekend, Rebecca had arranged for Scout to film Stella and had scripted some of the show, but, honestly, Stella on camera just glowed. And Mimi was already on track to be a fan favorite.

"I see you got the Fishwife sponsorship . . . Congratulations! Can you get me the special edition spicy one? I need fancy tinned fish to sustain Tor. He hasn't slept in a week. But the party is going to be incredible, of course."

"Of course it is. I'll see what I can do. They did send us a big box of product this weekend." Rebecca thought with satisfaction of the brightly colored tins scattered on the dining room table. "Also you still need to find me an outfit for Thursday." Tor had declared the *East River Review*'s sixtieth party to be 1960s themed, and New York was abuzz. She and Gabe had already spent an inordinate amount of time giddily speculating about who might attend.

"Are you thinking French new wave cinema or Mary Quant tights and a skinny-rib sweater?" Gabe asked.

"Uh, I was thinking sexy hippie?"

"You and every other basic editor in town! Fortunately, you have me to steer you past your pedestrian impulses."

"But I have that giant peace necklace from Halloween a few years ago. . . ." Rebecca knew it was a lost cause. "Fine! Then I hope you have a vision."

"I like an Edie Sedgwick vibe but your hair is impossible."

"Sorry I don't have a blond pixie cut! Also wasn't she Benzedrine skinny?"

"We'll think of something. Are you ready for the Lady's launch? The lineup is insane. Who would have thought a faux Brit from the Midwest would attract both *Good Morning America* and *The View*? I'm a genius!"

"I know! It better sell books, now that she bullied us into a glam hair and makeup budget," Rebecca said. "I still can't believe she's coming to the States. Also, the hair and makeup is clearly revenge for Avenue not covering the price of a Virgin Air Upper Class ticket so that she could drink some 'bubbly.'"

"At least she didn't say 'champers.'"

"True. You have to help me run interference so that Richard never gets close enough to stab her in the heart with a fountain pen when she's here signing books."

"Speaking of Richard, here comes straight man walking . . ." They turned to watch Richard's newest assistant striding across the office, typing one-handed on his laptop, earphones in, talking loudly. Why? There were maybe three straight men in publishing, and they were either old, still fixated on David Foster Wallace, or this guy, who was conducting some VERY IMPORTANT BUSINESS. Against her will, Rebecca thought of Ben. Undeniably hot. Not just hot for publishing but real-world hot. The hottest guy she had ever seen. But obviously in the worship of problematic dead white guys camp. And rude! And annoying! What did it mean that he had tended to the cactus?

Chloe, her hair in braids circa late-'90s Britney Spears, caught Rebecca's attention by miming a walk to Ami's office.

"Okay, I have to go meet with Ami to talk through the deal with the estate. We're Zooming with Rose and her lawyers. You wouldn't believe all the shit that has to happen to pull this off! Turns out the Lion's 'gentlemanly agreement' with Maury Kantor didn't always include signed contracts, so we have a lot to figure out."

"Look at you! Deign to have lunch with me later?"

"I can't: I'm meeting Trixie."

"Tell her I said hello." Gabe gave Rebecca an appraising look. "Okay, what about Jane Birkin?"

"I could straighten my hair!"

"And cut some bangs!" Gabe enthused.

"Or buy a wig?"

"Are you going to commit or not?"

"If you go as Warhol and dye your hair, I might consider it."

"I hope you give me more credit than that. Striped shirt, dark glasses, and a white mop on my head? I don't think so."

"You could be my bag. My Birkin?"

"I admire your brainstorming," Gabe said in such a manner that made it clear he did not actually admire her brainstorming.

"Okay, I have to go single-handedly make it possible for Avenue to keep publishing quirky little novels in translation. I guess you could say I'm paying your salary directly with my Lion coup."

"What I hear is that you're going to Ami's office to sit silently while she and Mel from Contracts hammer out a deal you have no interest in yet stumbled into thanks to a serendipitous series of events involving your mother?"

"When you put it that way, I have no choice but to have you fired." Rebecca took a big sip of her green juice, accidentally spilled a little on the desk—sorry, not sorry, Ben!—and grabbed her laptop.

"A sliver of power has corrupted you absolutely," Gabe said admiringly. "Wish me luck figuring out how to break it to the Lady that we will not be sending the requested stretch limo to meet her at the airport."

Gabe was gone before Rebecca could ask his opinion on the cactus development. On the other hand, best not to bring up anything Ben related because she knew she would fold under the slightest scrutiny and confess the shock of her attraction to him. She was lucky that the last few days had been spent launching Stella on YouTube, rehashing the remarkable discoveries about Jane and Rose, stressing about the missing manuscript, and gossiping about the upcoming party. It wouldn't be long until her friends sniffed out the unsettling developments in her desk sharing drama, as Gabe had been on track to this morning. She would *never* mention Ben. And if the day safely passed without either of them possessing the Lion's stolen manuscript, she would never have to see him again. And that was totally for the best!

"So it's totally for the best that I never have to see him again!" Rebecca announced to Trixie a few hours later. They were eating turkey burgers and splitting a plate of fries at the bistro located halfway between their offices. They had met years ago at a professional lunch when Trixie was too young to represent many authors and Rebecca was too young to have the power to acquire them and had immediately liked each other so much that Rebecca had gone to a club to hear Trixie's boyfriend Ike's band play that night. She and Trixie stood in the back nonstop talking to fill in as many details as they could about each other's lives.

"Sure. I haven't seen you this worked up since . . . since . . . ever?" Trixie speared cherry tomatoes into her mouth with the ease of someone who never spilled food or smudged her lipstick. She was so beautiful, it was almost unfair that she was also the nicest person Rebecca knew. But often enough she let her wicked humor flash, and that was when Rebecca loved her most. "I mean, were you ever this passionate about what's-his-name? The boring lawyer who dumped you? The one with the semicolon?"

Max's text had gone viral among Rebecca's friends and family. Her sister-in-law Emma had printed it out and taped it to the fridge to remind herself how grateful she was not to still be single. "Ugh. Max."

"Right, Ugh Max. And the one before that? The start-up bro who made us all go watch his truly awful improv? And how about your foray into dating a woman who turned out to be a stalker? And that guy who told you he was moving to Barcelona and then turned up in your Uber Pool three months later? What about the one with the loft in SoHo who called you Becky?"

"Jesus, Trixie! This is an appalling assault on my dignity! But also, I guess, thank you for paying such close attention?"

"What I'm saying is that during your long and active past—and I've really only been around for five years of it—"

"Oh, it wasn't much better before that either." Rebecca took a fistful of fries. "Please don't ask Stella about the Rat Bastard or Eduardo the Co-op Dude."

"My point is not to question your taste or luck, and we will certainly circle back to the Rat Bastard at some point, but the level of passion you just displayed describing all the reasons you hate your desk share guy is impressive. Should I order more fries?"

"Yes, obviously. To fries. Not to passion."

"Back to your desk share guy . . ."

"He's not my 'desk share guy.' Truly, that phrase does not convey the irritation—no, loathing—that I feel when I think about Ben Heath." As her mouth formed his name, Rebecca experienced a wave of weakness in her lower stomach—okay, like *really* low, like the almost sexual thrill of standing on the very edge of a cliff or, in her case, watching an amusement park ride that she refused to get on.

"Wait, your desk share guy is Ben Heath?"

"Yes, I told you."

"No, you just said 'desk share guy.' I hate to break it to you, but I'm on the phone with Ben Heath all the time."

"All the time? What are you even saying?" Rebecca glared at Trixie, who laughed at her.

"He's adorable! Smart and funny. He was bidding on that short story collection I told you about. I'm supposed to meet with him in person next week. Now I *really* can't wait to get a look at him!"

Rebecca did not care for this turn of events. "We're done talking about this! We're here for business. And you know what I'm going to bring up, right?"

"I'm pretty sure. Like, 85 percent sure."

"Tell me what you think it is."

"You say it first!" Trixie demanded.

"We say it at the same time," Rebecca countered. "One, two, three..."

"You quit your job and work PR for Stella," Trixie said at the same time as Rebecca blurted, "We let Alice do the sci-fi book."

There was a short, astonished silence.

"I'm sorry, excuse me?" Trixie began at the same time as Rebecca said in disbelief, "Quit my job and what?"

"Okay, I'll go," Trixie said. "I've never seen you as committed as you are to Stella's breakout. And you've been managing it all—from *salute!* to her Insta account and now the YouTube channel. I mean, it's obviously going to take off: people are already subscribing. You're good at it! You love it! You're almost as energized about promoting Stella as you are about Ben Heath."

"Ha ha." But Rebecca's mind was racing. Trixie's words were clicking something into place, something Rebecca had been trying to name for a while. Was doing what she did for Stella even a job? How would she get paid? What would her mom say if she left Avenue? Was it crazy to think about leaving—especially now, after the triumphant meeting with Ami and Mel from Contracts? Sure, it was not far off from what Gabe had described, but, no matter the circumstances, Rebecca was in the room; she was the one getting the credit. On the other hand, she remembered her mother's words: that she had no "fire in her belly" when it came to her career. And what about the conflict keeping her up at night? She was desperate to find and destroy the Lion's warped tell-all to protect her mom; at the same time, she was supposed to be representing his estate.

"Once you get even more eyes on Stella, you get a job and bring her with you. I can think of some cool branding agencies to meet with. Think about it."

"I don't know," Rebecca mused. "It's tempting, for sure. But that whole space seems kind of nebulous. I mean, I'm pretty sure I'm going to be promoted at Avenue thanks to the Lion coup."

"Look, just think about it. Do some research. Of course, it's fine if you stay at Avenue. And you're a really talented editor! But it's obvious what you love the most about your job is the author care part, the strategic part. I do not refer to Lady Paulette, obviously, but remember when you got L.L.Bean to sponsor Alice's last tour? They sent her all over the country in duck boots! And that's what you'd do for Stella and for all the other brilliant people you'd find. I just think you should be doing what lights you up. Just like you should be doing *who* lights you up . . ."

"Stop! You sound like Stella with her endless stream of sexting emojis. I'll think about it . . . a new job, I mean. If I can figure out what that would look like," Rebecca promised. "I know you agents always want to bring us editors over to the dark side."

"Speaking of the dark side . . ." Trixie made space for the waiter to deposit their second order of fries. "Do tell, please, what you're thinking about Alice. I'm sure I must have misheard you."

"First of all, have you read the draft?"

"No! I think I was too negative about the idea. I can't believe she sent the whole thing to you first. You recall we had an agreement to dissuade her? A little 'Keep Alice in the box' pact between colleagues?" Trixie picked up her phone and started scrolling through her texts. "I have the proof here somewhere . . ."

"I remember! But then I read it . . . Alice is on this insane so-called lifestyle program and she eats nothing but grass and cold brew, and it's making her really sensitive and hyperfocused. And anyway, right after our meeting last week, she emailed me the manuscript and said she was going to wait by the computer until I read it."

"That doesn't sound like Alice," Trixie said. "Alice is never in a hurry. The trilogy took her a hundred years."

"Well, she was insistent, so I read it . . ." Rebecca paused dramatically.

"And?"

"It's kind of a tour de force." Alice's draft had delivered on her promise of intergalactic tear-jerking romantasy. A well-written intergalactic tear-jerking romantasy.

"But what about her brand? Would Avenue publish it? Even if it's by Alice Gottlieb?"

"The way I see it is, her loyal audience will read it because they loved the trilogy, and she'll attract a whole new group who will come for the genre. I mean, what about that insanely popular series about hot trolls?"

"'Hot trolls' is an oxymoron. Look, if you think it will sell, who am I to argue?" Trixie signaled for the check. "We'll just need to figure out how much I make you pay for it."

"Over another lunch," Rebecca said. "Frank French should pay for our meals. After all I did for him!"

"What are you wearing to the party? I hope Gabe is helping you."

"Well, apparently I'm not allowed to be a sexy hippie."

"Weren't you a sexy hippie a few Halloweens ago? Right before the pandemic? The year Ike went as the Joker and I almost broke up with him because of it?"

"That was horrifying." Rebecca shuddered. "Gabe is going to plan something. What about you?"

"I think I'm going to go as Mrs. Robinson."

"You're going to wear a pointy leopard bra at the *East River Review* party?"

"No! Of course not! It's a work party! I have a leopard coat and some cigarettes, so I'm good."

"Oh, I never thought for a moment that you would be wildly inappropriate at a work party. What would give me that idea? Just recalling the time you forced the CEO of Random House to do a karaoke duet of 'Shallow' with you at their holiday after-party. Which you weren't even invited to. Also, that leopard bra is something Chloe would 100 percent wear to work."

"Glad you remember my one teeny lapse and bring it up every single time I see you." Trixie unnecessarily reapplied her lipstick while Rebecca put down her credit card. "Thanks, sweet pea. Even though now I have to read rom-com sci-fi all night."

"Oh, there is no 'com' about it. You'll weep, mark my words."

"At least tell me there's some scorching sex and potential for a sequel?" Trixie raised her eyebrows.

"Ask yourself if you want to read graphic sex scenes from the brain of Alice Gottlieb," Rebecca scolded. "Just a lot of tasteful yearning and some moderately spicy alien lovemaking. As for a sequel, all things are possible on the planet Eros." Rebecca gave Trixie a hug. "I'll see you Thursday in the Hamptons. La-di-da!"

"Thursday in the Hamptons! As for the planet Eros, I haven't forgotten about Ben Heath. We shall revisit."

"Ben Heath who?" Rebecca said airily. Between the party and Trixie's surprising but increasingly interesting suggestion about her career, Rebecca had no time for her obsessive annoyance regarding Ben Heath. Unless he showed up with the Lion's manuscript, she would never have to see him again. Only his cactus. She waved goodbye to Trixie and headed back to the office.

She was in the elevator when she got a text from Gabe.

Gabe:
strapping AND scrappy! scrappy AND strapping! 🔥🔥

Rebecca:
WTF?

Gabe:

> don't be coy with me, miss

Rebecca:

> i have no idea what you

The elevator doors opened before she could finish her text. And there in her place of work on a day that was NOT HIS DAY, standing in front of her desk that was NOT HIS DESK TODAY, was Ben Heath in all his admittedly strapping hotness, taking her breath away.

CHAPTER FOURTEEN

MONDAY
WORK/HOME, REBECCA

Rebecca stepped through the elevator doors at the last minute, fumbling her phone and trying to process the sight of Ben in her space. She was immediately convinced that everyone in the office was staring at her. Everyone in the office *was* staring at her. Okay, at least Gabe, Chloe, and Mrs. Singh were staring at her. *Pull yourself together*, she admonished herself. *Act like a professional adult in your place of work.*

In a gross invasion of privacy, Ben was opening her desk drawer and rummaging around.

"What do you think you're doing?" Rebecca hissed.

"Oh, well, I was looking for something to wipe up what appears to be cow cud on the desk."

"'What appears to be cow cud'?" Rebecca mimicked him. "How would you know?" So much for acting like a professional adult.

"I grew up in Vermont," Ben said, clearly trying to wield this fact—if it *was* a fact, and Rebecca didn't put it past him to lie—to his advantage.

"Well, here in New York City," she replied icily, "we can identify freshly pressed green juice."

"Oh, I'm sorry." Ben found a napkin left over from last week's lunch and began swiping at the tiny green puddle—actually, more like a few drops. "I might have recognized it as such if it was in an actual container and not spilled all over the desk." He wadded up the napkin and tossed it at the recycling bin and missed.

"Nice. I'm sure you didn't come all the way up just to litter." Rebecca inched past Ben, taking care not to actually make contact, and put her bag on the chair.

"Saving a seat?"

"I don't have to. It's Monday, and this is Avenue, in case you're confused. On Wednesday, when it's Hawk Mills, then you can sit there. I thought you had memorized the rules, seeing how you're the teacher's pet of the Collaborative Whatever Committee."

"Do you mean the Desk Share Cooperative Community Group Committee?" Ben asked primly.

Rebecca wanted to murder him. He probably had the fucking manuscript from Atticus too. Mrs. Singh was making little friendly gestures and getting up as if she was about to head over. Gabe and Chloe were making no pretense whatsoever of doing anything but staring. And eavesdropping.

Rebecca seethed. "Let's not do this here."

"Do what?" Ben asked innocently, picking the napkin up and tossing it into the bin on his second try. "I just came by to sign some HR documents that are due today." He smiled charmingly at Mrs. Singh, and Rebecca's heart skittered as she remembered him turning that smile on her at the town house. What a faker! She knew he must have the book in his messenger bag. Mrs. Singh had stopped to clatter some teacups on her desk. Did she really think they were going to have tea together? When had Mrs. Singh ever offered Rebecca a cup of tea?

"Follow me!" Rebecca snatched her phone out of her bag in case she had to bludgeon him with it and headed to her former office, a.k.a. the "Synergy Room." It took a lot, but she didn't look back to make sure he was following her; she tried hard not to flounce but, honestly, she was furious. She didn't believe his bullshit about HR documents for one minute. He had come to gloat. He had invaded the sanctity of her workspace and made her lose her professional cool in front of everyone. Maybe she wasn't known for her professional cool, but still. There were rules! Desk sharing rules! She hadn't read them, but she knew they existed.

Ben had in fact followed her into what was a much smaller space than Rebecca remembered. He closed the door behind them. Rebecca couldn't even spare a moment's thought for her office; there was nothing left of it but a small table, a few binders, and someone's half-eaten lunch. All she could do was back up until she stumbled against the table in an effort to put some distance between them. She assiduously avoided his eyes. His dark blue eyes. Her heart had started hammering, and she began talking so that he wouldn't hear it. "Why are you really here? Do you have it?"

"I told you. HR documents that need to be dated today."

Because she was refusing to look at his face, Rebecca had to scan the bulk of him in dark jeans, a close-fitting gray T-shirt, and a casual blazer. His boots were cool. Eyes on boots! "So it's just a coincidence that we had a bet come due today? Do you have the manuscript or not?"

"I take it, then, that you must not have it?" Ben folded muscular arms over his broad chest. For fuck's sake, focus! Rebecca stared at the boots.

"So you don't have it either? Where is it?" she asked the boots.

"Monday's not over till midnight," Ben said. "And I'm meeting Atticus tonight." He was leaning closer. Why? To gloat?

"Prove it."

"I don't have to prove anything; I'll just show you the manuscript after I get it tonight. And demonstrate my superiority, as you so maturely said."

"Whatever. You showed up empty-handed is all I'm saying. And we have no idea where the book is or if he's shown it to anyone." Rebecca was starting to sweat. He was way too big and the room was way too small. How had she ever considered this an office? It was a mousehole!

"I haven't heard anything. How would we know?" Ben smelled good. Of course he did. It was just like him to smell good and be the most vexing person on the planet. Rebecca took a deep breath but all that happened was that she could smell him more clearly. He smelled clean and soapy. Kind of like citrus but also fresh-cut grass? And with an undertone of something muskier, like Ben himself. Was she just going to just stick her nose under his arm and start sniffing? WHAT WAS HAPPENING? "Wait, I have an idea," Ben was saying. Was the idea to wrap his arms around her so she could bury her face in his fresh, soapy Ben-smelling shirt? "Do you follow BLURB? We could check and see if there's anything about Atticus?"

"Yes!" Rebecca practically yelled. She pulled up BLURB on Instagram with shaking hands. "Okay, okay." She was able to focus on her phone as Ben moved EVEN CLOSER and bent down to watch her scrolling. "Got it!"

BLURB Zadie Smith in from London; Franzen from Brooklyn; DeLillo speaking; Kingsolver a maybe; will Rushdie show? ♡

BookishBabe too much security needed for rushdie—they'll zoom him in 💥 🎤 ☮️ ♡

SichelPress they should donate the $$$ instead ♡

Anon, please what and not gatsby it up? LOL ♡

BLURB Atticus has lion manuscript: deets please ♡

HOT DESK

MargaretTate No one will touch it

BLURB But who has read it?

bookguy2030 [meme of man walking away from a burning car]

s+medonovan there are legal issues obvi

NYCpoodle heard he made the rounds tho

ANON ok guys fr we got one page copied from a legal pad it is written in first person from perspective of 23 year old woman

NYCpoodle WTabsoluteFFFF??

ANON not gonna lie i took photo

litthicc can confirm my boss got it too—i had to meet atticus in lobby he smelled like whisky it was 11am.

litthicc i was ordered to shred

BLURB please say you did not shred

litthicc of course i shredded. I also took notes

BLURB HERO

ANON SHERO here. "My eyes widened in pleased surprise as I took in his girth . . ."

litthicc "I had finished reading the notes for his latest novel and was filled with the satisfaction of a doula."

MBeeWrites NOOOOOOOOO

adrieangeloublossom i mean props to EDA for knowing what a doula is i guess??

skyelovesbooks everyone filled with girth and satisfaction WHAT A POS

butterchickenbookclub no wonder his widow wants it buried LOL

BLURB anymore where that came from??

ANON more of the same but not much of it

litthicc happy to be of service but that's all i got

Sneedsfam has he gone to tabloids?

bookguy2030 [meme of man walking away from a burning car]

Rebecca couldn't read any more. Ben was breathing on her neck. She turned off her phone. "Is this good or bad?"

"Good *and* bad?" Ben hadn't moved back to a respectable distance. *Was* there a respectable distance in this space?

"At least people seem to know they can't publish it. But it's not good if anyone is actually reading it. Let alone leaking it! And what if Atticus *does* take it to the media?" Rebecca felt a surge of panic as she imagined her mother's secrets and EDA's lies plastered on the front page of the *Post*.

"I can ask him tonight."

"I can't believe he never texted me back," Rebecca found herself saying, and immediately regretted it. Why show weakness?

"Look, I've been texting him nonstop since last Wednesday. He just responded this morning. It's not you, it's him."

"I've heard that before," Rebecca couldn't resist saying.

Ben smiled, which she experienced full force as she had forgotten not to look at his face. "Hard to believe," he said, and if she had to construe his tone, she would say gentle teasing. He kept smiling and she kept looking up at his face, unwillingly meeting his eyes. Danger! But also, he was so fucking handsome!

Rebecca tried to think of a response that would be simultaneously light and witty while also establishing the upper hand in a situation that was rapidly careening out of control. The sustained eye contact made her wish that, like Calista, the alien heroine of Alice Gottlieb's draft that had kept her up until 2 a.m., she could shape-shift into one of the four elements and be reconstituted elsewhere. She would choose fire. There was a sprinkle of light freckles across Ben's nose that she was, unwisely, close enough to count. Was he going to kiss her??

The door to the Synergy Room flew open with a bang, and Rebecca leaped backward, smacking her hip against the table. It was Paul from Production, come to reunite with the remains of his chopped salad. Apparently unable to recognize the fact that Rebecca was about to literally burst into flames—fine! she wasn't using "literally" correctly this time—Paul, whose social IQ at the best of times was, Rebecca thought ungenerously, a two out of ten, blundered into the tight space.

"I didn't know you had booked a meeting in here," he said peevishly.

"I forgot my tuna." He brandished a small Tupperware container, its lid emblazoned with PROPERTY OF PAUL L.

"Meeting's over," Rebecca announced. She moved briskly past Ben, her face hot, and past Paul, who was still holding the tuna aloft. Mrs. Singh, Gabe, and Chloe were staring as if they had been watching the closed door the entire time. Although she was hyperaware of Ben behind her, Rebecca mustered superhuman resolve, waved a quick goodbye over her shoulder without looking back, and kept walking all the way to the restroom. There, she applied cold wet paper towels to her cheeks and gazed at herself in the mirror. Who was that flushed and wild-eyed person? On the side of the sink, her phone vibrated with a text. It was from Atticus Adams: **Let's meet up tonight.** Maybe Ben thought he was going to win, but *he* was going be the jilted one waiting by his phone. Rebecca was back, baby.

"So let me get this straight," Stella said, pausing for a moment to inhale deeply over a jar of homemade kimchi. "You are meeting Atticus Adams tonight, hoping that he gives you the only copy of the Lion's deeply problematic unpublished manuscript so that you can win a bet with your hot desking partner—as in your *hot* hot desking partner—and save Jane from ruinous exposure? Did I get that right?" She began slicing Mimi's cold brisket, popping a carrot slice into her mouth. Stella was concocting a kimchi, yogurt, and palm wine sauce for the brisket, testing it out for the next installment on her YouTube channel. They were in the kitchen while Mimi finished her cocktail in the living room, no doubt rehearsing what she claimed was an extremely amusing brisket story.

"Correct." Rebecca had been tasked with dicing parboiled sweet potatoes.

"Girl."

"I know."

"Gochujang or sriracha?" Stella answered her own question. "Gochujang, obviously." She spooned some into a bowl. "Here, mix with the sweet potatoes and turn on the broiler, please."

"How are you incorporating the Fishwife haul?" Rebecca asked.

"Mimi's doing a tinned smoked salmon with pickled onions, dill labneh, and bagel toasts. Of course she has a story about 'shenanigans' with Moe Greengrass, son of Barney the Sturgeon King."

"That one I've heard. And you and Miles are still flying to Atlanta next month to see Grandma June?"

"Yes! And she's promised to show me how she makes lard pastry."

"What about Nonna? Have you FaceTimed her for recipes?"

"Of course. The cousins have been showing her the YouTube channel. She's really excited."

"All the grandmas are ready for fame. I'm so proud of you." Rebecca scraped sweet potatoes into the bowl. For the first time since she had come face-to-face with Ben, her pulse calmed. Tonight, one way or the other, the Lion's novel would be in safer hands; she would make sure of it. After that, it was totally for the best that she never see Ben again. It was too confusing. They shared a professional workspace! They were competitors. He would probably be pissed that Atticus blew him off and chose her to meet with tonight anyway. They could go back to exchanging snipes on the Office Life Inbox. *That would be just fine*, she thought dejectedly. What was wrong with her? She'd have to snap out of it before implementing her scheme to charm Atticus.

"It's all you, baby!" Stella splashed a few drops of wine into the sauce.

"Well, not *all* me," Rebecca replied. "Somebody has to conjure the recipes, cook the food, be nice with the banter, and look magnificent."

She thought again about Trixie's idea. Before she brought it up to Stella, she would do some research. Whatever the fuckety fuck it was that had happened between her and Ben in the Synergy Room had sidetracked her.

"And I owe you for the chance Tor is giving me Thursday night." Stella was working with a catering company to serve one of her desserts for the *East River Review* party. True that Rebecca had called Tor to ask, but also true that he was genuinely into the idea; she knew, because Gabe was always honest with her. "I'm going to do pineapple upside-down cupcakes," Stella enthused. "Classic sixties. Bananas Foster is too complicated for a big party, and even I can't work magic with Jell-O molds."

"Perfect. Did you make a decision about what you're going to wear?"

"As you know, my first choice is Angela Davis, but I don't want to scare all the white folk away from my cupcakes. So, it's Eartha Kitt as Catwoman. Black leather pants, some cat ears from Abracadabra, and copious eye makeup. Gabe's not going to approve sexy hippie, is he?"

"He is not. I think Jane Birkin? Low-slung bell-bottoms, crochet dress or peasant blouses, short skirts, high flat-heeled boots . . . the original boho chic."

"You are totally describing your own wardrobe. Didn't she have bangs?"

"Bangs were her thing. I'll get a wig. I have too much hair for bangs."

Stella smacked Rebecca's ass with a wooden spoon. Rebecca slid the tray of sweet potatoes under the broiler.

"Now, seriously, tell me more about Atticus Adams."

"He's a mess. Like on-his-way-to-rehab-any-second mess. And I know he's got finance bro vibes, but it must have really sucked to be the Lion's son. I honestly felt sorry for him when he was, like, 'It's my dad's book' right before he stole it. Even though he's a dick for actually showing it to people when he hasn't read it. At least he only handed out single pages. So far." Rebecca thought about the photo of Atticus in that sailor suit.

"What makes you think it would be any different if he *had* read it? Sounds like a desperate man to me. Be careful."

"I'm not going on a date with him! I'm winning a bet."

"Make sure those don't burn." Stella began serving onto three plates. "Are we going to talk about Jane? Any new developments?"

"It's complicated—reading that book and seeing her with Rose was like understanding my mom as a person for the first time, if you know what I mean."

"Well, as the only child of a very European mother, I had a pretty good idea of my mom's past. Lissa Marino is an extreme oversharer."

"She does love to make it awkward," Rebecca agreed. "My mom was never like that. It's crazy to think about this wild year she had in the city, in the same space as I'm in now, but, let's admit, much cooler. And then the trauma that she never shared with me. I can't imagine what it was like for her. I mean, I've told you how her mother was terrifying, right? Everything was sin, sin, sin. It was like Jane denied herself the friendship with Rose for some kind of penance. And I never knew she was a writer! Even though she was always pushing me toward English and books and publishing."

"Talk about vicarious living." Stella picked up the plates. "Poor Jane."

"And I was a clueless, self-absorbed little monster who knew nothing about her!"

Stella put down the plates and gave Rebecca a hard squeeze. "But you're my favorite clueless, self-absorbed little monster!"

"Thank you? I just feel bad that I never asked any questions!" Rebecca hugged back, then disentangled herself from Stella. "And even now, when I try to talk about her writing, she changes the subject."

"It's not too late, right? Though, from what you said, that secret book explained a lot."

"More than I needed to know. Like, Lissa Marino–level revelations but worse because it was the Lion telling the story. 'His girth'—ugh!"

"Men." Stella shook her head, curls flying.

"Men," Rebecca agreed.

"Still, though, time to get back on it."

"On it?"

"You know what I mean." Stella raised her eyebrows suggestively.

"Not a clue." Rebecca put the plates on the table and shouted into the living room, "Mimi! Dinner!"

After they ate, Stella jotted some notes down about tweaking the sauce, Mimi finished up her amusing brisket story, and they disappeared to smoke out of Mimi's bedroom window. Rebecca picked up her phone to text Jane, then decided she would actually call her.

"Hello, sweetheart." When Rebecca heard her mom's voice, it sounded exactly the same as it always did: a little brisk but happy to hear a full accounting of Rebecca's activities and feelings and opinions. Rebecca could imagine her reading in the blue chair in Philadelphia, but now she could also imagine her on the window seat at the East End town house. She felt protective of that young, dark-haired girl with all her dreams and insecurities. What was harder to imagine was Jane in Southampton with Rose.

"Just checking in," Rebecca said. She decided not to tell her mom about meeting Atticus in case she failed to get the manuscript. *Anyone* could google the masthead of the *East River Review* like Rebecca did, do a little forensics, and identify Janet the intern as Jane, Rebecca's mother from Philadelphia. She had to get the manuscript!

"I'm not an invalid yet," Jane responded.

"You're always complaining that I never call!"

"Well, you're sweet to check in again," Jane relented. "And I know all of this has been . . . surprising."

Rebecca thought that perhaps "all of this" was not the best way to describe the level of betrayal, assault, crushed dreams, and years passed. "How are you feeling about Rose?"

Jane's tone brightened. "It's not *exactly* picking up where we left off, but it's pretty close."

"I know I said this before, but I'm sorry. I'm sorry that your life wasn't what you expected or wanted." Rebecca couldn't help hoping Jane would contradict her.

"Rebecca. I've had a wonderful life."

"Still, though," Rebecca insisted, "it's not too late, right? I mean, now you're spending time with Rose? And for you to write? Though I guess you've been secretly writing?"

"It's never too late," Jane agreed, not taking the "secretly writing" bait.

"I'd love to read anything you write, okay?"

"We'll see." Jane laughed a little, and she sounded young. "Anyway, what did you and Trixie decide about Alice?"

"Mom, seriously," Rebecca persisted, "stop deflecting. We can talk like adults, you know. I have things to talk to you about, and you obviously have things to talk to me about. I'm not a baby."

"Well, you're *my* baby."

"Mom!" Didn't she know that Rebecca was about to head out on a mission to retrieve the stolen manuscript? Before Atticus sold it to the highest bidder? Or leaked it to the *Post*? Oh, right, she hadn't told Jane. "Try to hear me!"

"I know we have a lot to discuss. And I'll try, I promise. It's just, I've spent almost a lifetime not talking about it. It never occurred to me, for years, that what happened between me and Teddy was anything other than my fault. As Rose said, I didn't have the language you have now: there was no #MeToo movement. But I never want you to think I regret my life with your father, with you and the boys. I don't." Jane's voice softened, and Rebecca swallowed a sudden lump in her throat. In time, she thought, her mother would continue to process it all, and Rebecca was determined to be there for her. For now, she could at least offer up something Jane would appreciate.

"I know, Mom. I know. Also, and don't tell anyone, but Alice has been writing a crazy sci-fi love story."

"Romantasy is very popular these days," Jane said with authority. "Thank you for telling me."

"Well, I hope your book club will forgive her." Rebecca checked the time on her phone. "I have to go, but I love you!"

"Rebecca, I do hear you. I promise. Things will be different now that I have Rose again. Now that she knows everything. I love you too."

Rebecca said goodbye and went to brush her teeth so she wouldn't reek of kimchi while relieving Atticus of the manuscript. She would make it quick and painless, and then she would figure out how to lord it over Ben. Which wasn't the point, obviously, but she needed to keep her wits about her to make sure that stupid book ended up doing no harm.

After her second and a half glass of what Atticus assured her was VERY FINE WINE, Rebecca had to admit that her wits were not exactly about her. He had picked her up in a black car that was idling at the curb in front of Mimi's apartment. She looked suspiciously at the tinted windows and hesitated before getting in, but Atticus had pointed out that she got into Ubers all the time and that they would be chaperoned by Leon. Leon ignored them both all the way downtown.

Atticus was a type of man familiar to Rebecca: the charm that attractiveness and money and social ease gave him was offset by the wheedling pressure he exerted to have another drink, stay out a little later, be a good sport, be a fun girl. His longish hair fell rakishly into his eyes, so he had to keep brushing it back. She didn't care for his signet pinkie ring. But she admitted to an undeniable little glow of satisfaction that he was focusing his attention on her. Pathetic, she knew. How old was he, anyway? His vibes were less finance bro and more reckless, aristocratic boarding school teacher who was sleeping with his students. What was she doing? Part of her yearned to be at home in sweats and glasses, but part of her was tempted to be that fun girl, to see which fabulous, moneyed, secret venues he had access to. He was also carrying a black leather bag that she assumed contained the manuscript—which, she knew from her BLURB sleuthing with Ben, he had no luck unloading yet, though not for lack of trying.

"It makes sense that Avenue would buy the unpublished novel along with the rest of my father's work. What you do with it is up to you. You know what I'm saying, right?" Atticus was doing a moderately successful impersonation of a sober person—better than the one he had tried at the town house. They were sitting next to each other in a curved booth near the bar at Frenchette, where Atticus had eaten a steak while Rebecca had watched; although tempted to order food, she was still too full of brisket. He was probably used to women watching him eat while they sipped lemon water. Maybe she could choke down a crème brûlée?

"I'm happy to take it to Ami Ito and see what she says," Rebecca lied. She protested weakly as the waiter poured her more wine. Aside from one of Mimi's tiny cocktails and the *salute!* nights, she was not usually a weekday drinker. Atticus had already gone to the bathroom twice, bringing his bag with him; she had watched each time as he engaged in very close talking with the stunning hostess, then returned, energized and glassy-eyed.

"Now, you see, I'd really like to trust you on that." Atticus pushed his plate away, leaned back, draped his arms in a power move across the back of the booth, then wrapped and unwrapped a piece of Rebecca's hair around his finger. It happened so quickly that by the time she had jerked away, he was smirking, hands held up in a "What, me?" gesture.

This wasn't a business meeting. Nor was it a date. Rebecca had to stay focused on the task at hand. Not one more person was going to read about her mom playing strip pool with the Lion. And worse. It was doubtful Atticus knew that Jane was her mother or even that the book featured versions of Jane and Rose. Was it to her advantage that his father had had sex with her mother and that he had no idea? Atticus dropped his hand lower and brushed it against Rebecca's collarbone. Seriously? They were almost related! She shrugged him off and looked longingly at the leather bag.

"I think you'll take the book right to Rose is what I think." Atticus leaned farther back, his knees apart in a classic manspreading-on-the-subway stance. Rebecca inched away from his dangling hand. Obviously she would give the book back to Rose. If *she* knew it and *he* knew it, was it really a lie to say she would run it by Ami first? She had begun the night attempting to reason with him, but at this point maybe telling him what he wanted to hear was the wiser course?

"I think the book ends up with Rose regardless," she heard herself saying instead. Maybe he would just forget his bag the next time he did coke in the bathroom and she could execute a heist. That would be easier than whatever this was. Atticus was about to say something when his phone lit up. He bent over it, entranced. Rude. But also she had to pee. Rising to her feet, Rebecca realized she was a tiny bit drunk. She made her way to the restroom, focusing on putting one foot in front of the other. Why had she worn such high-heeled boots? Who was she trying to impress? Oh, right: Atticus. She nodded nonchalantly at the stunning hostess.

When Rebecca made it back to the booth, Atticus was still texting, but he had paid the bill and procured two shots. He looked up from his phone, giving Rebecca a slow, thorough once-over that she found both enraging and flattering. If he thought she was going to hook up with him just to get her hands on the book, he didn't know shit about her. Yes, she would drink his, to be fair, very fine wine, and, yes, she would most likely go to wherever the next one-percenter venue was, but, first of all, he was not her type; number two, she had established that they were practically siblings; secondly—no, wait, number three—she would not stoop to using what Mimi called her "feminine wiles" just to win a bet; number four, Ben; number five, what? Hang on and back it up to number four, or maybe it was thirdly? Scratch that! Ben was *not* a reason.

Still standing, Rebecca took the offered shot, tried not to cough as she downed it, and smacked the shot glass on the table. She was Fun Girl now! After she shared a meaningful goodbye with her new friend, Stunning Hostess, she crawled clumsily into the black car. Atticus slid in beside her, somehow in possession of a rocks glass filled with amber liquid that he must have taken from Frenchette.

Rebecca batted his hand from her thigh, and he went back to texting. Wherever they were headed had better be worth it. And she still had faith that by the end of the night the manuscript would be hers. She spared a quick, satisfied thought of Ben Heath waiting in vain for Atticus to text him. One thing was certain: she would not be riding home in this car with Atticus. She was sick of dodging his half-hearted advances, he was smoking out the window despite her protest, and he kept cranking up truly unbearable electronic music. "Where are we going?" she yelled over the painful percussions.

"Have you ever been to Ibiza?" she thought he yelled back.

Did he think she would go with him to Ibiza? Would she? She would not! For a fleeting moment, she imagined herself by a turquoise sea in one of those plunging one-pieces while Atticus, still in a gray suit and white shirt, handed her the manuscript with an umbrella drink. She turned him into Stella in her wide-brimmed beach hat, then Stella morphed into Ben Heath, tan and muscular. Fine! She would go to Ibiza with Ben if she had to! Atticus offered her a key bump that she refused—was cocaine really coming back now? She would have to ask Chloe—and just as her head was about to explode from the noise, the car stopped and she hauled herself out onto the relatively peaceful Lower East Side sidewalk.

"After you," Atticus slurred gallantly, miraculously still in possession of his full drink. He was gesturing toward a neighborhood dive bar that looked exactly like the kind of place where she, Stella, and Miles would play pool and fight over the jukebox during college. Maybe you walked through the dive part to a secret door that led down to a hidden bar where all the cool people lounged behind velvet drapes and sipped champagne? You did not. Betty Jack's was a self-contained familiar world, its fanciest patron an old man in a white hat. Rebecca's drink-addled brain snapped to attention when she caught sight of the tall, incredibly good-looking bartender.

"I thought I would call my own meeting," Atticus said, steering her forward. "Benjamin! My man!"

Ben's face lit up when he saw her; she was not mistaken about that. Then it darkened a little as she evaded Atticus. The bar was almost empty, but Ben was in the middle of opening and pouring beers. He kept his eyes trained on her while he worked efficiently. "What can I get you?" he asked, his voice neutral. *Oh, okay, so that's how he was going to play it*, Rebecca thought, perching unsteadily on a barstool. She too could be indifferent.

"Look here," Atticus announced. "I'll have a Manhattan with Rittenhouse, if you please." He plunked the Frenchette glass on the bar. It seemed as if Ben was about to say something, but he didn't and instead poured half the rye into a shaker.

"Water, please?" Rebecca asked in what she hoped was a chilly tone.

"Becca will have a glass of your top-shelf red," Atticus said grandly. He was starting to totter and reached out to steady himself by gripping Rebecca's shoulder. Ben watched intently as she peeled Atticus's fingers off. He put a glass of water in front of her and poured Atticus a small drink. "Stingy, what? And here I am helping you both out." Atticus was losing the exaggerated control he had displayed in the restaurant.

"Why don't you sit down," Ben told Atticus rather than asked him. Surprisingly, Atticus obeyed. He leaned against her, but this time it was more to prop himself up than to continue his relentless yet uncommitted groping. Ben raised an eyebrow.

"Benjamin. Benny. Can I call you Benny, my man?"

Ben slid Atticus's drink off the bar and smoothly replaced it with a glass of water; Atticus didn't seem to notice. "Why are you here?" Ben asked. Rebecca jerked her head toward the bag Atticus had slung onto the bar. She tried to convey with her eyes that the manuscript was right there. "Are you okay?" Ben gave her a concerned look. Why was he so dense?

"Listen," Atticus continued. "Listen." He stopped and looked around as if unsure where he was and why. Then he perked up. "There's a lot of interest in *Sun Run*. A lot of interest. Someone is going to make a lot of money. Why not you two?" He turned suddenly to Rebecca. "Heyyy. You're really beautiful, you know that?" It seemed possible that he had no idea that they had arrived together.

"Okay," Rebecca said, trying not to look at Ben. "We know you went around to different publishing houses. But Rose is the executor." It was time for some tough love.

"But what you don't know . . . Erica"—Atticus retrieved the wrong name with some effort—"is that I met with an agent. Talk about monnnnnnneyyyyy. I think Rose is making a big mistake, and guess what? The agent agrees with me."

This was an unpleasant development. The deal with Avenue to represent the Lion's estate was not actually signed. She didn't think Rose would ever work with an agent, but it was true that she was probably leaving some monnnnnnneyyyyy on the table by not doing so. Did Ben know about this? Maybe he set it up? Maybe it was a plot to have an agent cut out Avenue and go with Hawk Mills. Rebecca was about to cry just thinking about it: having her triumph, however undeserved, yanked away at the last minute. What would Ami say? What would her mom say?

"Agent or publisher doesn't matter," Ben said. "The terms of the will give Rose the authority to do what she wants with the manuscript. With all of it."

"Not everyone is as screw-pew-lusss as you two," Atticus warned, exhibiting for the first time tonight a flash of wounded anger that seemed real. "I have plenty of media contacts. I could start a Slubshack. A Subscrap. Self-publish, right?"

Rebecca was sure that Rose had more than enough money. But maybe she would be tempted? She was single-handedly supporting the *East River Review*, for example. That wasn't cheap. *Could* Atticus start a Substack? He could hardly stand upright!

"It's not going to happen," Ben said firmly. He sent a bowl of pretzels down the bar to the old man in the hat. "That book is not going to print. There's plenty of other writing he left behind. Stories, letters. Those will be the Lion's last word."

"But the book is the big one." Atticus fumbled in his pocket and pulled out a vial of coke. "And it just so happens to be the one I have in my possession, my man."

"Nope. Put that away." Ben tapped on the bar. "Right now."

"Aw, c'mon." Atticus continued trying to get the vial open, but his hand-eye coordination was failing.

"Not inside. You need to head out."

Atticus stood up suddenly, stumbled, and took firm hold of Rebecca's arm. "S'all right, s'all right, chill, my man. We were just leaving."

Rebecca tried to pull away, but Atticus was both dragging her off the stool and using her for support. There was a loud smack as Ben flipped the section of the bar that allowed him to get out from behind it. "Take your hands off her, *my man*. Let's go." As Ben was maneuvering Atticus toward the door, Rebecca had the presence of mind to snatch up the bag and remove what was, indeed, the manuscript, loose and a little worse for wear. She looked around wildly, then sat on it. Atticus was protesting, so Ben turned back and motioned to Rebecca, who tossed the now empty bag to him. They disappeared out the door. Her pulse was thudding in her ears.

After a few minutes, Ben came back. "We're closing a little early," he announced to two women snuggling in the red booth and to the man in the hat. "Finish up, please. First drink is on me the next time you come in." There was some grumbling (man in the hat), but soon the bar was empty. Ben locked the front door and turned off the neon "Betty Jack's" sign. Then he came over to Rebecca where she perched on a slippery pile of papers. She was ready to share the good news of her heroic, quick thinking. "I'll call you an Uber" was what he said.

Stung, Rebecca snapped, "I can call my own Yuber. I mean Uber." Now that Atticus was gone, she was the drunk one.

"I got it." Ben pulled his phone out. Why was he trying to get rid of her? Why was he so hot? "I'm sorry if your ride left without you," he said stiffly.

It took Rebecca a minute to clock his tone. What was his point? Did he think she *wanted* to be hanging out with Atticus? Wait, was he jealous? She tried to peer at his face, but he kept his eyes down. "What's your address?" he asked.

Was he seriously going to send her home like a naughty child? While she was literally (literally!) sitting on the manuscript they had both been trying to find? Seriously? Fine! She gave him her address. "What?" he said, after typing it in. "Six minutes."

"What 'what'?" Rebecca retorted.

"You're glaring." Ben reached over the bar to grab a sweater and a book. "I'll walk you out."

She was being dismissed. She tried to dismount gracefully from the barstool but slid awkwardly, a few sheets of papers floating down. In a reaction based wholly on necessity, Rebecca (like Atticus before her but not at all creepy!) grabbed at Ben so that she wouldn't fall. He was still wearing the gray T-shirt, and it still smelled good. He had instinctively held her to steady her, and Rebecca felt his muscles tense under her hand. She looked up at him, at his dark blue eyes and smattering of freckles. She would *not* kiss him! The jukebox started playing the old T. Rex song "Bang a Gong (Get It On)." She would *not* "get it on" no matter how many times the chorus suggested it. Even though her body fought her, Rebecca gathered the strength to let go and draw away. Looking anywhere but at Ben, Rebecca's eyes lit on the book he had tossed back onto the bar. Virginia Woolf's *Mrs. Dalloway*.

"Are you reading that book?" she demanded.

"Yes, when it's quiet in here," Ben answered.

Okay, fuck it! Rebecca crashed into Ben, who swept her up and deposited her on the bar, her legs on either side of him, and then they were kissing, *finally*; she wanted to inhale him; she could not get enough of his warm mouth, his hands tangled in her hair, the strength of his arms. He groaned against her lips and she felt her body answering. Her body was saying yes! Her body was saying, "You're dirty and sweet, oh yeah," or maybe that was T. Rex. Their teeth clashed and Rebecca sank her fingers into his biceps. Ben started kissing down the side of her neck, and she opened her throat to him as if waiting to be made a vampire. She felt his none-too-gentle bite reverberating in every part of her. Clamping her legs around his hips, Rebecca pressed herself against the length of his chest. A small sound of protest escaped her when he leaned back. He tipped her face up and they stared at each other, gasping for breath. The Uber honked outside, and pages of the Lion's book littered the floor of the bar all around them.

JANE

NEW YORK CITY
MAY 1982

After her father died of a heart attack when she was eleven, Jane refused to go back to church, but she still remembered the relief she had felt during confession when the priest assigned penances that eased the knot of self-condemnation for her childish sins. Since Rose had returned from Paris, Jane had been unable to tell her what had happened with Teddy. She knew she would, she knew she had to, but with each passing week, the whole encounter seemed more unreal, until she almost didn't believe it. Only the leaden combination of guilt and shame that settled deeper and deeper reminded her that something had come between her and Rose. What that "something" was faded like a strange dream.

Only a few days after the freak blizzard, Teddy won the Pulitzer Prize in fiction for *The Coldest War*. That was thrilling for everyone, of course, but Jane and Rose had also celebrated Sylvia Plath's posthumous win for poetry by reading *Ariel* to each other by candlelight. It was one of the few nights Jane had stayed uptown with Rose; instead, she had been spending more time in her East Village apartment with the excuse that she was using it as a studio for writing. She sat at the kitchen table gazing between the bathtub and the blank page. She had written nothing.

Rose was coming downtown to meet her at the Cupping Room Cafe on West Broadway for brunch. Jane arrived first and ordered Rose a cappuccino and herself a black coffee. She was determined to tell Rose, to clear the air, to do her penance. At the same time, Jane wondered if the incident—which, much as she tried, had not shaped itself into a funny story—might be better completely buried. Only two people knew, and neither would tell. Jane was good at keeping quiet. Teddy was busy, his star brighter than ever after the Pulitzer: *The New York Times* had just run a front-page Arts and Leisure article that anointed him a true literary lion. Everyone had chipped in to buy a big stuffed lion from FAO Schwarz, and he had appeared truly moved when Ellen presented it to him. Jane could live with the secret if it meant that Rose would never know. There she was now, in her bright oversize sweater (Drew called it "jelly bean" colors, and only Rose could pull it off) over striped tights and riding boots. Everyone turned as she came in, even the man at the end of the bar with spiky blond hair, who Jane was almost positive was Rod Stewart. Jane's heart swelled as her friend moved toward her, smiling, undistracted by the murmurs and stares. She would never tell.

"I'm so glad you sat at the bar," Rose exclaimed, hugging Jane. "Did you order me the chocolate chip pancakes?"

"Not yet," Jane answered. "But here is your coffee, Your Highness."

"Oh, I love you!" Rose enthused, taking a sip and leaning in close. "Is that person who looks like my aunt Helen with frosted hair and the plaid scarf Rod Stewart?" she whispered loudly into Jane's ear.

"Shhhhhh! You're the worst!" Jane started laughing, pushing Rose away. "Your hair is tickling me!"

"Oh, so you can still laugh?" Rose, teasing, picked up the menu as if she didn't know it by heart.

Jane sobered immediately. "What do you mean?"

"Oh, c'mon, Jane, you know." Rose looked at her searchingly. "You don't stay over. You don't seem happy. You've been weird ever since I got back from Paris."

"What? What do you mean?" Jane couldn't help her defensive response. Rose had complained about Jane's not staying with her at the co-op, but she had never been this direct.

"Don't insult me," Rose said seriously. "It's me, Jane."

Jane flushed. "I'm not. I mean, I'm sorry."

Rose dropped the menu and took Jane's hand. "I have to ask you something." Jane's heart sank, but at the same time the possibility of coming clean fluttered in her stomach. "And you have to promise to tell me the truth, okay? This is really hard. But I don't want you to protect me, okay?" Rose pressed her forehead against Jane's, and they locked eyes. "Do you promise?"

"Yes," Jane whispered. It wouldn't be the end of the world. Rose would forgive her and everything would go back to the way it had been before.

"Did . . . did something happen with my dad? Did he try anything? Did he do something? To you?" Each word sounded as though Rose had wrenched it from darkness. "When I was gone?"

Jane drew back, stung. "No! Rose, no!" She watched Rose's face, a battle playing out between suspicion and hope. "I promise," she added.

Rose let out a long breath and relaxed her shoulders. "Okay. Okay. I believe you." She brightened and flagged down the bartender. "Chocolate chip pancakes, side of bacon, eggs Benedict with fruit salad instead of home fries. Did I get it right?"

"Yes, of course," Jane said. "English muffin extra-toasted." The black coffee churned in her stomach. Her mind was whirring, still trying to process what had just happened. She wanted to claw back the chance she had to confess, to make things right. She had been so close that the words were still in her mouth, the relief almost tangible.

"Rose . . ." she began.

"Jane . . ." Rose teased, all smiles now. Jane steeled herself. What had happened with Teddy wasn't as bad as what Rose had imagined, was it? She knew Rose liked Teddy, but Jane would never be an impediment to that. Everyone loved Teddy, but Rose was Rose. The bitter coffee was rising in her throat, but she could see the way forward. She would find the words. The best words in the best order. She opened her mouth, but before she could speak, Rose blurted out, "Oh, I keep forgetting to give this to you!" and searched her bag, pulling out a book. "I bought this for you in Paris at the Bouquinistes—you know, those booksellers along the Seine? It's our favorite book! In French! For you to practice . . ." She handed Jane Marilynne Robinson's *Housekeeping*, the eerie, remarkable novel that had gripped Jane when she'd first read it. Rose was the only other person she knew that had read it and, of course, had felt its gorgeous chill in her bones too. *La maison dans la dérive*. "It means 'The House in the Drift,'" Rose explained. "Kind of perfect, right?" Jane looked at the book in despair. She would let go of the truth if it meant she could keep Rose close, even for one more day. She swallowed it all back down.

"Drew!" Rose exclaimed. "There he is! I invited him to join us: he was at Paco's last night, and I have news!"

Drew, in sunglasses with his jacket collar turned up, flopped on the bar chair next to Rose. "I'm tragically hungover! I need a Bloody Mary immediately! I need it intravenously!" he proclaimed.

"Oh my god, you are so dramatic." Rose smiled at the bartender who turned away from Rod Stewart and hurried over. "Jane? Bloody?"

"No, thanks," Jane said.

"Why is Jane cranky?" Drew pulled his sunglasses down his nose and looked over them at Jane.

"I don't know!" Rose ordered two drinks. "I'm trying to get it out of her!"

"I'm fine!" Jane insisted. "How's Paco?"

"Not great." Drew took his sunglasses off. "Jermaine is really sick. The nurse told Paco it's like a gay cancer or something."

"What does that even mean?" Rose put her hand on Drew's arm.

"I don't know. They're starting a Gay Men's Health Crisis here to raise some money and figure out what's going on. They threw a beach party last night." He took a long sip of his drink. "Hence the hangover."

"I'm sure they'll figure it out," Jane said anxiously. She couldn't bear it when Drew was sad.

"I hope you're right." Drew smiled reassuringly at Jane as if he could read her thoughts. "Anyway, Rose, what's your big news? Why did I have to drag my ass off a comfortable couch and come all the way over here to watch you eat dessert for breakfast?" Rose was drenching her chocolate chip pancakes in syrup.

"Sooo," Rose drawled. "Guess who called me? To ask me out to dinner? For a real date!"

"Mick Jagger?" Drew guessed. He leaned in to whisper conspiratorially, "I only said that to make Rod jealous. That's Rod Stewart, right? Kind of sexy even though he looks like my aunt Jang-mi."

Rose and Jane burst out laughing. "Not even close," Rose said. "Better."

"Better than Jagger," Drew mused. "Your guess, Jane."

Jane knew. Of course, she knew. "Paul Newman?"

Drew scoffed. "What is your obsession with Paul Newman? He's old!"

"Jagger is no spring chicken," Jane argued. She wanted to stall Rose.

"What do you both have against older men?" Rose speared a strawberry off Jane's plate and ate it. "Fine, I'll tell you. Teddy!"

"Finally!" Drew cheered. "I knew it! Who could resist you? Tell us everything!"

"Tell us everything," Jane repeated. It wasn't completely unexpected, was it? Rose and Teddy had been flirting, right? But still. A phone call? A date? Was he even officially divorced from Clara? Jane's mouth was suddenly so dry, she couldn't swallow. This made it real. Now Jane could never tell Rose.

"He's taking me to Lutèce. He wants to go somewhere really special, not like Elaine's or the Odeon. He said he's been thinking about me ever since we had that lunch where we went over my edits on his work. He said not even Maury Kantor sees what he's trying to do. Not like I did." Rose was so shyly pleased that her skin was almost translucent.

"You are the best editor," Jane said honestly. Her eggs Benedict looked disgusting.

"I'm so happy!" Rose sang. "Okay, I'm going to the bathroom, and when I come back, we'll plan my outfit for the date!" She slipped off her chair and walked away.

"Jane." Drew leaned across the empty space between them. "Two things. Quickly. One, I know why you're upset."

"You do?" Jane leaned toward Drew.

"Yes. Because Teddy hasn't said anything about your story, right? It's been months, and he took Rose out and he arranged the Keith Haring visit. He's had your story the whole time and hasn't said shit. It's not cool."

"I . . . I, well . . ." Jane thought furiously about how to respond. "I guess it does bother me," she relented, and with those words, her hope drained away. Once she omitted the truth, that looming event, she had to lie and lie. She was an idiot for thinking she could bury it and go on as if nothing had happened.

"Listen," Drew said earnestly. "You should ask Rose to mention it to Teddy. I mean, it's pretty obvious that he's crazy about her. And now that they're going out, it makes sense, right? He'll do whatever she wants."

"No!" Jane couldn't bear it. With every word, Drew was drifting further away. Rose was drifting further away.

Drew flinched. "You don't have to yell," he said. "Calm down! I think it's a good idea."

"I'm sorry." Jane pushed the eggs around her plate, trying to stop the tears. "Please don't mention it to her. Just don't, okay?"

"I won't, I won't. I'm sorry I snapped. I'm just very fragile right now." Drew sighed. "Too-many-piña-coladas fragile."

"What else were you going to say?"

"Okay, you know how Paco is still friendly with Clara? Or at least he doesn't shun her like everyone else?"

Drew had mentioned before that Clara still confided in Paco and that they had spent a lot of time together before her exile to London. "Yes?"

"Clara is pregnant! And she refuses to do anything about it even though Teddy is trying to divorce her."

"What?" Jane hadn't thought of Clara in months. "Does Rose know?"

"No! I was going to tell you both today, but with her big news I don't think I should, right?"

"No, don't ruin it for her," Jane agreed.

"She'll find out soon enough. Unless Clara gets smart. Even Paco is done with her. Why would she have a kid with someone who doesn't want to be with her?"

"Poor Rose," Jane said. She slipped the book into her purse. She wanted to protect Rose no matter what.

"Yeah, it makes it messy for everyone." Drew finished his Bloody Mary and took the celery stalk out of Rose's. "Here she comes!" Jane looked up to see Rose at the other end of the room, beaming at them.

"Jane." Drew touched her arm. She turned to him. "You're a great writer. You're the real writer, you know? Let her have this."

"What do you mean?" Jane stiffened.

"Jane," Drew said gently, which made it worse. "We all love Teddy. But you don't need Teddy. You have me and Rose. You have your writing. I'm not saying Rose needs him, but they make sense, right? Rose and Teddy."

Jane didn't say anything, but she managed a small smile. It was the least she could do for him. Relieved, Drew sat back to make room for Rose. "It's going to be great," he promised. "You'll see."

In the end, it was Ellen who arranged it all. "Teddy told me to keep an eye on you," she said gruffly, waiting for Jane when she came out of the bathroom at the office, pale and shaky from throwing up. She gave Jane the number of a Planned Parenthood clinic. She called Shirley the bookkeeper and handed Jane a fat envelope of cash, calling it a bonus for a job well done. She told Jane to be a "smart girl." She told Jane that there was a job for her at the *East River Review* if she wanted to come back as long as "everything was taken care of." She told her that Parker would write her a recommendation if she needed one—that even she, Ellen, would write her one. That she would say Jane had a great eye. Teddy would be happy to call his dear friend at the *Haverford Review* if she wanted to work there. She even gave Jane an advance copy of the spring issue and an *East River Review* tote bag filled with all the other issues Jane had worked on.

Drew thought she was jealous. Rose and Teddy were affectionate: Rose delirious with happiness, Teddy unctuous and solicitous of her. There were photos of the two of them in the *National Enquirer* and the *Post*, Teddy shielding his face, Rose radiant. When Jane first told Rose she was going back to Philadelphia, Rose wept. She begged Jane to stay; she gave Jane Polaroids and her silver necklace to remember her by but at the same time refused to believe that Jane would leave. Jane, numb, stayed calm and repeated obvious lies about having to help her mother in the store, about coming back after the summer. The last time she saw Rose, when she was saying her official goodbyes at the office, Rose was cool, distant. Her polite remoteness hurt Jane more than the tears because Rose's withdrawal gave Jane a glimpse of her future, bleak and Rose-less. Drew stayed upstairs; he was taking it all personally. Teddy had gone to London to end things with Clara for good this time. Deedle patted her on the ass. Parker got a little emotional. Jonathan was on the phone. Ellen walked her out the blue door and hugged her quickly, reeking of cigarettes.

Jane quit her job at the Apple on Madison. She broke her lease on the East Village apartment. She left *The Coldest War* on the kitchen table, with its inscription, "To Jane, who has 'it.' —Best, EDA." When she bought a *New York Times* from the kiosk near the subway, the old woman, whose name, Jane had learned, was Haleema, insisted again on giving her a blueberry muffin. Then Jane cried. She cried on the subway, not trying to stop, not caring who stared and who looked away, and she cried as she carried her tote bag and two heavy duffel bags all the way to Penn Station.

By the time Jane was aboard Amtrak, her tears had dried. As the train lurched in the dark tunnel out of the station, she looked coldly at her reflection in the window. It was only one year of her life. All of that in one year. One year was nothing. Nothing. She had filled five notebooks. The train emerged into the bright May sunshine. New York City was behind her now, literally. It was hardly real, she thought, hardening her heart. Her broken heart.

CHAPTER FIFTEEN

THURSDAY
WORK, BEN

There had been no Post-it yesterday. The desk was clean enough. Ben picked up the cactus in its new pot and examined it again. Rebecca Blume had watered it and upgraded it. What did it mean? Was she making an investment in their shared desk? After the surprising and unforgettable events of Monday night, Ben had spent an inordinate amount of time reliving them. Even now, his gaze drifted to the Synergy Room and he felt a rush of heat. Of course, he had texted her that night to make sure she got home safely in the inopportune Uber. He had texted her the next day to suggest they talk. He had wanted to text her yesterday, but Ava had advised him to take a break.

The rest of the time, Ben was reaching out to Jane and Rose, reading snippets of the material they had been sending him, editing it together into a proposal for Caro. The idea for the memoir project predated any real connection with Rebecca, he reminded himself. After a quick response to his first text—possibly drunken? Was that the issue?—she was ghosting him. Maybe he would reach out once more? Forget it. If she didn't want to see him again, he would respect that. It might kill him, but he would.

The computer dinged with a Blabber message from Howie, who was sitting at his desk.

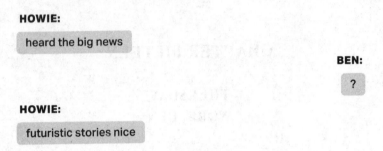

Ben's meeting had gone well, and Caro had let him increase his offer enough to win Marc Cooker's book in an auction run by the agent, Trixie Carter. His first acquisition at Hawk Mills! He would need to keep wins coming to make up for the loss of the Lion's estate. Caro was disappointed, obviously, but she was professional enough not to blame him, at least entirely, when Avenue had announced its acquisition of the estate.

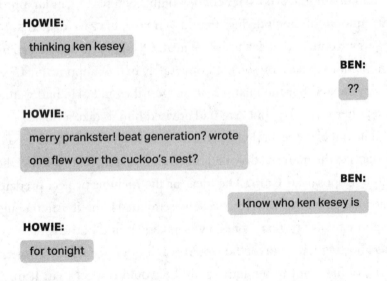

Rose had insisted that Ben come to the *East River Review* sixtieth party in Southampton. His invitation was the subject of much office gossip, according to Howie. Ben's feelings were mixed: he knew he didn't really deserve to be there as a junior editor, but he did want to pay tribute to the Lion, even though he had experienced a crash course in the toppling of idols. Also, it would be amazing to hear DeLillo speak. Who was he kidding? DeLillo was not the point. Seeing Rebecca again—she would be there, right?—was the point. Should he text her to see if she was going?

HOWIE:
costume would be mostly sideburns

BEN:
not wearing a costume

From across the room, Howie popped up in disbelief. He loped over and came to a halt at Ben's side. "It's a theme party!" he finally wheezed.

"It's optional," Ben argued. "And I'm not a costume guy." Howie's disappointment was hard to witness.

"I have two other very low-maintenance ideas." He coughed. "John Lennon glasses? Whaddaya think?"

"No." Ben checked his phone. Nothing. In half an hour he had a meeting. Then a call with Trixie, who was interested in looking at what they had collected so far and had generously agreed to explain to Jane and Rose how an agent could make selling their book easier and more lucrative. Rose and Jane were meeting with her next week, and if that went well, he hoped to get the go-ahead from Caro to present a proposal for their memoir to Hawk Mills. Jane, whose writing was unsentimental and original, had revealed that she had been working on a novel, and Ben was also going to bring that information, along with Rose's old *New Yorker* stories, to Caro. It would be gratifying to publish the memoir and then Jane's novel as Avenue was reissuing the Lion's work.

"Okay, hear me out," Howie persisted. "You go as Kurt Vonnegut. It's basically just a walrus mustache. Genius, right?"

"Not a costume guy," Ben repeated. He couldn't help the image that flashed into his head of kissing Rebecca while sporting a walrus mustache. Absolutely not. Of course they wouldn't be kissing at a work event. And judging by her silence this week, maybe ever again.

"What time is the Jitney leaving?" Howie asked. Ben's invitation had specified which Jitney he was to board to begin the exodus to Long Island. (Ava had helpfully explained that the Hampton Jitney was basically a tricked-out Greyhound bus for rich people not rich enough to have a driver.)

"Three p.m."

"We have time," Howie mused.

"Not. Going. To. Happen. Do you have the title comparisons I asked for? Any jointly written memoirs?"

"Boss, so far I've only got the Bush sisters. Will keep looking."

Howie went back to his desk to find what Ben needed. After sorting through an almost overwhelming number of emails, Ben joined Mrs. Singh for a quick cup of tea in the kitchen before his meeting. Because she had brought him a muffin, he was spared the indignity of rooting around the leftovers from a breakfast meeting: pale cantaloupe and cheese cubes, a few grapes and stray toothpicks strewn on a black plastic tray. The days of donuts were now few and far between. He learned from Mrs. Singh that thickened flaxseed was a desirable substitute for egg and that someone who used to work in Design had tried to expense a family vacation to Jamaica. He learned that Frank French was publishing an op-ed in the *Times* on the success of hybrid workplace management and the ability of hot desking to maximize space utilization. Their teatime was interrupted by a FaceTime call from Ava, who was at the Union Square farmers market.

"I was thinking you could ask Rebecca to ask Stella Marino-Miller about less meat, more mushroom loaf."

"*Mushroom loaf*? Also, as you well know, she's not answering my texts."

"You're seeing her tonight, right? Look how gorgeous this is!" Ava held up a bouquet of leeks.

"Don't forget, you have to stay with Butch. I'm going straight from here to Southampton."

"Abolish private property!"

"Ava, I'm at work. What else?" Mrs. Singh was rinsing the teacups and not even pretending not to listen.

"Get through this party for the Lion—try not to cry—and also move things along with Rebecca. Don't fuck it up!"

"I appreciate your support," Ben said, clicking off his phone and turning apologetically to Mrs. Singh. "Sorry about that."

"I do have a recipe for mushroom loaf, dear," she said helpfully. "Lentils and turmeric!"

"I'll tell my sister."

It was still early when Ben got another FaceTime call, this one from Jane and Rose, who crowded into the frame and waved at him. "What did you think of what we sent?" Rose asked.

"So good!" When Ben had first broached the idea of their writing a memoir in response to the Lion's work, he had been a little hesitant, especially after the shock of reading *Making the Sun Run* and of coming face-to-face with Rebecca. Rose and Jane had smiled at each other in their private way and agreed it was a good idea. And the more he thought about it, the more it seemed like a way to make something positive out of the whole mess. "Let me take this into a pod."

"Did you like the part about stuffed cabbage with Allen Ginsberg at Veselka?" Jane asked.

"And Jane's story that Teddy basically plundered to write *Hoydenish*?" Rose added.

"That was crazy." Ben shut himself in the spaceship. "And now that I've read Jane's version, it's hard to stomach the other."

"Although *Hoydenish* is a better title than 'Tomboy,'" Jane admitted. She didn't sound as bitter as Ben would have been. "And he got a whole novel out of it . . ."

"It's cathartic," Rose said. "And you can't imagine how wonderful it's been to be back with Jane, revising it all on our terms."

"I'm so glad," Ben said. "It would be helpful if you could both write some more about your lives after that time. I'm thinking it will be important for readers to see how the experience at *East River Review* was formative in different ways—how it resonated for both of you long after the fact."

"I'm not sure anyone wants to read about my life in Philadelphia." Jane's face was obscured for a minute as the camera dipped.

"No, that's *exactly* what people will want to read about," Ben promised. "It seems to me the heart of the story is the damage and the reclamation—for both of you: the version of what *really* happened. I think a lot of women will be able to relate. And a lot of men will have their eyes opened . . . I know I did." He winced a little. But that was why they were doing this. "Just keep sending me everything. I know it's moving quickly, but I want to get it all going concurrently with whatever Avenue has planned for the Lion's estate. Once you get everything to an agent, I'll be able to pitch it to Caro."

"We don't mind a fast pace," Rose assured him. "We already had so much material." She turned the cell phone away from her and Jane. "It's complete mayhem here right now." Ben could see hordes of people scurrying around outside a huge glass window. He could make out the ocean in the background. "We look forward to seeing you later!"

"Yes—I'll try not to talk business. But I'm impressed with how it's all taking shape."

"Thank you, Ben!" they both called out at the same time. After they disconnected, Ben sat for a minute in the soundproofed capsule. He felt a glow of pride. Even if nothing came of it—and he was almost positive something *would* come of it—he felt energized to be part of the process. Working with Rose and Jane gave him a tangible way to assuage the complex and mostly negative feelings about the Lion that he was still trying to process.

Ben was on a call with Marc Cooker, the former Google exec turned short story writer, when Rebecca texted him. His heart leaped, but he quickly discerned a negative tone. He averted his eyes and focused on Cooker. After the call ended, Ben took a few centering breaths. Maybe he had misinterpreted her intent in his swift glance?

Rebecca:

> why are you talking with rose and jane about their book WTF

> maybe you could lmk first

> what's your ndgurm

> endgame

> ????????

Ben's memory of Rebecca at Betty Jack's had sustained him since Monday. Every time he let his thoughts drift from work, he had been inundated with images of her that made it impossible to focus until he wrenched his attention back to whatever task was at hand. Her mouth, her hair, how soft she was, her powerful presence. But, looking at his phone, Ben recalled the Rebecca Blume of snark, temper, and chocolate-covered almonds strewn all over. Just because someone was beautiful and fierce and sexy and smart and, he admitted, kind of funny, it didn't mean they were a good person. Maybe he had fallen for a bad person. But he knew, on a bone-deep level, that she was a good person. An annoying good person who could be neater and learn better text etiquette.

Rebecca:

neither did you!! why are you involved? or calling trixie all the time??

Ben:

she's an agent!

Rebecca:

and my friend

Ben:

was unaware that publishing is a minefield of your personal relationships

looking out for jane and rose

Rebecca:

paternalistic BS!!!!

i suppose you plan to edit this book

Ben:

let the best person win

would think you of all people might support a competing narrative to center women's voices

if rose and jane disagree which i happen to know they don't they can tell me

Rebecca:

wow so you're centering women's voices now

Ben:

your point?

Rebecca:

lion apologist five minutes ago

Ben:
you have a lot of misplaced anger

Rebecca:
oh it's placed correctly

Ben:
i spoke to jane and rose more than once including this am and set up a mtg for them with trixie and no one at any point suggested i check with you just so you know

no doubt you'll be busy shepherding lion's estate

since you're such a fan

you know it can be both/and not just either/or

Rebecca:
EDA both sexist AND cheater

bad husband AND bad father

shall i go on???

Ben:
so you never separate artist from art

how are you the person handling the estate

Rebecca:
avenue will put him in his place, you'll see

Ben:
it's more nuanced and complex

Rebecca:

nope

Ben:

nope? srsly? that's all you have? nope?

Ben waited for a few minutes, but there were no more texts from Rebecca. He tossed his phone onto the desk. How was she the most frustrating person he had ever met? Texting was bullshit. He wanted to see her. Why? Because he couldn't stop thinking about her and recalling every moment of their encounter three nights ago at the bar. It wasn't just wanting her, although that was the most distracting part. It was also that he needed to talk to her, to argue with her, to learn more about her. Would he see her tonight? His phone buzzed and he practically dislocated his shoulder grabbing for it. It was not Rebecca.

Atticus:

hey man can you step outside for a minute

Ben:

?

Atticus:

i'm downstairs

Since escorting Atticus out of Betty Jack's on Monday, depositing him in the waiting car, and collecting the manuscript so that it could be returned to Rose, Ben had heard nothing. Atticus was lucky Ben hadn't decked him. He wasn't a violent person and, as a bartender, he had to make sure not to lose his cool even as he was dealing with drunk assholes. But watching Atticus basically maul Rebecca was hard to take. When they first walked in, he had been so happy: it was as if he had manifested her. But when Atticus touched her, Ben thought for a painful moment that they were somehow a thing. Which made no sense, he knew. But nothing about Rebecca Blume made any sense. Except for how he knew that they needed to see each other again. Even just to figure out what it was between them.

Atticus:

you there?

Ben:

what

Atticus:

just come down

Was Atticus here to confront him about taking the book back? Would Ben have to kick his ass in front of his place of work?

Atticus:

please

Ben looked at his phone. Who knew what Atticus was up to? Did Ben owe him anything? Maybe a little, since he had been playing up their friendship to Caro and Rose and using it to gain access to the Lion—to what was left of the Lion, at least. And Rebecca had snatched the stolen manuscript out of his bag, which Ben was pretty sure he wouldn't have had the balls to do.

Ben:

ok

When he got outside, Atticus was leaning against the wall of the building, smoking. He straightened up when he saw Ben and gave him a less bone-crushing handshake than last time.

"I want to apologize," Atticus said, looking, Ben realized, exhausted but clear-eyed. "I know I've been a dick."

Ben remembered the coaching Ava had given him about accepting apologies: Don't say it's okay unless it is. "I appreciate that," he said instead.

"I know you were just trying to do what's best for my dad. I've been pretty fucked-up since he died."

Ben cocked his head. "Fine," Atticus continued. "I was pretty fucked-up before that. But it didn't help."

"I'm sure," Ben said. "I know it must be rough."

"Rose sat me down last night. She promises my dad wasn't trying to screw me over or control me. Well, he *was* trying to control me. But she did promise me he really had my best interests in mind."

Ben examined Atticus for a hint that he was still manipulating, but if he was reading it right, Atticus was serious. "What made you listen this time?" he asked, thinking of the wink.

"Look." Atticus took a deep drag. "I know the Lion wasn't perfect. But he was a hero to me, you know? Everyone wanted something from him. And when he turned his focus on you, there was nothing like it." Ben remembered the Lion's heavy hand on his shoulder. He understood. "I guess I thought that maybe, because I was his son, he would *have* to give me something. I've been in therapy—shout-out to Dr. Cornell: that poor bastard has been analyzing me since I was eight—so I know what I wanted was attention, validation, something to prove that I mattered a little more to him than everyone else." Ben thought with a pang of what *he* had wanted from the Lion: attention, validation . . . something to prove that Ben mattered a little more than all the other fans who were no doubt clamoring for his time. Atticus continued: "I guess Rose finally got it through to me that he wanted me to go to rehab because he cared. And she was pretty adamant that

Sun Running was not a great look for the Adams brand. Not in this climate, if you know what I mean."

"I *do* know what you mean," Ben answered. They stood for a minute in companionable silence.

Atticus dropped his cigarette butt and immediately lit another one. "I'm in training for rehab. Saying my amends. And I hear they take it all away but the smokes."

"You're going to go? That's good." Ben knew that Atticus would have ended up at rehab, since his inheritance depended on it, but it seemed as though he might even show up sober. "When are you leaving?"

"Figured I'd head out tonight. An old friend is going to drive me to the airport to keep me honest."

It was hard to know what to say. *I'm proud of you? You're doing the right thing? Good luck?* Ben went with "I'm glad to hear it."

"You coming to Southampton?" Atticus asked.

"Rose invited me," Ben answered, catching sight of Howie out of the corner of his eye. Howie gave him an enthusiastic thumbs-up, vape pen protruding from the side of his mouth. It was a regular smoking section out here. "I'm catching the Jitney at three."

"Like hell you are." Atticus perked up. "You can come with me."

Ben wasn't sure he could bear more than five minutes in a car with Atticus's Ibiza playlist. "I'm good."

"Benjamin. Don't be a fool. Meet me at the Blade Lounge on West Thirtieth at five forty-five p.m. We'll be at the party by seven."

Ben wasn't sure if Blade was a helicopter, a jet, or a seaplane. He spared a quick thought for his carbon footprint and did the calculations. Atticus would be flying anyway. "If you're sure?"

"My man . . ." Atticus stepped on another cigarette, slapped Ben on the shoulder, and started toward the black car waiting at the curb. "See you there."

CHAPTER SIXTEEN

THURSDAY
WORK/"WORK," BEN

The helicopter to the Hamptons was a tooth-rattling ride that not even noise-canceling headphones improved. Ben's stomach had dipped with the copter as it rumbled above the gleaming expanse of Atlantic Ocean and the dense hedgerows and mansions lining the beaches below. At least it was only forty-five minutes. There was an overflow of traffic, security, and beautiful people outside the giant shingled estate that Atticus called "Oceaan House with two *a*'s like the Dutch" so that Ben wouldn't think it was a typo in the name chiseled into a high stone wall. Like one of the British royals, Atticus had their driver from the heliport sneak down a guarded private road around the side of Oceaan House, where they disembarked amid a caravan of catering, band, and florist vans. They made their way in through the back, dodging a stream of staff being directed by a slim, calm man in a headset.

"The party is out back on the porches, lawn, and pool deck." Atticus snatched a martini from one of the silver trays. "Chill," he said when he got a look at Ben's face. "It's for you."

Ben took the drink so that Atticus wouldn't be tempted. The last thing either of them needed was to get drunk. He wanted to see

Rebecca, so best he be sober. He put the martini back on another tray. Atticus kept leading Ben through a maze of hallways until they burst into a tremendous room with double-height ceilings and a wall of windows looking out onto the expanse of grounds below and the ocean beyond. The room was empty of people, but Ben could see a crowd milling outside around the dark blue pool and spilling over a series of decks and boardwalks that led to the beach. "If it gets too much for you, I give you permission to take refuge inside," Atticus said over his shoulder. "This place is crawling with every type of literary sycophant. The Lion would have loved it."

Ben moved next to Atticus by the massive windows. The sun was setting and everything was tinged with gold. "My mom read a scientific study once that claimed just looking at water for a few minutes a day calms you down, lowers your heart rate."

"Are you saying that between the East River and here, I should never have turned to stimulants? Or are you saying that obviously I would have turned to stimulants?"

"My mom bought us a fish tank," Ben said.

"I'll be looking at the Pacific Ocean this time tomorrow." Atticus pulled out a cigarette and tapped it against his wrist.

"Rose will fucking kill you if you smoke in here," a voice came from behind them. "I see you've come as Sinatra."

Atticus smiled in a way that made Ben wonder if he had ever seen him smile before. "Wilson! I see you've come as Sonny without Cher."

Ben turned to see a woman in baggy jeans and a bowling shirt. "Ben, this is Billie Wilson, townie. The shirt is not ironic."

"Nice to meet you, Ben. Adams, have you packed?" Ben deduced that this was the old friend making sure that Atticus got on the plane to rehab. He said hello. Billie marched up and grabbed Atticus's face, roughly turning it from side to side. "Look at you, getting a head start on sober. I love to see it."

Atticus shrugged her off. "Billie is immune to my charms," he told Ben.

"That's right," she agreed. "I know all his unsexy secrets."

"Also, you're gay," Atticus reminded her.

"That's *not* why I'm immune to your dubious charms," Billie corrected him. "For instance, I can see that your young friend Ben here is one good-looking man. While you're still giving douchebag vibes. C'mon, let's get you packed while I chaperone your ass. You don't want to miss all the suck-ups out there. I think I saw Charles Dickens."

"If it's not Stephen King, Billie doesn't give a fuck," Atticus said admiringly. "Well, gotta go smoke this ciggie out my bedroom window like the old days. See you for the speeches. I hear DeLillo is going to make nice."

When Atticus and Billie were gone, Ben scanned the crowd, looking for Rebecca. There was a black-and-white French New Wave film projected on the side of one of the outbuildings. Ben identified it as *Jules and Jim* thanks to repeated exposure while Ava was taking what she insisted on referring to as "cinema" classes. He could hear music muffled by the thick glass: he thought it was a Beatles song. There were long tables piled with food (he hadn't eaten since Mrs. Singh's vegan muffin) and flowers. There were *East River Review* covers strung in a colorful mass above everyone's heads. There was no sign of Rebecca Blume.

"Hello, Ben." Rose had slipped next to him. "I'm so glad you came."

It occurred to Ben that he was once again in one of Rose's private rooms without an invitation from her. "Atticus was right here . . ." he began. Jane appeared on the other side of him.

"I love how so many of the young people dressed in costume," Rose continued. "Deflates some of the pomposity, don't you think?"

In his jacket pocket Ben fingered the round glasses that Howie had pressed on him. Since Howie had missed a meeting in order to procure them, Ben had agreed he would at least consider it. He pulled them out and put them on. "John Lennon," he announced. A feeble gesture, but momentous for him. He was rewarded with a smile from Rose.

"Look at all the old men who broke out their seersucker suits for the Memorial Day weekend," Jane said, clearly less impressed with Ben's effort. "That one's smoking a pipe."

"Ah, Maury Kantor. I can't believe he made it."

"I can't believe he's still alive!" Jane laughed.

Ben was very aware of Jane as Rebecca's mother. Did she know where Rebecca was or even if she was there at all?

"We've made so much progress," Rose announced. "Even since this morning. Talking and writing!" She leaned forward and smiled at Jane. "Even more than we've sent to you."

"That's great," Ben said. "I know Trixie Carter is excited to meet with you both. You'll be in great hands with her."

"We can't thank you enough." Rose patted Ben on the arm. "It's been a tonic."

"And a few gin and tonics," Jane added. They both laughed.

"It would be wonderful to have you as the official editor," Rose said generously. "Though I agree that we should go the more conventional route and work with an agent first. But we certainly won't forget your enthusiasm."

"I would love that. Whatever agent you decide to go with, Trixie or someone else, I'm planning to push hard at Hawk Mills so we end up with it. Once it's finished, of course. No pressure."

"Trixie comes highly recommended from more than one source," Jane said. "My daughter, Rebecca—you met her at the town house—is a close friend of hers."

Ben felt his face redden. He gazed fixedly out the window at the last blaze of sunset on the water. He couldn't even hear her name without consequences.

"Well, I suppose I should mingle," Rose sighed. "There's a whole run of show I've been given by the *East River Review* staff and a lovely young man who's the party planner."

"He reminds me a little of . . ." Jane trailed off. Ben heard something break in her voice. He looked at her closely, but she had turned away.

"We had a friend," Rose told Ben. "Many years ago. He died when he was far too young."

"Oh, I'm so sorry."

"It was long ago," Rose said. "It still hurts, of course. But time makes it bearable. Now we have all this. And I have my instructions!"

"Have you thought more about what you want to say?" Jane asked. "I mean, if you decide to speak at all. Which, of course, you know you don't have to, no matter what that pretentious ass in the hat says."

"Tom O'Flanagan," Rose explained to Ben. "*East River Review*'s editor."

Ben nodded. He didn't announce that he agreed with Jane's assessment, but he thought it. "Pretentious ass in the hat" was something Rebecca might say. Which made sense, he guessed. He stole a sideways glance at Jane, who suddenly looked up at him with probing eyes. Did she know he was thinking about her daughter all the time, even at this very second? He knew she couldn't read his mind, but maybe Rebecca had told her something. What would she have said? She was hardly even returning his texts.

"I have some thoughts," Rose was saying. "We'll see."

"Ben, you're a millennial," Jane said. "What do you think about YouTube and TikTok?"

"Actually, I'm Gen Z."

"Even better. Do you think people can really make a career out of using social media?"

"Well, sure," Ben said. "Some people make a lot of money with branding and sponsorships. And they can have millions of followers. I know it's huge for book sales."

"Hmmmm." Jane turned back to gaze out the window again. "And I suppose there are people whose jobs are managing and handling all of these digital celebrities?"

"I don't know that much about it, but I would think so."

"What a world." Jane shook her head. "All right, Rose, into the Lion's den we go." She took Rose's arm. "We'll see you out there."

"Be sure to get something to eat," Rose added. "And if you want to spend the night, we certainly have enough room." Did Ben look hungry again? He *was* hungry again.

"You can stay in your own wing," Jane promised. "I do."

"It will be nice for Atticus to have you here to see him off." Rose and Jane headed to the French doors that led outside, Rose smiling at the security guard. Ben watched as they descended the wide gray steps flanked by hundreds of candles, their heads bent toward each other. It was getting more crowded, and Ben was determined to find Rebecca and get something to eat. He followed the path Rose and Jane had taken into the still-warm evening air.

After eating numerous deviled eggs and a mound of Swedish meatballs and washing it all down with a Sazerac cocktail, Ben finally caught sight of Rebecca. She was glowing in a white crochet minidress, carrying a wicker basket, and arguing with a handsome man in a white tuxedo with a red rose in the lapel. She was shaking what appeared to be a limp brown cat at the man. Theirs was clearly an intimate relationship. Ben's heart sank. So it wasn't just the fact that she was annoyed about his getting involved with the book idea for Jane and Rose. There was someone else. Fuck. Ben put his plate on a table, where it was immediately whisked away. He would walk down to the beach. The band launched into an instrumental version of Dylan's "Like a Rolling Stone." *How does it feel?* Ben thought. *It feels like shit.*

He would have to walk past Rebecca on his way to the beach, but he could take it. Before he set out, he pocketed the round glasses.

As he got close enough to discern that it wasn't a brown cat at all, Rebecca suddenly saw him, turned bright red, and stuffed what was apparently a wig into her wicker basket. All of Ben's plans about casually strolling by evaporated in the scorching heat that shimmered between them. She had to feel it too, right? He came to a halt. Every time he saw her—and, by his count, this was the fifth—she was more startlingly vivid than he remembered.

"Ben Heath!" the handsome man exclaimed. There was a small silver pistol that Ben assumed was a prop in the pocket of his tux. What did it mean that he knew who Ben was? Would Ben have to fight him? Was the gun really a prop? The man offered his hand to Ben, a good sign. "Name's Bond. James Bond." Ben shook. "*Goldfinger* era. Nineteen sixty-four."

"This is my friend Gabe." Rebecca was flustered. "He runs marketing at Avenue." Gabe was wearing a wide silver ring that could be a wedding ring. Jesus, was Ben now a person who noticed if people were wearing wedding rings? Gabe was clearly a stylish guy. Maybe he was just wearing a cool piece of jewelry. If he was *with* Rebecca, why would she introduce him as her friend? Why would she have launched herself at him at the bar? They were obviously just friends. He stared at Rebecca. He couldn't help it. She raised her eyes to his, and his breath caught.

"Well," Gabe remarked, after an awkward minute, "I'm going to find Tor and have a word with him about this very aggressive harmonica solo. It was a pleasure to meet you, Ben Heath."

"It was. I mean, nice to meet you too." Ben dragged his gaze from Rebecca.

"We'll talk later, kitten." Gabe plucked a martini, fittingly, from a passing silver tray and left.

"Kitten?"

"Walk with me." Rebecca turned sharply on her low-heeled boots and began weaving through the crowd without looking back. Was there any chance he wouldn't do exactly as she wished? He followed her away from everyone to a small hut with a bench facing the beach. She ducked inside, and they were hidden from the party. "Sit, please," she ordered him.

"Seriously?" He wasn't Butch, for fuck's sake.

"I did say 'please'!" Rebecca argued. Then she added more softly, "It's just that you're so tall, okay?"

Ben sat. As Rebecca dropped the wicker basket on the bench, she suddenly grabbed the wig out of it. "Shit!" Next, she retrieved from a napkin two slightly crushed cupcakes with pineapple rings and cherries embedded like flowers in the icing.

"Why are there cupcakes in your . . . uh . . . bag?"

"Do you think they're ruined?" she asked anxiously.

"I volunteer to investigate. As long as the wig didn't shed."

Rebecca examined the cupcakes and handed one to him. "Clean." She took the other one and sat down. They both looked straight ahead at nothing but water, sand, and sky. Even though they weren't touching, he could feel the vibration between them as they ate in an electrified quiet. Rebecca tossed her cupcake wrapper in the basket and took a deep breath. "Look, I'm sorry I was a dick about your being involved in the memoir, okay?"

It wasn't every day that not one but two people apologized to Ben for being dicks. "I can see how it might have taken you by surprise," he offered. "And I probably should have mentioned it to you, since it's your mom and all."

"No." Rebecca kept looking forward. "Rose and Jane are excited and inspired. I came out here yesterday and they were showing me all his journals and some of their letters. Then, after I rage texted you this morning, I had a long talk with them. I guess I was a little hard on you. I know your input has been important to them. They really do want to have a 'conversation' with the Lion. And now that they have *Making the Sun Run* back, they can do it on their own terms."

"I thought they would have torched it."

"Maybe they'll have a bonfire ceremony eventually. But, for now, it's been kind of a touchstone, a way to tell their story in reaction to the Lion's bullshit version."

"And do we know if Atticus leaked any more of it? He says he didn't, but he might not remember."

"He probably did. I'm sure we'll be reading about it on BLURB. But nobody can publish it, and people have short attention spans. Avenue will be flooding the market with sanctioned reissues and focusing on getting ahead of the criticism; I mean, we have a lot of ideas about how to amplify women's voices, as you so self-righteously said." Ben sneaked a look at Rebecca's profile. She was half smiling.

"I think I said 'center.' But 'amplify' works."

"And while I'm groveling here, you had a point about both/and. I know the Lion wasn't *all* terrible. Or maybe he *was* terrible, but Rose and my mom fell for him. And I've read *The Coldest War*. I get why people might, I don't know, admire his writing. His earlier writing."

"People?" Ben could tell this speech was hard for Rebecca, but, much as he appreciated it, he couldn't help himself. "You mean, like, *totally unevolved* people?"

"Exactly." Rebecca elbowed Ben in the side. She was still facing straight ahead, but her tone was light. Honestly, he couldn't take it anymore. Maybe she had only kissed him at Betty Jack's because she was drunk. Maybe—and he had started to put this theory together while obsessively going over every detail of the night—she had only kissed him because he was reading Virginia Woolf. Either way, he had to know if she would be interested in kissing him again. He took a deep breath. "Also," Rebecca continued before he could speak, "I, uh, I find you really distracting."

"*Distracting*? In what way distracting?"

"As in I can't stop thinking about you. Or thinking about the other night." Rebecca sounded almost agitated, and he saw color rising on her neck and cheek.

Ben reached over and gently tilted her face toward him. Her green eyes and dark lashes were intense in the furious blush of her heart-shaped face. "I can't stop thinking about you either. If that helps."

"It helps," she whispered.

Ben leaned down and Rebecca met him halfway. When his mouth covered hers, his body surged toward her. Relief and urgency flooded him at the same time. He wanted to devour her, to stay up all night talking with her, to learn everything about her. But mostly, right now, he wanted no space between them. When her tongue slipped into his mouth, he gathered her closer still.

"Oh my goodness! I beg your pardon!" a tall woman with bright red lipstick and a matching turban exclaimed in a British accent. "I was just searching for somewhere quiet to rehearse, and here I've put my foot in it!" She disappeared from view, her voice trailing after her. "Carry on!"

"I think that was Zadie Smith," Ben said. His hands were still in Rebecca's hair, cupping her head.

"I *know* that was Zadie Smith."

For the first time, Ben noticed that the music had stopped and someone was speaking into a mic. "And that might be DeLillo?"

"I don't care if we miss DeLillo." Rebecca pressed her hand against Ben's chest, where he could feel his heart thudding under her palm. "But we can't miss Rose."

"We can't miss Rose," he agreed. He didn't move except to smooth her hair back from her face.

"No, we have to go back." Rebecca also didn't move but gripped his shirt.

"Okay, we're going back now." Ben dipped his head to kiss her again until they both lost their breath. When they broke apart, he could hear, over the sound of his heart and the surf, a woman's voice. A woman's amplified voice.

"Rose!" Rebecca jumped up and adjusted her minidress down over her thighs. A maraschino cherry rolled out from under her. "Fuckety fuck!" she exclaimed. "I knew I shouldn't have worn white!"

Ben got up, winced, and grabbed her wicker basket to hold strategically in front of him. "I'll just carry this thing for you, if that's all right."

Rebecca laughed. It was the first time he had heard her full-throated laugh. He followed her white dress in the darkening blue. Rose was behind a lectern on a platform near the pool, while above her, on the outbuilding, a series of photos was projected: photos of the Lion reading, looming at his desk, squiring women, accepting an award, riding a bike on the beach with young Atticus. The large crowd had gathered, murmuring, glasses and plates clanking, waiting for Rose to continue speaking. Ben and Rebecca stood near the edge, with her just in front of him. He could smell her hair. Limes and basil.

"And I know that many of you are wondering what our plans are for the *East River Review*. This is something Teddy and I discussed at length. I'll be selling the town house, but I assure you that the magazine, with a new, improved, less underground office, will be well provided for." Here people laughed in relief, and Rose continued. "I'm committed to continuing to support, in all ways, this very special endeavor founded by my husband sixty years ago." There was a round of enthusiastic applause. Ben could see O'Flanagan in his stupid hat clapping harder than anyone. "Teddy would have been delighted that everyone is here to celebrate the magazine. And, of course, to celebrate him. He did love to be the center of attention. And I so appreciate all of you coming and those speaking in his honor. We're planning a more formal memorial service at St. John the Divine in about six months. Many of you will be called upon to speak then as well, and I'm grateful to Maury Kantor and PK Publishing for all their hard work." Rose gave a little wave, and Ben picked Maury Kantor out of the crowd: seersucker suit, pipe, somehow still upright.

"There are many things to be said about Teddy . . ." Rose paused and sought out Jane, who Ben could see was standing in the front. It was good to be tall. "But I think the best way to remember him is to listen to his own words. I'd like to read an old story, one of my favorites. I know that Teddy loved it too." Rose shuffled a few papers on the lectern in front of her and put on a pair of reading glasses. Ben realized he was holding his breath. Rose paused, then began to read. As soon as he heard the first paragraph, Ben was transported back to that night at Bread Loaf, the expectant audience, the stars through the barn window. As he listened to Rose's calm, measured voice, he heard a ghost echo below its surface, the Lion's words as he had read them, building the meticulous and powerful world of the story. A man, a girl, a horse. He couldn't help it: he blinked back tears.

Without saying anything, somehow sensing the swell of emotion in him, Rebecca reached back and her hand found Ben's. She held it until Rose read the last word. She held it while the crowd was silent for a beat, then applauded wildly. She held it while Rose left the lectern and hugged Jane. She held it while Zadie Smith made a few jokes to lighten the mood and described the Lion's use of metaphor as an inspiration. She held it as they walked back into the house, passing a huge sheet cake decorated with the iconic blue door, nodding to the security guard, who let them pass. She held it even as they said goodbye to Atticus, who shook Ben's other hand firmly, complained about Billie's truck, and was led out by Billie. She held it as they made their way up yet another wide, curving staircase, then down a long hallway lined with photographs, bright paintings, and charcoal drawings. She held it when they arrived in the suite of rooms where she was clearly staying (half-unpacked bag, clothes tossed on chairs, an empty kombucha bottle, another pair of boots collapsed in the middle of the rug). There were wraparound windows facing the sea, which he could make out beyond the crowd while the band segued into Marvin Gaye.

"I thought you might want to have a seat," Rebecca said. Without unclasping his hand, she gestured at the long, low couch under the windows. Very low. Seriously, how many of these things did Rose own?

"We might never be able to get up again," he pointed out.

"That works for me." Rebecca smiled up at him, and he drew her in. Everywhere that he was hard, she was soft. Their mouths found each other again as they stumbled toward the couch. It was a long way down, but she landed on top and inhaled sharply as Ben moved her roughly against him.

"Is it too much?" he asked hoarsely.

"No!" Rebecca breathed into his mouth. She tasted like pineapple. "More." She ran her hands up inside his shirt, her nails scraping his chest. He shivered.

"Is it too much?" she asked, straddling him, her white dress up around her hips.

"No." Ben felt too big for his body, as if he might burst through his skin into a thousand fragments. "More." Rebecca pulled her dress over her head, getting stuck for a minute, cursing and laughing as Ben tried to help, more of an abs exercise than he had anticipated. He shed his shirt gracefully in comparison, but it took them a while to yank off his pants, especially since Rebecca kept kissing every new part revealed. Finally, they were both naked. Her skin was luminous in the dark room. Ben had never felt this way before: delirious yet grounded, desperate for her yet able to slow down time. "You are so beautiful," he murmured as he slid his hand between her legs, and she was warm and wet, her breath coming in quick gasps that stirred him until he thought he might lose his mind. "We don't have to . . ." he started to say as she arched above him.

"We do! We do have to!" Rebecca exclaimed.

"I haven't done this in a long time," he admitted. "And never like this."

"What do you mean? Girl on top?"

"No! I mean . . ." Ben hesitated, but there was nothing he could hide from her. "Feeling like this. About you."

"Feeling like what?" Rebecca guided him into her and they both stopped moving in the shock of how good it was, how right.

"Crazy. Crazy about you. Your perfect mouth. Your stupid Post-its. Your annoying cactus. Your gorgeous skin. Your beautiful heart. I know you have one."

Rebecca leaned forward, moving slowly, her hair tickling his chest. "*Your* annoying cactus," she whispered. "*Your* stupid Post-its. *Your* beautiful heart. Ben."

There was a sudden explosion of bangs from outside and the windows lit up beside Rebecca, outlining her body in blue. The sound reverberated as a stream of silver sparks filled the sky. Their eyes locked and it was too much. It was everything. She was laughing. It was fireworks. Literally.

JANE

NEW YORK
2022

Jane *had* seen Rose, once, a few years after she left New York City. Her mother had given Ellen the phone number of Jane and Sam's rented house in West Philadelphia. Jane was working in the publications department at UPenn, where she had met Sam, in his first year as a history professor. Ellen had called to tell her about Drew. After Jane hung up the phone, she hardly knew what to do with herself. Pacing the kitchen, she needed to get outside, to walk. So much of what she had tried to forget but had not forgotten came spilling over the barriers she had erected. She had read about the wedding in *The New York Times*. (Reading it daily was a habit she had kept up since moving home; this was, of course, before the twins.) The black-and-white photograph of Rose and Teddy made them seem like impossibly beautiful strangers from another era. Jane processed the details about the custom Carolina Herrera dress, an intimate reception at Maxwell's Plum. She had steeled herself against the loss, and only when the paper trembled did she realize her hand was shaking.

When she was very young, she found a cat in the small park a few blocks from her house and carried it, unresisting, home. After feeding it scraps against her mother's wishes, Jane was distraught when it disappeared. Her father had told her that sick animals sometimes ran off so that they could die alone. Leaving New York, leaving the *East River Review*—leaving Drew and Rose—Jane finally understood that cat's instinct not to expose its hidden, fatal wounds. When she remembered her last month in New York City, Jane saw herself as that feral cat. Even when staying might have provided a cure, her urge to flee had been too powerful.

She hadn't been back to the city, but Jane couldn't bear to miss what Ellen had called a "celebration of life" for Drew. Apparently, there had been a service at his parents' Korean church in Queens, but this was for his friends. In her head, Jane replayed the phone calls she had had with Drew since she'd returned to Philadelphia. At first, he called as a sort of intermediary for Rose. He phoned next to tell her that Paco's boyfriend Jermaine had died, that another Cisneros story had been published, that Rose and Teddy had gone to Lake Como. In the last phone call, over a year earlier, Drew mentioned that he still expected her to come back—that, like him (he had been made an assistant art editor), she could officially join the *East River Review* masthead. But he had been preoccupied as well: other men he knew were sick; he had met Jasper Johns; Deedle's long-suffering wife, Marion, had left him for a woman. Drew had stopped asking if Jane wanted him to give a message to Rose.

The memorial was at a stone church in the West Village, one with a walled garden accessible to the street. It was drizzling. Jane couldn't bring herself to go inside. She had wanted to arrive early or late; either way, she planned to see Rose before Rose saw her. Her heart was skipping as if she were meeting a lover or having a heart attack; she remembered pressing her hand uselessly against her chest to calm it. Finally, she perched on one end of a bench under a broad tree where she could watch people arriving, a small black umbrella angled to hide her face. There was a steady stream of attendants ranging from men dressed in sparkly hats and high heels to Parker and Jonathan, hunched in overcoats. Was there a chance Rose wouldn't come? Had Jane missed her in the crowd? Was she inside already? Jane remembered thinking she could just slip in next to Rose as if the years had collapsed, as if the rented house in Philadelphia and gentle Sam were the dream and she was waking in the cool mist of her New York City life.

A church official had waited for stragglers, then closed the heavy doors. Not long after, as Jane tried to will herself to move, a black car pulled up outside the iron gates to discharge Rose and Teddy. Jane shrank back but they never looked her way. In all her imaginary reunions with Rose, Jane had somehow forgotten to factor in Teddy. But there he was, more imposing than ever, his handsome face serious as a statue. Rose looked (Jane remembered the word that stuck in her head) like an adult. She was wearing a long black belted coat and shiny boots. It was as if Rose had become even more glamorous, had matured into her role as the wife of a famous man, while Jane had somehow remained as she was that first day at the *East River Review*, awkward but eager to open herself up to these amazing new friends. Had she believed that Rose and Drew would stay the same? Drew was gone. Rose was moving far ahead. Jane caught only a glimpse as Rose sagged against Teddy and he gathered her under his arm, murmuring over her bent head. They moved together like one graceful dark animal toward the doors that opened as if someone had been waiting for their arrival.

Jane knew she would leave before Rose came out. She stared miserably at the church's stone facade. Rose and Teddy, as Drew had said, made sense. Once again, Jane could see no way back into the world she had so abruptly abandoned—one that, she realized while sitting in that garden, she missed with an overwhelming ache. One that was already irrevocably changed. She unclenched her hands and examined the crescents cut into her palms. Without her noticing, a small woman had slipped onto the other end of the bench. She was wearing a clear plastic rain bonnet tied over her hair, and she sat straight backed, her feet hardly touching the ground. Because of that, she seemed childlike, but Jane sneaked a glance and saw that she was older and that she had Drew's sharp cheekbones. All of Jane's agonizing about Rose evaporated in her certainty that this woman was Drew's mother.

"I'm sorry," Jane said, but the woman kept gazing ahead, as Jane had done before, training her eyes on the church. Had she not heard? Did she not understand? Jane dug in her bag and retrieved a handful of Polaroids. The faded images were a little distorted. What had she been thinking when she brought them from Philadelphia? That she and Rose would look at them together; that they would prove that Jane had some claim on Drew even though she had left him? Jane continued, "I was his friend." She placed the photos on the bench next to the woman, who didn't glance down at them but pulled a bedraggled tissue out of her raincoat pocket and held it delicately to her nose. The drizzle had become a soft rain. "Please take my umbrella." Jane held it out, but the woman made no move toward it. After a few minutes, Jane propped the opened umbrella carefully over the photos. In one of them Drew was striking a pose while Jane was moving toward the camera, her mouth open, talking or laughing. The church bells began to ring. Jane stood up. "I'm sorry," she said again, helplessly. She didn't remember anything else: how she got to the station, the train back to Philadelphia, what she told Sam, nothing. But she remembered the plangent bells and the woman waiting silently in the rain as if any minute the church doors would open to reveal her son, his mischievous arched eyebrows and his perfect swoop of hair.

"Mom!" Rebecca's voice startled Jane out of her memory. She was sitting on a love seat in the sun porch overlooking the ocean. There was almost no evidence of last night's party: an army of people had already broken down tables, folded up chairs, and spirited away the leftovers. Jane had stayed up late talking to Rose, but even though she had a large bed to herself, she had not been able to fall back asleep when she woke at 6 a.m.

"Good morning, sweetheart." Jane took in her daughter's wild hair, sweatpants, and oversize gray T-shirt. "You're up early." She patted the space beside her. "Come sit for a minute."

"Don't worry, I'm going back to bed," Rebecca claimed. "I'm just looking for something to eat first." She flopped onto the love seat, her legs curled up next to Jane. "Are you crying? Are you okay?"

Jane held one of Rebecca's bare feet. It was chilled, and her toenails were painted an iridescent blue. "I am crying," she answered. "But I'm okay." She cupped her fingers to warm her daughter's foot.

"It must be hard to be in his house," Rebecca asserted. She wiggled her other foot under Jane's hip. "You're really brave."

Jane, surprised, scanned the light-filled room, the tasteful neutral linens and soft cashmeres, the art books on wicker tables, the masses of blue hydrangeas. She saw nothing but Rose. "It's not hard to be here," she promised. "It's beautiful here. Rose has made it beautiful."

"True," Rebecca agreed. "Honestly, though, with this view, you'd have to try really hard to screw it up. But that's not what I meant."

Jane squeezed Rebecca's foot. "I know what you meant."

"You have a lot to process, Mom," her daughter announced. "It's all right to be upset. Or angry. *I* would be angry. I *am* angry for you!"

Jane had read Teddy's book with a mixture of shock and revulsion. She had laughed out loud in disbelief, had cringed with embarrassment for herself, for him. There were times that he had managed brilliant sentences, whole paragraphs that sang. But in his arrogant assurance that he could speak for her, he had only succeeded in creating a distant reshaping that she hardly recognized. Had she felt anger? Not quite. It was more, Jane thought, a desire to counter his narrative with her own, to find her own best words. Jane saw that Teddy's version, even steeped as it was in delusion and self-aggrandizement, had also recognized her power as a writer. He had tried to take something from her; he had tried to give something back. "It *is* a lot to process" was all she said to Rebecca. Her beautiful daughter prodded her with chilly feet, so self-assured and bossy, so confident that she understood everything.

"I think it's amazing that you and Rose are writing together." Rebecca yawned. "It's going to be so good."

"And you're sure you don't want to be the editor?" Jane couldn't help herself.

"Mom! We already talked about this. That's not how it works, anyway. Haven't you heard of the professional code of ethics?"

Jane very much doubted that Rebecca had spent any time perusing a professional code of ethics, but it was probably true that having her daughter edit this book—if indeed it turned into a book—was not a good idea. And she did trust Ben Heath, who so far had guided her and Rose with a reassuring mix of enthusiasm and professionalism. That first day back in the town house, after she had read *Making the Sun Run*, she and Rose had decided to write their own version; later when Ben came to them with the same idea, they took it as an auspicious sign. "Well, the whole project has been exciting so far, no matter what happens. And you *are* a talented editor."

"You keep saying that! I know you think it's a bad idea that I try something new." Rebecca, agitated, pulled her feet out from under Jane.

Rebecca *was* a talented editor. Saying it didn't mean that Jane was harping on her baffling notion that she might leave Avenue Publishing just as she was finding real success. In their phone calls since

Jane had arrived in Southampton, they had been making progress toward what Rebecca had wanted: that they talk like adults. Jane told Rebecca more about what had happened with Teddy, with Rose. She had talked haltingly, then more easily, about the novel she was working on. Rebecca had confided that she was thinking of leaving her job at Avenue. Jane was trying hard not to react negatively to what sounded, frankly, like a dubious and difficult new venture. She did understand why Rebecca wasn't thrilled about handling Teddy's estate. She wanted to be supportive. Rebecca was young enough to take risks, old enough to make her own decisions. Jane also believed in Stella, could see how the two of them brought out the best in each other, fiercely prioritized their friendship, had always balanced each other.

Looking backward was dangerous for Jane, even as she and Rose pored over the journals and read each other's letters, as they compared notes on their own memories. She tried not to dwell on what leaving had cost her; Teddy loomed so large that she couldn't imagine how she and Rose could have ever made their way out from under him even if she had stayed. Still, to have had a friend like Rose . . . Jane gave her head a single sharp shake. Not everyone got a second chance. She would seize it.

"Are you mad that I'm thinking about leaving Avenue? I know you don't understand social media, but, trust me, I'm good at it."

Jane smiled. "I know you are. *I'm* the one who doesn't get it! And I do trust that you're passionate about this, and I believe that you and Stella are a great team." And if the whole thing turned out to be a disaster, Jane would be there for Rebecca, would try not to give a whiff of *I told you so*. "I'm sure you've saved a lot of money by living with Mimi."

"Are you saying I should move out?" Rebecca sprang up from the love seat. My lord, she was hotheaded sometimes.

"Rebecca," Jane said, keeping her tone calm. "You'll be fine. One big decision at a time. Focus on this new venture, then you can worry about finding your own place or anything else that comes along. You don't need any distractions."

"Okay, but just so you know . . ." Rebecca was suddenly blushing furiously. "Um. So. Ben stayed here last night."

"Ben Heath?" Jane peered closely at her daughter. Obviously, Ben Heath. Ah. The gray T-shirt hanging to her knees. Her tangled hair.

"Do you think Rose will be mad?" Rebecca asked anxiously. "I mean, was it rude?" She pressed the back of her hand to cool her red cheek in a gesture that Jane recognized as one of her own.

"I recall he was invited, so no. And this house is certainly big enough for privacy, if that's what you're worried about."

"Ugh! Mom!" Rebecca put both her hands over her face, but she couldn't hide her joy. Oh, she was so young! Jane stood up and gave her daughter a quick hug.

"I'm happy for you," she said.

Rebecca, her face still aflame, hugged Jane back, then moved away. "Do you think it's all right if I try to find us something to eat?"

"Of course! I know they packed away so much food from last night. And Rose has plenty of breakfast things. Help yourself." Jane couldn't resist adding, "I'm sure you need your strength."

"Mom!" Rebecca fled, but not before Jane could enjoy the mix of chagrin and happiness in her expression.

She picked up her phone from the side table to call Sam, moving to look out the windows at the ocean, still tinted pink from sunrise. "Good morning, my love," he answered. There were clicks and whirs in the background, and she knew he was navigating the espresso machine, the only technology he had mastered in their many years together. "How is it in *Great Gatsby* country?"

"So beautiful," she answered, watching as birds skittered across the sand, darting in and out of the waves. One of the *East River Review* covers came loose from where it was strung and blew into the pool.

"Are you happy to be there?"

"Yes. Very happy." Jane understood that Sam didn't require a rundown. He needed to know that she was fine but had no interest in a detailed description of the party. "I think Rebecca has met someone special."

"Has she?" Sam scraped a spoon against what she knew was a yogurt container.

"Yes. The young editor I told you about. Ben Heath?"

"Mmmmmm . . ." Sam, she imagined, was nodding his head, almost certainly having no clear recollection of her telling him about Ben Heath.

"Did we get the bill from the landscaping company yet?"

"I believe so."

"Just put it in the basket, all right? I need to call them about the azaleas."

"When will you be home?" Sam asked, then his attention shifted to Fergus. "Who's a good old boy?" he murmured kindly.

"You are, my love," Jane replied. "I think next week."

"Ethan and Emma are picking me up for the barbecue at Andrew and Gabrielle's on Monday. Early, so I'll get some time with the boys."

"Lucky you!" Jane said. "Don't forget to bring that little red shirt they left. It's clean and folded on the dryer." She knew that it would still be there when she got home.

"We'll miss you," Sam said, a little wistfully. It was as much as he would offer over the phone about this new development in their lives, this rush of memories and revelations, the trips to New York, Jane's tears and joy.

"Give my love to everyone, of course." Jane imagined that Sam too was gazing out a window, the one over the kitchen sink, its sill crowded with plants, little glass vases, a jar of shells. He would see, if he noticed, the pink blooms of the plum tree they had planted when Rebecca was born.

"I'll see you next week," Sam said. He was ready to start the day now, to head out for a long walk with Fergus.

"Talk to you tonight." Jane resisted reminding him to wear a sweater. She ended the call and watched another *East River Review* cover become unfastened in the wind and whirl across the lawn. She should go out to gather them up before the string broke.

"Here you are." Rose's voice lilted behind her, and Jane turned to see her friend crossing the room with a tray that held two cups and a silver pot of coffee.

"Here I am." Jane smiled and moved toward Rose. They had all day ahead of them. There was so much to say.

EPILOGUE

SUNDAY
HOME, REBECCA AND BEN
EIGHTEEN MONTHS LATER

The New York Times

NONFICTION · A ROAR OF ONE'S OWN

By Cadbury Andrews
Nov. 26, 2023

"Inside the Lion's Cage" by Rose Bergesen Adams and Jane Kinloch Blume

When someone as monumental as Edward David Adams dies, the world braces itself for the inevitable onslaught of posthumous work—the unpublished diaries, self-serving correspondence with notable intellectuals of the day, perhaps a wisely abandoned first attempt at fiction, or the last musings of a mind not only in decline but dangerously out of step with contemporary life. Which is why seeing how Rose Bergesen Adams, Edward David Adams's widow, has managed his estate and, consequently, his legacy, has been astounding. Under her direction, Avenue Publishing has reissued four of Adams's novels so far, with another four scheduled over the next two years. Cover designs featuring vivid paintings from some of the most prominent mid-century women artists seem designed to widen Adams's mostly male fan base, but the truly revolutionary act is that each novel is introduced by a notable female critic. Far from the usual fare, these introductions don't function as a hagiography but rather actively interrogate Adams's work.

Reckoning with a writer who has become synonymous with postwar male malaise in a world thankfully now more interested in the power dynamics that allowed such narcissism to be possible, it would be easy to dismiss Adams. But these introductions manage the near impossible—to celebrate the beauty of Adams's sentences, and his almost unrivaled ability to plumb the pathos of the American male, while at the same time taking him to task for his casual misogyny and arrogant assumptions about institutional power. Never has such a major writer been so thoroughly contextualized, his undeniable genius balanced so carefully with his blind spots. The recent #liontalk and LionTok phenomenon on social media feature mostly young women reading profound passages from Adams's fiction and crying in recognition but also laughing at the clumsy, dated lines that mar other sections of his work. The trend has not only launched all four of these reissues onto the best-seller list, but also, since each introduction takes pains to measure his work against less commercially successful but no less important women writers working contemporaneously, the sales of Vivian Gornick, Paula Fox, and Doris Lessing have seen a welcome boost.

But by far the most exciting literary event surrounding Adams's legacy is the publication of "Inside the Lion's Cage" (Hawk Mills), the joint memoir by Rose Bergesen Adams and Jane Kinloch Blume, who met as young women reading the slush pile at Adams's famed East River Review. Fast friends, and giddy with being at the center of such an intoxicating literary scene, the women eventually take divergent tracks. Rose becomes Adams's third wife, and Jane returns to her home in Philadelphia, channeling her ambitions into raising a family. I won't reveal here the incident that set them on their respective paths and paused their friendship for four decades, but it has all the power and dramatic flair of a Douglas Sirk movie, even more stunning for being true.

"Inside the Lion's Cage" is told in alternating chapters. We see Rose, caught up in the cyclone of Adams's fame, her own writing and publishing career pushed to the side so she can play hostess, wife, and, eventually, nurse to the difficult man she married. As for Jane, her traumatic exit from New York reverberates for years in her quiet suburban life, her accomplishments as a wife and mother at times overshadowed by the unrealized promise of her literary talent. Ingeniously woven throughout are journal entries, the women's letters, and snippets of prose from Rose and Jane, making "Inside the Lion's Cage" a brilliant tapestry of thwarted ambition, a moving portrait of friendship interrupted, and an unparalleled examination of the sacrifices women of a certain era felt compelled to make for the men in their lives. Sensitively and masterfully edited, this book draws the cage around Adams a little tighter. We can still admire his majestic beauty, but the danger and the neediness and roaring self-regard are kept at a necessary distance.

What transpired to keep these two women silent for so long is a familiar, unacceptable devastation. But it is thrilling to learn that Jane Kinloch Blume's first novel will be published next year by Hawk Mills. Her editor? Rose Bergesen Adams, who is now, at the age of 66, an editor at large for the venerable publishing house. Forty years in the making and not a moment too soon.

Entertainment WEEKLY

EW.COM

TV

The Lady and the Brain makes a dazzling leap from page to screen: Lady Paulette extends her reign and confirms a six-episode Season Two

By Christopher James | Published on August 1, 2023 3:01AM EST

Lady Paulette was "over the moon" during the filming of *The Lady and the Brain*, Netflix's popular drama series adapted from the posh Iowa native's memoir of her long liaison with noted British philosopher Chester Wineskin.

"It takes three actresses to play me," Lady Paulette told EW. "And I was and will be a trusted adviser to each one." Lady Paulette described the experience of watching her life unfold on the screen as "truly smashing," adding that she had to "mop up tears" as Henrietta Constable, fresh from her acclaimed performance as Diana in *The Royal Wives*, embodied the young American when she first ensnares the older, more conventionally brilliant Wineskin (played with bumbling charm by Benedict Cumberbatch). "I did so fret that the portrayal would be rubbish," Lady Paulette confided. "But Henrietta was quite attentive to my many suggestions and notes." Constable, who has been nominated for an Emmy for her portrayal of the Lady, recalled how grateful she was for Lady Paulette's tutelage, previously telling EW that she would be "gutted" to pass the role on to Charlize Theron, who will take up the mantle in Season Two, streaming next year on Netflix.

National Public Radio Online Edition

NPR.org

Author Interviews

FRESH AIR from NPR

Alice Gottlieb's Marvelous Transformation

March 28, 2023 · 11:30 AM

Heard on *Fresh Air*

By Galvin Tucker

Her new book, *Elemental Eros: Book One of the Calista Chronicles* (Avenue), has catapulted Alice Gottlieb to a stratosphere of fame and fortune previously unimaginable for this National Book Critics Circle Award winner, whose trilogy following four generations of New England women garnered critical acclaim and a small but loyal book club fan base. Currently holding strong at number one on *The New York Times* Combined Print & E-Book Fiction Best Sellers List and winner of the 2023 Goodreads Choice Awards for Best Fantasy and Best Science Fiction, *Elemental Eros* introduces alien heroine Calista Abellona, who must balance her intergalactic duties as Flame Princess with her passionate, illicit love for her royal father's sworn enemy's son, Tanim, the cyborg merman. Gottlieb is working on Book Two of the Calista Chronicles quartet. She is also a regular contributor to *The Kirkus Romance Reviews* and a spokesperson for Caffeine and Green, a lifestyle program that was recently acquired by GOOP.

Listen: 44 minutes

bon appétit

— CULTURE —

Stella Marino-Miller, the enormously popular social media star, is cooking up a new way to connect with fans

An exclusive interview and first look at the culinary influencer's forthcoming plans

BY ISADORA PLUMKEY
November 26, 2023

The explosive growth of cooking content creators on TikTok and Instagram shows no sign of slowing down, and nowhere is that more apparent than in the multipronged success of Stella Marino-Miller. We caught up with the talented Marino-Miller just after the launch of her latest venture on YouTube. This interview has been edited and condensed.

BA: What a year you've had! Did you ever imagine you'd already have over half a million subscribers for your new YouTube channel?

SMM: We were doing really well with the shorter-format YouTube show, so we were hoping the extended version would take off. We're so grateful to all the people watching! [Marino-Miller works closely with her best friend and manager, Rebecca Blume, founder of the branding firm People Who Love to Eat.]

BA: Part of your success has to do with the grandmas—can you talk a little about that?

SMM: I think the experience of learning from and cooking with someone you love—whether it's a childhood memory or aspirational—strikes a chord.

BA: And your varied platforms allow viewers and followers to be a part of those relationships.

SMM: Exactly—I get a lot of feedback from people wishing they could make kugel with Mimi.

BA: And of course, The Pie. [Marino-Miller's spin on her grandmother June's cherry pie went viral; everyone from this editor to Michelle Obama tried their hand at it.]

SMM: The Pie! That was amazing. I think my nonna is a little jealous—she's really trying to make her chive gnocchi happen. But it doesn't have quite the same ring to it.

BA: I think it sounds delicious. What's next for you?

SMM: The new longer-format YouTube show gives me a chance to cook complete meals, which is exciting—and I'm working on an old-school cookbook that will be a mash-up of recipes, stories, photos, and dinner party templates.

BA: The key to a perfect dinner party?

SMM: Lose the expectation it will be perfect and embrace the chaos. Great company helps. Candles. Curated playlists. It's not rocket science.

BA: Recommended kitchen tool?

SMM: A cherry pitter for obvious reasons.

BA: Favorite meal?

SMM: Tinned razor clams on crackers spread with garlic herb butter. Eaten over the sink late at night. Wait. Can I choose another one too? Ritz crackers, extra-sharp cheddar cheese, Castelvetrano olives, and a strong gin cocktail in a tiny etched glass.

Page Six

GOSSIP EXCLUSIVE

Atticus Adams, son of literary lion Edward David Adams, reveals plans for a "Sober Nightclub" in Ibiza after his second stint in rehab:

SEE THE EXCLUSIVE PHOTOS OF ADAMS WITH A MAKEUP-FREE CHARLI XCX

By Sanja Porter-Bowman
May 3, 2023

Sources told Page Six that after his well-documented struggles, Adams is "in a better place" and using a chunk of his hefty inheritance to open a multifloored club with terrace level, open roof dance patio and convenient cryptocurrency for clubbers. Adams was spotted frolicking on the Spanish beach near mega pop star Charli XCX during his latest visit to outfit the new space with pyrotechnics. "They're just pals," an insider told us. "Charli is engaged to a rock star and is focused on building her brand right now." The two appeared separately at a lavish evening drone show where Adams donned an apple-green tie and gray suit. Charli, resplendent in a micro dress crafted entirely from fish scales, kept her distance.

FILED UNDER: Atticus Adams, Charli XCX, Ibiza, Nightclubs

"'Sensitively and masterfully edited'!" Rebecca yelled from her own small but cheerful office in the Lower East Side apartment she shared with Ben. It turned out that Betty Jack was the neighborhood landlady and had been happy to move Ben and Rebecca into a more spacious apartment in a building next door to his old place.

"Come in here and read it with me!" Ben yelled back from the bedroom.

Rebecca closed her laptop, went into the mostly separate kitchen, and turned on the electric kettle. They were both tea drinkers now. While waiting for the water to boil, she texted Stella about the *Bon Appétit* interview. She put a few pieces of homemade biscotti on a plate for Ben, who was no doubt hungry. The rest she wrapped in parchment paper and stored in a tin to bring uptown to Mimi's for their weekly dinner. The rustling roused Butch from his chair perch and he lumbered over to sit on one of her bare feet.

"Ouch—off! Fine—here you go." Rebecca slipped Butch some biscotti.

"Don't feed him people food!" Ben yelled, displaying once again an uncanny ability to sense what she was doing through at least two walls. "You and Ava are going to make him sick!"

"Good boy," Rebecca murmured to Butch. "You stay out here. Sorry your dad's so mean." She gathered two mugs and balanced the plate precariously. Butch padded down the hallway after her, but she closed the door with her hip. "He's making sad whale eyes."

Ben was lying in bed, reading on his phone. "He'll be okay. He loves to give us privacy." There was a thud as Butch, crestfallen, positioned himself on the floor outside the bedroom door.

Rebecca deposited the mugs and plate on the pile of books in lieu of a bedside table. She tucked herself under Ben's arm and touched his face. "I love you so much that I don't even mind that your stubble is basically ginger."

Ben didn't look up from his phone. "I love you so much that I still want to have sex with you even though you're wearing a Sixers shirt that belonged to your brother."

"Ha ha. Ava says she's going to meet us at Mimi's."

"Yeah, tell her to bring the leftover tofurkey for herself. We should call Rose and Jane. They've got to be so happy with the review."

"It's not tofurkey," Rebecca corrected him. "It was Stella's recipe for mushroom loaf, it was delicious, and you know it. My parents stayed in the Hamptons with Rose after Thanksgiving. We should have gone there straight from Vermont."

Ben kissed the top of Rebecca's head. "I promised Mimi when you moved out that we wouldn't miss too many Sunday dinners."

"I guess we'll always have Oceaaaaaaaaan House," Rebecca replied. "And thank you. But you don't have to be afraid of Mimi."

"I promised her," Ben repeated. "Hey, Stella's interview was great. You're going to get even more business now. You'll need another assistant."

"I know, right?" Rebecca pressed her foot against Ben's calf. "Now read me the review. I want to hear it again. You're the star, baby . . ."

Ben read the review out loud, then dropped his phone next to the bed.

"Masterful and sensitive! Sensitive and masterful!" Rebecca pinched Ben delightedly. He caught her hand and pinned it with the other one above her head. "I'm going to print it and frame it for your desk."

"Chloe will definitely approve. She owes me after the scented candle debacle." Rebecca's departure and Chloe's promotion had resulted in Ben and Chloe sharing the desk. Ben found her a much neater partner but one with an unfortunate predilection for perfumed everything from tissues to what Ben believed might be scratch-and-sniff notepaper.

"She owes both of us after the great cactus deception." Rebecca squirmed a little and Ben rolled on top of her. Chloe and Howie had revealed themselves as what Howie referred to as the "cactus yentas"—interested only, Howie claimed, in bringing together two people whose happiness would result in making the workplace more pleasant if the cactus didn't die first. Ben knew that Howie would have also been interested in more than a matchmaking scheme with Chloe, but now that he was in graduate school, his texts to Ben were less pining about Chloe and more enthusiastic about a Chomsky scholar named Clementine.

"Speaking of succulent . . ." he said, kissing Rebecca's neck.

"So corny." She shivered. Ben released her hands and she clasped her arms around him. He thought about his incredible luck and Rebecca's perfect mouth. She thought about how she couldn't tell the sound of her heart from the sound of his.

On their windowsill, basking in the late morning sun, the cactus thought it kind of missed workplace drama. And that it was somebody's turn to water it.

THE END

ACKNOWLEDGMENTS

Writing a book is one thing, while bringing it into the world is something else entirely. I have been so fortunate to have such smart, committed publishing people seeing it through. Thank you to my agent, the lovely and talented Elisabeth Weed, and to my two editors: Alison Callahan at Gallery Books, whose passionate advocacy was nothing short of miraculous, and Lily Cooper at Penguin Michael Joseph, who made the book better every time she touched it. Thank you to my enthusiastic foreign rights agent, Jenny Meyer; designer of the perfect cover, Sara Wood; copyeditor David Chesanow; and the incredible team at Gallery: Sally Marvin, Lucy Nalen, Mackenzie Hickey, and Taylor Rondestvedt.

I appreciate the encouragement from my early readers: Rachel Dickerman, Jen Gates, Mary Beth Holcomb, Chris Jenko, Andrea Sarvady, Lucy Seward. Nina Premutico for sharing that text.

My women friends have sustained and enriched me for my entire life—in different cities, states, and countries. Uncontrollable laughter, long lunches, dinner parties, late nights, book clubs, dog walks, texts, emails, phone calls, and letters before that. I am thankful beyond measure for your kinship, advice, and humor. I love all of you crones.

To my best friend, Jen Gates: you are generous, gracious, and fiercely supportive. Dare I say you are the wind beneath my wings.

Thank you to my phenomenal parents, who gave me confidence and unconditional love—if you hadn't provided such a happy childhood, maybe I would have written more books.

I have two wonderful brothers, one of whom happens to be a brilliant editor. Without Colin, there is no *Hot Desk*: thank you for the intellectual property, the nagging, and the threats. Doing this with you has been incredibly fun. I'm sorry you made me cut all the sexiest parts. Thank you for bringing Peter into my life, especially since he does everything.

Thank you to my other brother, James, for calm, wise counsel; for introducing my children to drunk cigs; and for bringing Ann, Rachel, and Jules into my life. Thank you, Rachel, for answering all my questions with your millennial wisdom, such as no one's cell phone ever rings unless it's an old person or spam.

Lucy and Isabel: being your mother is the most important thing I've ever done. I'm so proud of your empathy and spark. You are my favorite people.

Finally, thank you to my amazing husband, Bill. I'm sorry that when we first met you were under the impression that I was a person who might run with the bulls. You always champion me, you are my astute and most ardent reader, you make me laugh, and you bring the fireworks. Thank you for your family, including your parents, whose marriage is an inspiration. You make everything possible, my love. I am grateful every single day for our life together.

ABOUT THE AUTHOR

Laura Dickerman has an MA in fiction from NYU and an MA in English from Middlebury College's Bread Loaf School of English. She has taught high school English at Hopkins School, Collegiate School, and Germantown Friends School. She was an intern at *The Paris Review* many, many years ago. At her lowest point, she spent a month temping for her youngest brother, who was critical of her photocopying skills. She's been a book club leader, a tutor, and a recipient of an NEH grant. She lives in Atlanta with her husband. They have two grown daughters. *Hot Desk* is her first novel.